**family handyman**

# BEST
# TIPS
# & PROJECTS
# 2019

**family handyman**

# BEST TIPS & PROJECTS 2019

by The Editors of *Family Handyman* magazine

**FAMILY HANDYMAN BEST TIPS & PROJECTS 2019**
(See page 288 for complete staff listing.)
Editor-in-Chief: Gary Wentz
Project Editor: Mary Flanagan
Contributing Designers: Mariah Cates
Contributing Copy Editors: Donna Bierbach, Peggy Parker
Indexing: Lisa Himes

Vice President, Integrated Sales: John Dyckman

Trusted Media Brands, Inc.
President & Chief Executive Officer: Bonnie Kintzer

*Warning:* All do-it-yourself activities involve a degree of risk. Skills, materials, tools, and site conditions vary widely. Although the editors have made every effort to ensure accuracy, the reader remains responsible for the selection and use of tools, materials, and methods. Always obey local codes and laws, follow manufacturers' operating instructions, and observe safety precautions.

ISBN 978-1-62145-434-2 (dated), 978-1-62145-435-9 (undated)

Address any comments about *Family Handyman Best Tips & Projects 2019* to:
Editor, Best Tips & Projects
2915 Commers Drive, Suite 700
Eagan, MN 55121

To order additional copies of *Family Handyman Best Tips & Projects 2019*, call 1-800-344-2560.

For more Trusted Media Brands products and information, visit our Web site at tmbi.com.
For more about Family Handyman magazine, visit familyhandyman.com.

Printed in the United States of America.
1  3  5  7  9  10  8  6  4  2

# SAFETY FIRST—ALWAYS!

Tackling home improvement projects and repairs can be endlessly rewarding. But as most of us know, with the rewards come risks. DIYers use chain saws, climb ladders and tear into walls that can contain big and hazardous surprises.

The good news is, armed with the right knowledge, tools and procedures, homeowners can minimize risk. As you go about your projects and repairs, stay alert for these hazards:

## Aluminum wiring

Aluminum wiring, installed in about 7 million homes between 1965 and 1973, requires special techniques and materials to make safe connections. This wiring is dull gray, not the dull orange characteristic of copper. Hire a licensed electrician certified to work with it. For more information go to cpsc.gov and search for "aluminum wiring."

## Spontaneous combustion

Rags saturated with oil finishes like Danish oil and linseed oil, and oil-based paints and stains can spontaneously combust if left bunched up. Always dry them outdoors, spread out loosely. When the oil has thoroughly dried, you can safely throw them in the trash.

## Vision and hearing protection

Safety glasses or goggles should be worn whenever you're working on DIY projects that involve chemicals, dust and anything that could shatter or chip off and hit your eye. Sounds louder than 80 decibels (dB) are considered potentially dangerous. Sound levels from a lawn mower can be 90 dB, and shop tools and chain saws can be 90 to 100 dB.

## Lead paint

If your home was built before 1979, it may contain lead paint, which is a serious health hazard, especially for children six and under. Take precautions when you scrape or remove it. Contact your public health department for detailed safety information or call (800) 424-LEAD (5323) to receive an information pamphlet. Or visit epa.gov/lead.

## Buried utilities

A few days before you dig in your yard, have your underground water, gas and electrical lines marked. Just call 811 or go to call811.com.

## Smoke and carbon monoxide (CO) alarms

The risk of dying in reported home structure fires is cut in half in homes with working smoke alarms. Test your smoke alarms every month, replace batteries as necessary and replace units that are more than 10 years old. As you make your home more energy-efficient and airtight, existing ducts and chimneys can't always successfully vent combustion gases, including potentially deadly carbon monoxide (CO). Install a UL-listed CO detector, and test your CO and smoke alarms at the same time.

## Five-gallon buckets and window covering cords

Anywhere from 10 to 40 children a year drown in 5-gallon buckets, according to the U.S. Consumer Products Safety Commission. Always store them upside down and store ones containing liquid with the covers securely snapped.

According to Parents for Window Blind Safety, hundreds of children in the United States are injured every year after becoming entangled in looped window treatment cords. For more information, visit pfwbs.org or cpsc.gov.

## Working up high

If you have to get up on your roof to do a repair or installation, always install roof brackets and wear a roof harness.

## Asbestos

Texture sprayed on ceilings before 1978, adhesives and tiles for vinyl and asphalt floors before 1980, and vermiculite insulation (with gray granules) all may contain asbestos. Other building materials, made between 1940 and 1980, could also contain asbestos. If you suspect that materials you're removing or working around contain asbestos, contact your health department or visit epa.gov/asbestos for information.

---

For additional information about home safety, visit mysafehome.org.
This site offers helpful information about dozens of home safety issues.

# Contents

## 1. INTERIOR PROJECTS, REPAIRS & REMODELING

Home Care & Repair ........................... 10
  *Renew Cabinets, Resurface Bad Walls,*
  *Loose Studs in Plaster Walls and more*
Fire Blocking Basics............................ 17
5 Myths About Mold .......................... 21
Swing-Out Storage............................. 24
Ultimate Container Storage................ 29
Laundry Room Pedestal...................... 34

No Cutting Corners.............................. 41
Plaster and Lath Tear-Off.................... 47
Handy Hints......................................... 51
  *Easy-to-Make Wine Rack, Two Nail*
  *Lengths in One Gun and more*
Cleaning! .............................................. 56
  *Simplify Bath Cleaning, Gutter Cleaner,*
  *Quick Fix for Marker Mistakes and more*

## Special Section: PAINT & STAIN .................................................................................58

## 2. ELECTRICAL & HIGH-TECH

Home Care & Repair ........................... 68
  *9 Simple Tips for Faster Wi-Fi,*
  *Add Solar Power to Your Shed,*
  *An Electrical Panel Myth and more*

Electrical Cable Basics......................... 77

## Special Section: WELDING .......................................................................................80

## 3. PLUMBING, HVAC & APPLIANCES

PAUL TESSLER/SHUTTERSTOCK

Home Care & Repair ........................... 90
  *No-Wiggle Toilet, Mini-Split Systems*
  *and more*
Toilet Tune-Ups ................................... 97
Stay Warm When the Power's Out... 101

No Water? Now What? ..................... 104
Prevent Frozen Pipes......................... 109
Handy Hints....................................... 113
  *Self-Draining Dehumidifier and more*
Great Goofs......................................... 114

## 4. WOODWORKING & WORKSHOP PROJECTS & TIPS

Get the Best Plywood for
  Your Buck........................................ 116
Flip-Top Bench.................................... 122
Quick & Easy Cabinet Doors.............. 130
Easy Crate Shelf................................. 136
Viking Long Table............................... 140
Cedar Bath Mat.................................. 148
French Cleat Tool Wall....................... 150
Floating Shelf
  (with a Secret Drawer).................. 156

Make Your Own Barn Wood.............. 160
Backyard Cantina................................ 165
Bottle Caddy....................................... 169
Wipe-On Poly...................................... 173
Compressor Cart................................. 179
Handy Hints......................................... 180
  *Quick Mixing Surface, No-Wait Glue,*
  *Convenient Bench Clamps and more*

Special Section: SECRET HIDING PLACES.................................................184

## 5. EXTERIOR REPAIRS & IMPROVEMENTS

Home Care & Repair ........................ 190
   *Stop Mice Before They Come In,*
   *Installing Gutters and more*
Easier Paver Patios ........................... 192

Finding & Fixing Roof Leaks............. 196
Handy Hints........................................ 201
   *Easy Concrete Mixing and more*

Special Section: HOLE SAW SMARTS.................................................202

## 6. OUTDOOR STRUCTURES, LANDSCAPING & GARDENING

Home Care & Repair ........................ 208
   *Multipurpose Garden Tools, Planning a*
   *Retaining Wall and more*
Restore a Weedy & Patchy Lawn...... 213
Sprinkler System Fixes ..................... 218
Living Wall ......................................... 224
Digging Holes .................................... 230

Concrete Basics ................................. 234
Choose a Lawn Tractor ...................... 237
Install an Irrigation System .............. 242
Handy Hints........................................ 247
   *Chimney Flue Planters, Measuring*
   *Stick for Firewood, Easy Apple*
   *Cleanup and more*

Special Section: CAR & GARAGE.................................................250

## 7. USING DIY TOOLS & MATERIALS

Home Care & Repair ........................ 262
   *Is Your Square Square?*
Cordless Brad Nailers........................ 263
8 Easy Ways to Cut Metal Fast.......... 269

Choosing Caulk.................................. 273
Handy Hints........................................ 277
   *The Money Wrench Trick, Compressor*
   *Creeper, Pocket Magnet and more*

Special Section: 28 THINGS HOMEOWNERS MUST KNOW.................................278

Index ........................ 284    Acknowledgments................................. 288

# 1 Interior Projects, Repairs & Remodeling

## IN THIS CHAPTER

Home Care & Repair ...................................10
*Renew Cabinets, Resurface Bad Walls,
Loose Studs in Plaster Walls and more*

Fire Blocking Basics ..................................17

5 Myths About Mold ..................................21

Swing-Out Storage ....................................24

Ultimate Container Storage......................29

Laundry Room Pedestal............................34

No Cutting Corners ....................................41

Plaster and Lath Tear-Off..........................47

Handy Hints ...............................................51
*Easy-to-Make Wine Rack, Two Nail
Lengths in One Gun and more*

Cleaning! ....................................................56
*Simplify Bath Cleaning, Gutter Cleaner,
Quick Fix for Marker Mistakes and more*

# HomeCare&Repair

**TIPS, FIXES & GEAR FOR A TROUBLE-FREE HOME**

## MAKE A SMALL ROOM **LOOK BIGGER**

You may not be able to add to your square footage, but with creative decorating and a few shortcuts and tips, you can make a room look like you did.

■ **Furniture with Legs Showing.** This draws the eye upward and creates the illusion of more light and open space.

■ **Ditch the Clutter.** Removing knick-knacks, artificial plants and other decorative items makes a space feel open and larger.

■ **Sheer Window Treatments.** Use the windows in a small room to bring light into every corner. Sunlight will make the room seem larger.

■ **Less Furniture.** Open floor space gives the appearance of more square footage.

■ **Choose a Light Color Scheme.** Lighter color palettes create the illusion of a larger area. Dark colors, although trendy, are best used in larger areas.

■ **Try Monochrome.** Choose a paint scheme using one color in varying shades and/or textures. This will keep the room open and airy.

UNITED PHOTO STUDIO/SHUTTERSTOCK

## LOCATE STUDS IN PLASTER WALLS

Finding a stud behind plaster and lath is hit-or-miss with a typical stud finder. Here's a better method. Tape a rare earth magnet (about $4 for a 10-pack at home centers) to a piece of dental floss. Slowly drag the magnet across the wall surface. The magnet will "hang up" a bit over the nails used to fasten the wood lath to the studs.

DENTAL FLOSS

RARE EARTH MAGNET

## NO CORKSCREW? NO PROBLEM!

**Insert a key**
Push a key into the cork at a 45-degree angle until the key's teeth are all the way in the cork. Then twist and pull the cork up and out.

—Tina Watrud

## PORTABLE CLOTHES PODS

Here's a cool way to pack your clothes for moving. First, cut a hole in the center of the bottom of a large trash bag. Grab a handful of clothes by the hanger hooks and slip the bag over it, pulling the hooks through the hole. Use a zip tie or wire to hold the hooks together, and then tie the open end shut. Your clothes stay clean in these easily portable pods, and you never have to take them off the hangers!

—Sophie Rehbein

# HomeCare&Repair

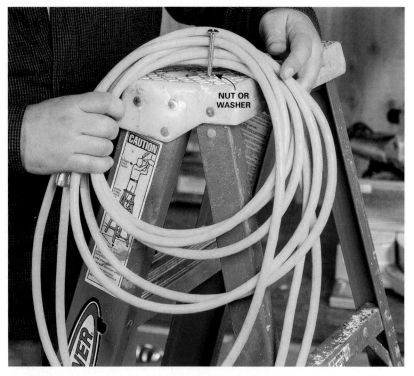

## CARRIAGE-BOLT LADDER HOOK

Sometimes there isn't room to set all the stuff I might need at the top of my ladder. So I attach a bolt to the top surface through one of the existing tool holes. You'll need a nut and washer on top and underneath. It's perfect for hanging an extension cord, a tool belt or even a bucket.

—Mark Ammons

## RESURFACE BAD WALLS

You can patch cracks in plaster walls, but there's a good chance they'll come back. Wall liner, on the other hand, can bridge cracks and flex with seasonal movement. It's basically wallpaper but much thicker and paintable. Some versions are smooth, others textured. Find it at home centers and online.

## CHOOSING THE BEST THIN-SET FOR THE JOB

Thin-set is the cement-based go-to adhesive for most tile projects. As you're perusing your options, you'll notice a price range of $8 to $30 per 50-lb. bag. The least expensive thin-set is just Portland cement and graded sand, and it has worked for centuries. It's appropriate for porous tile over concrete substrates.

However, most modern floor tile is porcelain. The more expensive "modified" thin-sets have various levels and types of polymer additives, which increases their adhesion and flexibility—as well as their price. They were developed to bond impervious tile, such as porcelain or glass, to most any substrate.

I use the best possible thin-set available for any given circumstance. Coverage for a 50-lb. bag is about 50 sq. ft., and a typical bathroom takes one bag. An extra 20 bucks to ensure that the tile will stay stuck is cheap insurance.

### MEET AN EXPERT

**Dean Sorem, our tile expert, has been installing tile for nearly 40 years.**

# KEEPING CROOKS OUT:
## THE BASICS MATTER MOST

Small security measures are a huge deterrent. Most home break-ins aren't the work of criminal masterminds; burglars just want to steal stuff with minimal time, effort and risk. Unfortunately, there are lots of easy targets in any neighborhood. But that's good news for you. If you make your home just a little harder to get into, you greatly increase the odds that crooks will bypass your house and look for an easier job.

### Focus on windows and doors

All the usual security advice (install exterior lighting, ask the neighbors to watch your house, etc.) is worth following. But above all, know this: Most break-ins occur through ground-level windows and doors. So strengthening them is crucial. For help with that, search for "home security" at familyhandyman.com.

### Daytime is crime time

Most of us think of burglary as a nocturnal activity. That used to be true. But these days, most burglaries occur between 10 a.m. and 5 p.m. In many cases, the crooks get in through unlocked doors or windows.

### What about window bars?

Window bars are almost impossible to get past, making them the toughest type of window security. But before you install the bars, ask the local police if they're necessary. In many areas, crooks avoid breaking glass. It makes a racket and is dangerous to the thief. As one cop put it, "When we find broken glass, we usually find drops of burglar blood."

# HomeCare&Repair

## WHERE TO KEEP FIRE EXTINGUISHERS

Common sense dictates that you keep fire extinguishers wherever there's a potential for an accidental fire, such as in kitchens and garages. But some fire experts also recommend keeping them in places like laundry rooms and workshops and at the tops of basement stairwells.

Extinguishers should never be more than 75 ft. away from a Class A (ordinary combustibles) hazard, and no more than 50 ft. from a Class B (flammable liquids) hazard. When you mount a fire extinguisher to a wall, keep it high enough so kids can't reach it, near an exit, and away from any kind of heat source. Also place the extinguisher a safe distance from items and areas with the highest risk for fire so you can get to it when you need it most.

## POCKET STORAGE

Hang-up shoe organizers let you add easy-access storage just about anywhere—fast! Find them for about $15 at discount stores.

SECOND HOLE

## SIMPLE WINDOW LOCKS

The latches on most double-hung windows are no match for a burglar with a pry bar. Pin locks are an easy solution. To install one, all you have to do is drill a hole. If you want to lock the window in a partially opened position, drill a second hole. Pin locks cost about $5 at home centers and online. They work well on sliding doors too.

## RENEW CABINETS

Cabinets are the largest cost on many kitchen remodeling jobs. But most old cabinets can be refreshed, even if they're in terrible shape.

### Paint

You can make old cabinets look great, often for less than one-tenth the cost of new cabinets. If you're willing to do some tedious prep work, you can get beautiful, long-lasting results. To see how, go to familyhandyman.com and search for "paint kitchen cabinets."

### Reface

Refacing starts with a layer of real wood veneer applied to the frames. Add new doors and drawer fronts, and the cabinets will look entirely new. The pro cost is typically less than half the cost of new cabinets. For a step-by-step DIY guide, go to familyhandyman.com and search for "reface cabinets."

## HIDE CABINET DAMAGE WITH BACK PLATES

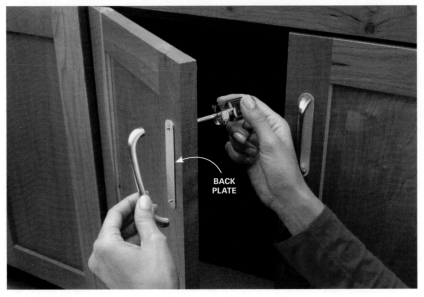

BACK PLATE

New cabinet hardware that includes back plates can hide the wear that occurs around cabinet knobs and pulls. You'll find a small hardware selection at home centers and an endless selection online.

BACK PLATE

# HomeCare&Repair

## DRAWER STOP

To keep a drawer from being pulled all the way out, create a drawer stop with a 3-in. strip of 1/8-in. metal bar stock. Drill a 3/16-in. hole 1 in. from one end. Screw the metal strip to the back of the drawer about 1 in. from the top so it'll swing freely. Tip the strip and slide the drawer in. The heavier end of the strip hangs down and keeps the drawer from falling out.

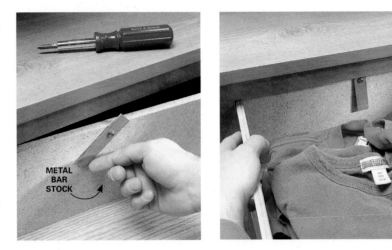

METAL BAR STOCK

## FIX NAIL POPS—AND KEEP THEM FROM COMING BACK

Nail pops happen when drywall nails or screws break through the surface. They're usually caused by shrinking and swelling of the wall studs. If you just pound them in and patch them, they'll be back. Here's how to fix them permanently.

SMASHED DRYWALL

NAIL POP

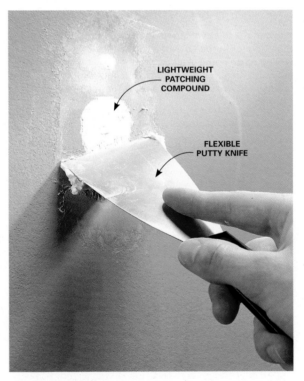

LIGHTWEIGHT PATCHING COMPOUND

FLEXIBLE PUTTY KNIFE

**1 Prepare for patching.** Drive drywall screws into the stud above and below the pop. Don't use nails. If the drywall has puckered around the pop, slice it out. If the area is flat, leave it alone. Remove the popped nail or screw.

**2 Patch the holes.** Fill the depressions with joint compound. Let the compound dry and coat it again (and probably again!) until the patch is flat. Smooth the patch with 100-grit sandpaper, then prime and paint.

# FIRE BLOCKING
## BASICS

**Holes and gaps in wall and ceiling cavities allow a fire to spread rapidly. They also allow airflow, which feeds a fire. Sealing these gaps slows or may even stop the spread of flames, smoke and gases.**

Fire blocking aims to prevent or at least slow the vertical movement of flames, smoke and gases by sealing off concealed spaces like stud cavities and soffits. Smoke and gases readily travel horizontally as well, so preventing horizontal air movement, such as within a dropped ceiling, has its own name: draft stopping.

Code requirements for adding fire blocking and draft stopping apply mainly to new construction. But if you're finishing a basement, putting on an addition, remodeling a room, or just running pipes or wires through a plate, you'll need to include fire blocking.

We'll show you the most common fire blocking applications on the following pages so you can apply the principles to your project.

**AIRFLOW**

**AIRFLOW**

### The Problem
Flames spread easily through holes and gaps in wall or ceiling cavities. The airflow through the gaps adds more oxygen to feed the fire.

## Figure A
## Whole-House Fire Blocking

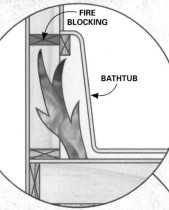

FIRE BLOCKING

BATHTUB

**Drop-In Tubs**
If the wall behind a drop-in bathtub is finished, no blocking is required. If the wall isn't finished, install 2-by material between the studs, flush with the top of the tub. Insulation batting in the wall extending at least 16 in. above the tub is also sufficient.

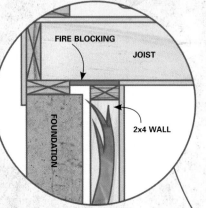

FIRE BLOCKING

JOIST

FOUNDATION

2x4 WALL

**Basement Walls**
The gap behind a 2x4 wall has to be sealed off from the joist bays above the wall.

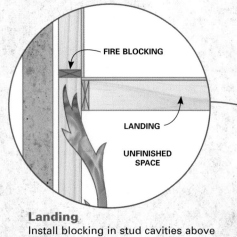

FIRE BLOCKING

LANDING

UNFINISHED SPACE

**Landing**
Install blocking in stud cavities above a landing over an unfinished space.

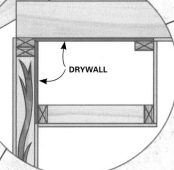

DRYWALL

**Soffits**
Soffits provide an easy path to floor and ceiling joist bays if they're not fire blocked. Without a soffit, the top plate provides the fire blocking.

**Soffit with a Finished Back**
If the wall and ceiling were drywalled before the soffit was put in, no further fire blocking is needed.

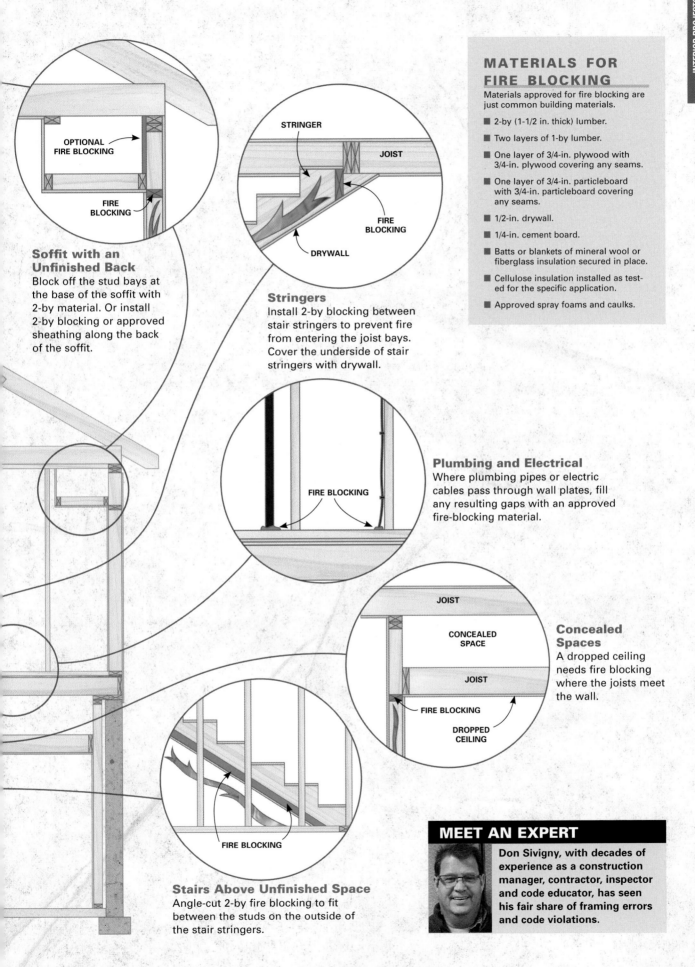

## MATERIALS FOR FIRE BLOCKING

Materials approved for fire blocking are just common building materials.

- 2-by (1-1/2 in. thick) lumber.
- Two layers of 1-by lumber.
- One layer of 3/4-in. plywood with 3/4-in. plywood covering any seams.
- One layer of 3/4-in. particleboard with 3/4-in. particleboard covering any seams.
- 1/2-in. drywall.
- 1/4-in. cement board.
- Batts or blankets of mineral wool or fiberglass insulation secured in place.
- Cellulose insulation installed as tested for the specific application.
- Approved spray foams and caulks.

**Soffit with an Unfinished Back**
Block off the stud bays at the base of the soffit with 2-by material. Or install 2-by blocking or approved sheathing along the back of the soffit.

**Stringers**
Install 2-by blocking between stair stringers to prevent fire from entering the joist bays. Cover the underside of stair stringers with drywall.

**Plumbing and Electrical**
Where plumbing pipes or electric cables pass through wall plates, fill any resulting gaps with an approved fire-blocking material.

**Concealed Spaces**
A dropped ceiling needs fire blocking where the joists meet the wall.

**Stairs Above Unfinished Space**
Angle-cut 2-by fire blocking to fit between the studs on the outside of the stair stringers.

## MEET AN EXPERT

**Don Sivigny**, with decades of experience as a construction manager, contractor, inspector and code educator, has seen his fair share of framing errors and code violations.

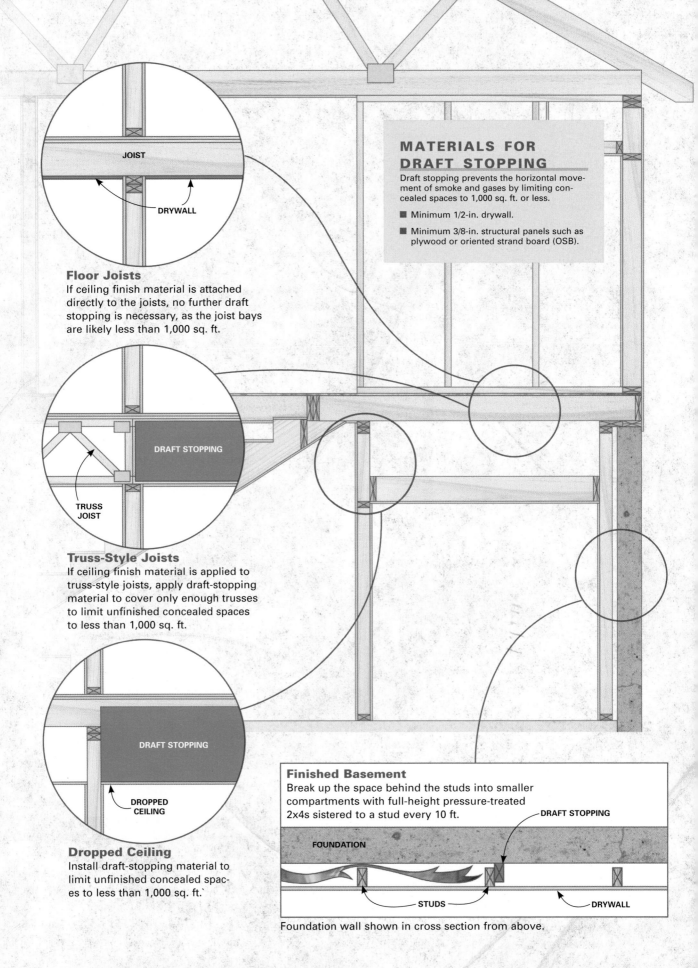

**JOIST**

**DRYWALL**

## MATERIALS FOR DRAFT STOPPING

Draft stopping prevents the horizontal movement of smoke and gases by limiting concealed spaces to 1,000 sq. ft. or less.

- Minimum 1/2-in. drywall.
- Minimum 3/8-in. structural panels such as plywood or oriented strand board (OSB).

### Floor Joists

If ceiling finish material is attached directly to the joists, no further draft stopping is necessary, as the joist bays are likely less than 1,000 sq. ft.

**DRAFT STOPPING**

**TRUSS JOIST**

### Truss-Style Joists

If ceiling finish material is applied to truss-style joists, apply draft-stopping material to cover only enough trusses to limit unfinished concealed spaces to less than 1,000 sq. ft.

**DRAFT STOPPING**

**DROPPED CEILING**

### Dropped Ceiling

Install draft-stopping material to limit unfinished concealed spaces to less than 1,000 sq. ft.`

### Finished Basement

Break up the space behind the studs into smaller compartments with full-height pressure-treated 2x4s sistered to a stud every 10 ft.

**DRAFT STOPPING**

**FOUNDATION**

**STUDS**

**DRYWALL**

Foundation wall shown in cross section from above.

# 5 MYTHS ABOUT MOLD

**W**e're exposed to mold spores in the air every day, both indoors and out, and most of the time that's no cause for concern. But given moderate temperatures, a food source (nearly any building material) and moisture, mold can grow on almost any surface inside our homes. Left unchecked, that can mean real trouble. Mold can harm health and destroy the building materials it feasts on. Unfortunately, there's a lot of misinformation about mold and how to handle it. So let's separate myth from fact and look at solutions that work.

## MEET AN EXPERT

Dan Tranter is the supervisor of the Indoor Air Unit at the Minnesota Department of Health. The Indoor Air Unit conducts research, education and outreach concerning indoor air quality, especially for radon, mold and carbon monoxide.

## MEET AN EXPERT

Kelly Smeltzer works as an indoor air quality specialist with the Minnesota Department of Health. She handles education and outreach on the topics of mold, carbon monoxide and healthy homes, along with enforcement of Minnesota rules pertaining to air quality in sports arenas.

ISTOCK.COM/DARREN TOWNSEND

ISTOCK.COM/ANDREYPOPOV

## WHEN SHOULD YOU CALL A PRO?

- If you can smell mold, but you can't find the mold or moisture problem.
- If there is so much mold that you can't remedy the problem easily.
- If there are highly susceptible individuals in your home. This could include those with respiratory conditions such as severe asthma or allergies, and those with a weakened immune system caused by HIV, chemotherapy or an organ transplant. Young children and elderly persons may also be more susceptible to mold-related health issues.
- If there are other hazardous materials present, like asbestos or lead, that will be disturbed or removed along with the mold. Hire a contractor who is licensed for those hazards.
- If moisture has created structural problems. Consult a qualified contractor to do the repairs or a structural engineer to advise you on what needs to be done.

### If you call a pro, do your homework

- Get several quotes.
- Ask for references.
- Ask about their experience, accreditation and training, particularly in indoor air quality.
- Ask if they hold any professional certifications or licenses. Certifications are voluntary, but they're a good indication that a contractor has basic knowledge and participates in continuing education. A few states require licensing for mold testing and remediation contractors, but most don't, so check with your state or local government.
- Ask if they use accredited labs and testing equipment. Lab accreditation is typically done through the American Industrial Hygiene Association and/or the American Association for Laboratory Accreditation.
- Ask if the testing company is also involved with the remediation process; that could be a conflict of interest.

**1** **Mold testing is critical.**

Surprisingly, this isn't the case. Testing gives you a snapshot of the quantity and type of mold present. But all types of mold (there are more than 100,000!) need to be removed, so it's not essential to identify the type. Also, there are no health-based safety standards for mold levels, so testing doesn't necessarily give valuable information, and it's expensive.

MOLD UNDER CARPET

ISTOCK.COM/VISUALCOMMUNICATIONS

**2** **No odor, no mold.**

Wrong! Odor is one telltale indicator, but just because you can't smell mold doesn't mean it's not there. Actual inspection is always best. If you don't smell mold but suspect there may be a problem, check likely areas first. If you know of any roofing or plumbing leaks, that's a good starting point. Bathrooms, basements, crawl spaces and sink cabinets are other likely areas.

ISTOCK.COM/LLEEROGERS

**3** **Black mold is deadly.**

This is a popular misconception; toxicity isn't related to mold color. Some types of mold, given the right conditions, can produce mycotoxins. It's not well understood which molds produce these poisonous substances, and even the ones that can produce them don't always do so. And when they do, it doesn't amount to much.

### 4  You must clean with bleach.

This isn't true either. Bleach does kill mold, but it's hard on your lungs, and it doesn't do a good job of removing mold. Scrubbing with soap and water is a safer and more effective way to eliminate mold from hard surfaces.

If porous surfaces like drywall or carpet get moldy, you can't clean them; you have to get rid of them. Bleach is necessary only if the moisture that caused the mold is from sewage. In this case, use 1/4 to 1/2 cup of bleach per gallon of water. Scrub the area and leave the bleach solution on for at least 30 minutes before rinsing it off. Thoroughly dry the area afterward.

SOAPY WATER

BLEACH

### 5  Mold-killing products are the solution.

Products such as mold-killing chemicals, paints and air filters help, but they're temporary fixes. Even if they do kill the mold, it'll keep coming back until moisture issues are corrected.

ISTOCK.COM/HEIKO KUVERLING

ISTOCK.COM/FONRIMSO

**The Bottom Line: It's All About Moisture**

Moisture is the essential ingredient for mold to thrive, and it can come from many sources. If an area has gotten wet for any reason, dry it within 24 to 48 hours, before mold has a chance to grow. The most common sources of moisture are plumbing leaks, roof leaks, wet basements, poor yard drainage, window condensation and high humidity. Search for each topic at family-handyman.com to learn how to deal with it.

If porous surfaces such as carpet, drywall or ceiling tiles have gotten moldy, remove and replace them. Your house's humidity should be 30 to 60 percent from spring to fall, and about 20 to 30 percent in the winter. If it's high, use air conditioners or dehumidifiers. Use an exhaust fan ducted to the outside when you're cooking. Install and use a timer on your bathroom exhaust fan. It should run for at least 30 minutes after showers.

For in-depth information on mold and mildew removal, search for "mold and mildew" at **familyhandyman.com.**

# SWING-OUT **STORAGE**

**Triple your cabinet space!**

By Jeff Gorton

INTERIOR PROJECTS, REPAIRS & REMODELING

**If** your wall cabinets are so full that you can't find anything without constant reshuffling, we have the perfect solution. This swing-out cabinet provides two extra layers of shelving for great visibility and easy access.

We chose to make shallow shelves on the front for spices and wider shelves on the back for bottles or cans, but you can configure your swing-out however you like. Narrow adjustable shelves behind the swing-out provide even more storage space.

## Tools and materials

You'll find all the materials for this project at home centers or lumberyards. The plywood has to be cut accurately into the parts for the swing-out, and the 1x3s ripped into 1-in.-wide strips for the shelf edging. A table saw and power miter saw are the best tools for these cuts.

We used an 18-gauge brad nailer and 1-1/2-in. brad nails to connect the parts. But if you don't own a brad nailer, you can use screws or drive finish nails by hand.

## Plan the swing-out size

Since there are so many different sizes of wall cabinets, we can't give you an exact plan for building a swing-out to fit in yours. However, since most wall cabinets are about the same depth, you should be able to make the cabinet 8 in. deep like ours, and you'll only need to adjust the width and height to fit. Start by

**3 Tiers of Shelving**
Keep your most-used spices on the front shelf for instant access. The two inner shelves (p. 24) are perfect for items you use less often.

FRONT SHELF

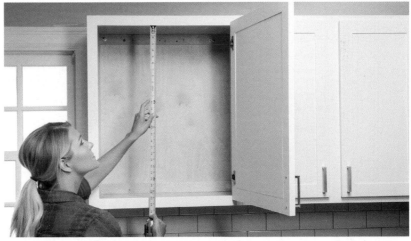

**1** **Measure your cabinet.** Measure the height of the opening and subtract 1/2 in. to determine the height of the shelf unit. Also measure the narrowest width from protruding hinges or door parts.

CARDBOARD TEMPLATE

**2** **Check for clearance.** Subtract 2 in. from the width measurement and cut an 8-in.-wide cardboard template to that dimension. Position the template as shown here. If the template won't clear the door or hinges, reduce the length.

## WHAT IT TAKES

**TIME: 1 day**
**COST: $110\***
**SKILL: Beginner to Intermediate**
**TOOLS: Table saw, miter saw, hacksaw, drill and 1/4-in. bit, carpentry hand tools. A nail gun is optional.**

*\*Approximately, depending on size.*

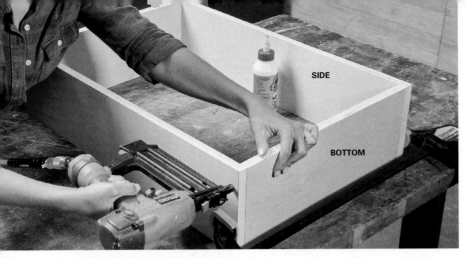

**3 Build a box.** Assemble the sides, top and bottom with glue and nails. Or, if you use screws rather than nails, you can skip the glue.

measuring the height of the opening (**Photo 1**) and recording the measurement. Subtract 1/2 in. from the height to get the length of the sides (A).

Determining the width is trickier because you have to subtract from the width measurement to compensate for the diagonal width of the swing-out. There are formulas you can use, but it's easier to simply make a cardboard template and adjust the size until it fits. Cut a piece of cardboard 8 in. wide and 2 in. shorter than the width of the cabinet and see if it fits diagonally (**Photo 2**). Trim the cardboard until you have about 1/2-in. clearance. Now measure the cardboard and subtract 1-5/8 in. to determine the length of the top and bottom (B).

## Figure A
### Swing-out Shelf

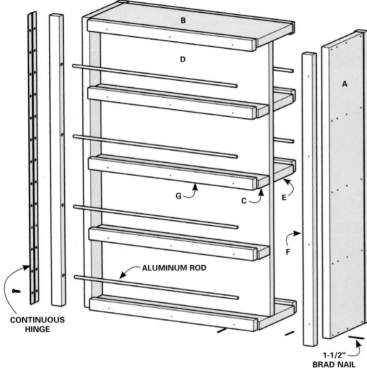

CONTINUOUS HINGE

ALUMINUM ROD

1-1/2" BRAD NAIL

## Figure B
### Stationary Shelf

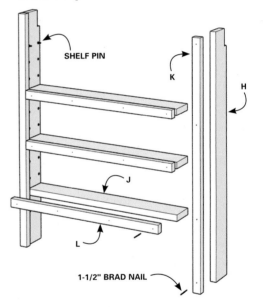

SHELF PIN

1-1/2" BRAD NAIL

## MATERIALS LIST

| ITEM | QTY. |
|---|---|
| 3/4" x 4' x 4' plywood | 1 |
| 1x3 x 8' board | 1 |
| 1x3 x 10' board | 1 |
| 36" x 1-1/2" continuous hinge | 1 |
| 36" x 1/4" aluminum rod | 4 |
| 1/4" shelf pins | 12 |
| Magnetic cabinet catch | 1 |
| Small package of 1-1/2" brad nails | 1 |

## CUTTING LIST

| ITEM | QTY. | MATERIAL | DIMENSIONS | PART |
|---|---|---|---|---|
| A | 2 | 3/4" plywood | 3/4" x 6-1/2" x 26-1/2" | Sides |
| B | 2 | 3/4" plywood | 3/4" x 6-1/2" x 17-1/4" | Top/bottom |
| C | 3 | 3/4" plywood | 3/4" x 2" x 17-1/4" | Shallow shelves |
| D | 1 | 3/4" plywood | 3/4" x 25-1/16" x 17-1/4" | Divider |
| E | 2 | 3/4" plywood | 3/4" x 3-3/4" x 17-1/4" | Deep shelves |
| F | 4 | 3/4" boards | 3/4" x 1" x 26-1/2" | Vertical edging |
| G | 9 | 3/4" boards | 3/4" x 1" x 16-7/8" | Horizontal edging |
| **SHELVES AT BACK OF CABINET** | | | | |
| H | 2 | 3/4" plywood | 3/4" x 2-3/4" x 27-1/2" | Side supports |
| J | 3 | 3/4" plywood | 3/4" x 2-3/4" x 21" | Shelves |
| K | 2 | 3/4" boards | 3/4" x 1" x 27-1/2" | Vertical edging |
| L | 3 | 3/4" boards | 3/4" x 1" x 20-1/2" | Shelf edging |

**Note:** These sizes are for a swing-out for a 24-in.-wide wall cabinet. To fit your cabinet, adjust the sizes according to the instructions in the article.

## Build the carcass

Start by cutting out the sides, top and bottom and nailing them together (**Photo 3**). Then determine your shelf spacing and nail in the shallow shelves (C). Leave enough space for your tallest spice containers. We spaced our shelves about 5-1/2 in. apart.

Next, measure the inside height and width dimensions and cut the interior plywood divider (D) to fit. Press the divider against the shallow shelves and nail through the sides to hold it in place (**Photo 4**). Flip the carcass over and measure from the face of the divider to the edge of a side to determine the width of the deeper shelves (E) on the back of the swing-out. We added two shelves, leaving one tall space for bottles, with two shorter spaces above. If you have a lot of bottles, you could simply divide the space in half and install only one shelf. Cut the shelves to fit and nail them in.

When the plywood carcass is finished, install the 1-in.-wide solid wood edging. After ripping the boards to 1 in. wide, cut the vertical pieces (F) to length, mark the hole locations and drill holes for the rods (**Photo 5**). Then nail the vertical edging pieces to the carcass, letting them hang over the outside edge about 1/16 in. (the width of a quarter; **Photo 6**). Cut the horizontal edging pieces to fit between the vertical pieces and nail them in. Install these with the bottom edges flush to the plywood to create a 1/4-in. lip on the top of the shelf. Repeat this process on the opposite side to complete the swing-out construction.

## Apply finish and install the swing-out

We used spray cans of polyurethane to finish our swing-out before installing it. Cover the aluminum rods with masking tape. Then apply several light coats, sanding the dried polyurethane with 400-grit sandpaper between coats.

**4** **Install the divider.** Position and nail the narrow shelves. Measure the inside width and height of the swing-out and carefully cut the 3/4-in. plywood divider to fit. Drop the plywood divider into place and nail through the sides, top and bottom to hold it. Flip the carcass over and install the wider shelves.

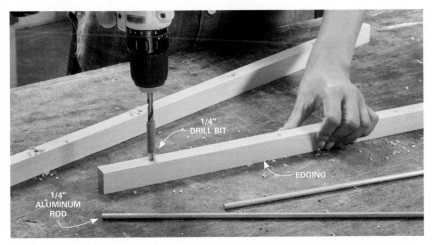

**5** **Drill holes for the rods.** Set one edging piece on the swing-out and mark the rod positions 2 in. above each shelf. Drill 1/4-in. holes in the center of the edging at each mark. Use this as a pattern to mark and drill the opposite edging piece.

**6** **Add the edging and rods.** Nail on the first edging piece. Then install the rods and nail on the second vertical edging. Measure and cut the horizontal edging boards. Glue and nail the edging to the carcass. Repeat on the opposite side.

Cut a continuous hinge to the height of your swing-out cabinet with a hacksaw. Determine which side of the swing-out is opposite the cabinet door and mount the hinge to this side (**Photo 7**). **Photo 8** shows how to attach the swing-out to your wall cabinet.

## Finish up with more shelves

Install shelves at the back of the cabinet. Measure the depth of the cabinet and subtract 8-1/4 in. to determine the depth of the shelves. Subtract 3/4 in., the thickness of the edging, from this dimension to determine the width of the plywood sides and shelves.

Cut two strips of plywood for the sides, and cut as many shelves as you want. Cut the side supports (H) to fit top to bottom in the cabinet. Then drill a series of 1/4-in. holes in the plywood sides for shelf pins. Use a shelf-pin jig or a strip of pegboard with 1/4-in. holes as a drilling guide.

**Figure B** shows how to install the edging pieces on the shelves and side pieces. Finish up by screwing the side shelf supports to the sides of the cabinet and installing the shelves. Mount a magnetic catch to the top of the wall cabinet to hold the swing-out in place.

**7** **Attach the continuous hinge.** Cut a continuous hinge to the height of the swing-out using a hacksaw with a fine-tooth blade. Position the hinge so that it can fold over the front of the swing-out and drive a screw at the top and bottom. Then drive the remaining screws.

**8** **Hang the swing-out.** Prop up the swing-out so that there's equal space on the top and bottom. Align the continuous hinge with the front of the hinge pin (the rod-shaped center section) flush to the cabinet face. Attach the hinge with the small screws provided.

**9** **Add adjustable shelves.** Cut the shelf supports and shelves to fit. Add the edging strips and drill the shelf-pin holes. Then screw the shelf supports to the side of the cabinet and drop in the shelves. Screw a magnet to a block of wood at the top of the cabinet.

# ULTIMATE CONTAINER STORAGE

## No more digging for the right lid!

By **Jeff Gorton**

It's always a challenge to find matching containers and lids. This rollout solves the problem by keeping them all neatly organized and easily accessible. The full-extension drawer slides are the key.

To simplify tricky drawer slide installation, we've designed an ingenious carrier system that allows you to mount the slides and make sure everything is working smoothly before the unit is mounted in the cabinet.

**1** **Measure the opening.** Measure from any protruding hinges or door parts to the opposite side to find the opening width. Also check to make sure the cabinet is at least 22 in. deep.

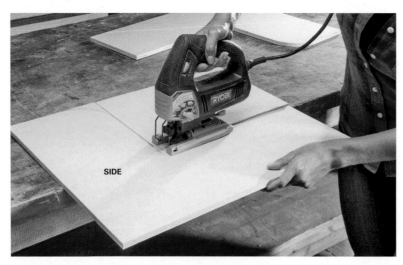

SIDE

**2** **Cut the side panels.** Cut each panel to size. Then cut the notch to form the L-shape. Start with a table saw or circular saw for the straight cuts. Finish the inside corner with a jigsaw.

**3** **Cut the curves.** Mark the curves on the side panels by tracing along a gallon paint can. Mark the dividers using a quart-size paint can. Then cut with a jigsaw.

## Tools and materials

Our 24-in. base cabinet required a 4 x 4-ft. sheet of 1/2-in.-thick plywood for the rollout, plus a 2 x 3-ft. scrap of 3/4-in. plywood for the carrier. Yours may require more or less. We found high-quality birch plywood at a home center for this project. If you have trouble finding nice plywood, consider ordering Baltic birch or ApplePly plywood from a home center or local lumberyard. The carrier fits under the rollout and isn't very conspicuous, so almost any flat piece of 3/4-in. plywood will work for that.

In addition to the lumber, you'll need a pair of 22-in. full-extension ball-bearing slides (about $22 at home centers or woodworking supply stores) and a 1/4-in. aluminum rod.

We used a table saw to cut the plywood parts, but if you're careful to make accurate cuts, a circular saw will work. You'll need a jigsaw with a plywood-cutting blade to cut the curves on the sides and dividers. We used a finish nail gun and 1-1/4-in.-long brad nails to connect the parts, but you could substitute trim-head screws if you don't mind the larger holes they leave.

## Measure the base cabinet

Most base cabinets are about 23 in. deep and will accommodate this rollout, but measure yours to be sure. If the measurement from the back of the face frame to the back of the cabinet is less than 22 in., you'll have to build a shallower rollout and use shorter drawer slides.

The other critical measurement is the width. Measure the clear opening width; that is, the width from any protruding hinge or door parts to the opposite side of the cabinet opening (**Photo 1**).

**WHAT IT TAKES**
**TIME: 1 day**
**COST: $65**
**SKILL: Beginner to Intermediate**
**TOOLS: Table or circular saw, jigsaw, drill and 1/4-in. bit, hand tools. A brad nail gun simplifies the construction.**

Subtract 3 in. from this measurement to determine the width of parts B, C, D and E.

## Cut out the parts

After adjusting the size of parts B, C, D and E for the cabinet width, you can cut out all the parts except the carrier bottom. If you're using a table saw, make partial cuts to form the L-shaped sides. But remember, you can't see how far the blade is cutting on the underside, so be sure to stop short of your inside corner marks by at least an inch. **Photo 2** shows how to complete the cut with a jigsaw.

Trace along the edge of a 1-gallon paint can to draw the radius for the curve on the side panels. Trace along a quart-size can to draw the radius on the dividers. Cut the curves on the sides and dividers with a jigsaw (**Photo 3**). Smooth the curved cuts with 100-grit sandpaper.

## Build the rollout

Mark the location of the 1/4-in. rod on the side panels using **Figure A** as a guide. Wrap tape around a 1/4-in. drill bit 1/4 in. from the end to use as a depth guide while drilling. Drill 1/4-in.-deep holes at the marks. Use a hacksaw to cut an aluminum rod 1/2 in. longer than the width of the bottom.

Apply wood glue to all edges that meet, and arrange the sides, bottom, front and back on a workbench and clamp them together. Work the aluminum rod into the holes. Tap the parts with a hammer to align the edges perfectly before connecting them with brad nails (**Photo 4**). Take your time aiming the nail gun to avoid nail blowouts.

Finish the rollout by adding the dividers. First decide how many dividers you want and calculate the width of the space between the dividers. Cut a spacer block to that dimension and use it as a guide to install the dividers. Attach the dividers to the shelf (**Photo 5**). Then measure down 7-1/2 in. from the top and make marks to indicate the top edge of the divider shelf. Line up the divider assembly with these marks and nail it in. Draw divider center lines on the back of the rollout as a nailing guide. Then attach the dividers (**Photo 6**).

**4** **Assemble the rollout.** Glue and clamp the parts together. Don't forget to install the rod. Align the edges by tapping on the panels with your hand or a hammer. Then nail the parts together.

ROD

BRAD NAIL GUN

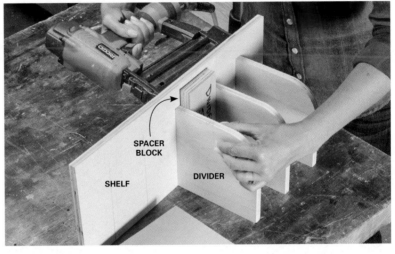

SPACER BLOCK

SHELF

DIVIDER

**5** **Nail the dividers to the shelf.** Cut a spacer the width of the desired space between dividers and use it to position the dividers as you nail them to the shelf.

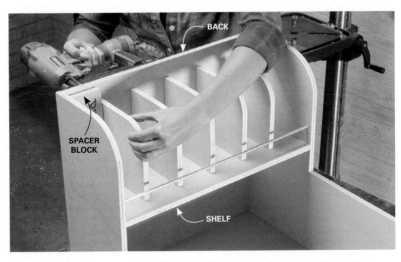

BACK

SPACER BLOCK

SHELF

**6** **Nail the dividers to the rollout.** Position the shelf and nail through the sides into the shelf. Then use the spacer block to align the dividers and nail through the back.

## CUTTING LIST

| ITEM | QTY. | MATERIAL | DIMENSIONS | PART |
|------|------|----------|------------|------|
| A | 2 | 1/2" plywood | 1/2" x 22" x 18" | Sides |
| B | 1 | 1/2" plywood | 1/2" x 7-1/2" x 18" | Front |
| C | 1 | 1/2" plywood | 1/2" x 22" x 18" | Bottom |
| D | 1 | 1/2" plywood | 1/2" x 17-1/2" x 18" | Back |
| E | 1 | 1/2" plywood | 1/2" x 7-1/2" x 18" | Shelf |
| F | 5* | 1/2" plywood | 1/2" x 6" x 6" | Dividers |
| G | 1 | 3/4" plywood | 3/4" x 20" x 22" | Carrier bottom |
| H | 2 | 3/4" plywood | 3/4" x 2-3/4" x 22" | Carrier sides |

**Note:** These sizes are for a 24-in.-wide base cabinet. To fit your cabinet, adjust the sizes according to the instructions in the article.

## MATERIALS LIST

| ITEM | QTY. |
|------|------|
| 1/2" x 4' x 4' plywood | 1 |
| 3/4" x 2' x 3' plywood | 1 |
| Pair of 22" full-extension slides | 1 |
| 36" x 1/4" aluminum rod | 1 |
| Small package of 1-1/4" brad nails | 1 |

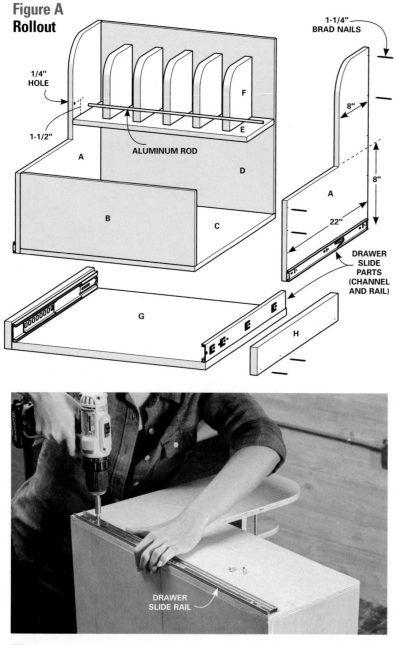

**Figure A
Rollout**

Drawer slides require 1/2-in. clearance on each side, so making the carrier exactly 1 in. wider than the rollout will result in a perfect fit. Measure the width of the completed rollout and add exactly 1 in. to determine the width of the carrier bottom. Cut the carrier bottom from 3/4-in. plywood. Then screw the carrier sides to the carrier bottom to prepare the carrier for mounting the drawer slides.

### Mount the slides

Follow the instructions included with your drawer slides to separate the slides into two parts: a channel and a rail. Usually, pressing down on a plastic lever releases the parts and allows you to separate them. Screw the rails to the drawer (**Photo 7**) and the channels to the carrier sides (**Photo 8**).

When you're done installing the slides, check the fit by carefully aligning the rails with the channels and sliding them together. The rollout should glide easily on the ball-bearing slides. If the slides seem too tight, you can adjust the fit by removing one of the carrier sides and slipping a thin cardboard shim between the carrier side and carrier bottom before reassembling them.

### Mount the rollout in the cabinet

**Photo 9** shows fitting the carrier assembly into the cabinet. There will be a little side-to-side play, so you can adjust the position to clear the hinge and door. This will probably require you to offset the carrier slightly away from the hinge side. Screw the carrier to the bottom of the cabinet and you're ready to install the rollout (**Photo 10**). Since you've already checked the fit, it should operate perfectly. Now load it up with containers and lids and enjoy your neatly organized container rollout.

**7** **Screw the drawer slide to the rollout.** Separate the drawer slides and attach the rail to the rollout. Align the rail flush to the bottom and flush to the front before driving the screws.

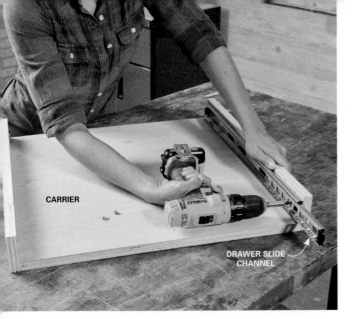

**8** **Screw the drawer slide channel to the carrier.** Rest the drawer slide channel on the carrier and align the front flush to the front of the carrier side.

**9** **Install the carrier.** Position the carrier so that the rollout will clear any hinge or door parts. Drive screws through the carrier bottom into the cabinet.

**10** **Install the rollout.** Line up the rails and channels and slide the rollout into the cabinet. Slide it back and forth a few times to make sure it rolls smoothly.

# LAUNDRY ROOM
# PEDESTAL

## Save your back without spending an arm and a leg.

By **Jeff Gorton**

**SPACE FOR BASKETS**

**STOCK MOLDINGS**

**STANDARD BOARDS OVER PLYWOOD**

**F**ront-loading appliances have a lot of great features, but being easy on your back isn't one of them. That's why manufacturers offer matching pedestals that raise the machines to a comfortable height. But these pedestals cost up to $250 each, and you still won't have a place to stash laundry baskets. With our plan, you can build your own unit for about half the cost, and get a functional pedestal that will look great in any laundry room.

You can choose from the three versions we show here—contemporary, Craftsman and classic. They differ only in the amount of trim and moldings you add to the basic plywood carcass.

## WHAT IT TAKES
**TIME: 1 weekend**
**COST: $80 to $200**
**SKILL: Beginner to Intermediate**
**TOOLS: Basic DIY tools, including a circular saw. A table saw, a miter saw and a finish nail gun would make the job easier.**

## CHOOSE YOUR STYLE!

Build it basic or deck it out with moldings.

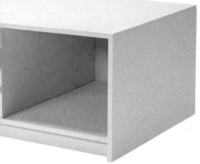

### Contemporary

Leave off the trim and you have a sleek and functional pedestal. This version doesn't require any miters, so even a beginner can build it.

### Craftsman

Adding trim on the face and sides transforms the pedestal with minimal additional cost and work. Most of the trim cuts are simple right angles, so even this version is easy.

### Classic

If you prefer a traditional look, add moldings. You'll need to cut a few miters to fit the moldings where they meet at the corners, so this version requires slightly more skill.

### Figure A
### Contemporary

**Overall Dimensions:**
**58-1/2" Long x 31-1/2" Deep x 18-1/4" Tall**

23" LONG
15" WIDE
10-1/2" TALL
SUGGESTED BASKET SIZE

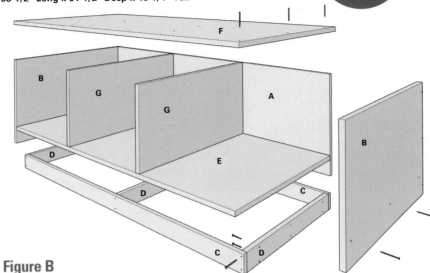

### Figure B
### Craftsman

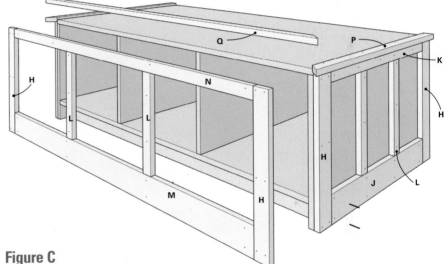

### Figure C
### Classic

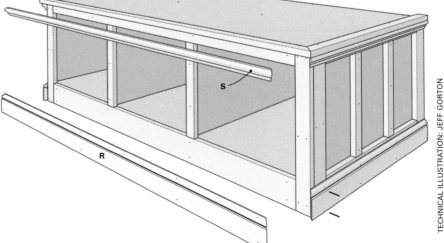

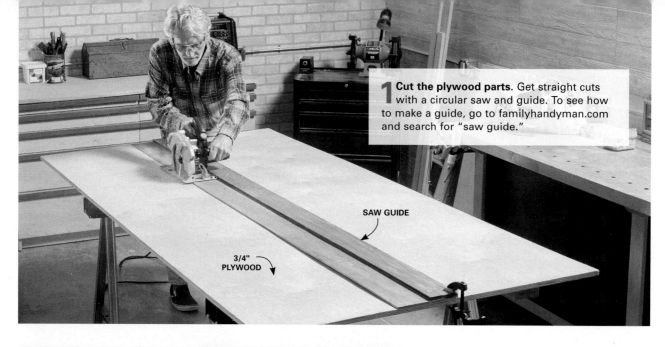

1 **Cut the plywood parts.** Get straight cuts with a circular saw and guide. To see how to make a guide, go to familyhandyman.com and search for "saw guide."

SAW GUIDE

3/4" PLYWOOD

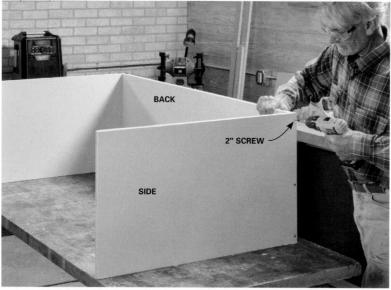

BACK

2" SCREW

SIDE

2 **Screw the sides to the back.** Drill 3/32-in. pilot holes through the sides into the back. Then drive 2-in. screws to connect the sides to the back.

## Skill, time and materials

The skill required goes up a little as the versions get fancier. Including painting, expect to spend a weekend on this project. In addition to standard DIY tools, you'll need a circular saw and a straightedge guide or table saw to cut the plywood. A miter saw would make cutting the trim for the Craftsman version easier, and is necessary if you want to add the moldings. And a finish nail gun would simplify all the trim work.

The pedestal requires two sheets of plywood, and some trim boards and moldings if you want to add them. You'll find all these at any home center or lumberyard. Remember, you can always ask to have the plywood cut into smaller pieces to fit in your vehicle. See the **Materials List** on p. 37.

3 **Add the toe space frame.** Cut the parts to length from the plywood strips. Drill pilot holes and join the parts with 2-in. screws. Set the frame into place and connect it to the sides and back with 1-1/4-in. screws.

TOE SPACE FRAME

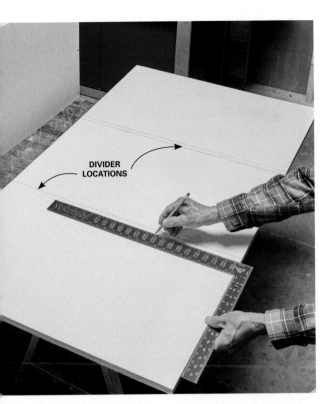

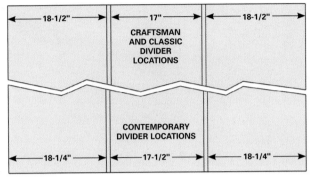

## Figure D
## Divider Locations

### PEDESTAL TOP

| 18-1/2" | 17" | 18-1/2" |

CRAFTSMAN
AND CLASSIC
DIVIDER
LOCATIONS

CONTEMPORARY
DIVIDER LOCATIONS

| 18-1/4" | 17-1/2" | 18-1/4" |

### PEDESTAL BOTTOM

| 17-3/4" | 17" | 17-3/4" |

CRAFTSMAN
AND CLASSIC
DIVIDER
LOCATIONS

CONTEMPORARY
DIVIDER LOCATIONS

| 17-1/2" | 17-1/2" | 17-1/2" |

DIVIDER
LOCATIONS

**4 Mark the divider locations.** Mark the positions of the two dividers on the top and bottom. Draw light pencil lines to indicate the edges of the panels. Turn the panels over and make a single line to indicate the center of the dividers. Use this line as a guide when you drill the screw holes. You can wash off these lines or paint over them after the pedestal is assembled.

## CUTTING LIST

| ITEM | QTY. | MATERIAL | DIMENSIONS | PART |
|------|------|----------|-----------|------|
| A | 1 | 3/4" plywood | 3/4" x 54" x 17-1/2" | Back |
| B | 2 | 3/4" plywood | 3/4" x 30" x 17-1/2" | Sides |
| C | 2 | 3/4" plywood | 3/4" x 54" x 2-3/4" | Toe space frame front and back |
| D | 3 | 3/4" plywood | 3/4" x 25-3/4" x 2-3/4" | Toe space frame sides and middle |
| E | 1 | 3/4" plywood | 3/4" x 54" x 29-1/4" | Bottom |
| F | 1 | 3/4" plywood | 3/4" x 55-1/2" x 30" | Top |
| G | 2 | 3/4" plywood | 3/4" x 14" x 29-1/4" | Dividers |

### ADD TRIM FOR THE CRAFTSMAN VERSION

| ITEM | QTY. | MATERIAL | DIMENSIONS | PART |
|------|------|----------|-----------|------|
| H | 6 | 1x3 board | 3/4" x 2-1/2" x 17-7/8" | End stiles |
| J | 2 | 1x4 board | 3/4" x 3-1/2" x 25" | Bottom end rails* |
| K | 2 | 1x2 board | 3/4" x 1-1/2" x 25" | Top end rails* |
| L | 6 | 1x2 board | 3/4" x 1-1/2" x 12-7/8" | Interior stiles* |
| M | 1 | 1x4 board | 3/4" x 3-1/2" x 52" | Bottom front rail* |
| N | 1 | 1x2 board | 3/4" x 1-1/2" x 52" | Top front rail* |
| P | 2 | 1x2 board | 3/4" x 1-1/2" x 31-1/2" | End nosings* |
| Q | 1 | 1x2 board | 3/4" x 1-1/2" x 58-1/2" | Front nosing* |

\* Cut to fit

### ADD MOLDING FOR THE CLASSIC VERSION

| ITEM | QTY. | MATERIAL | DIMENSIONS | PART |
|------|------|----------|-----------|------|
| R | 3 | Baseboard molding | Cut to fit | Trim at base |
| S | 3 | Base cap molding | Cut to fit | Trim under cap |

## MATERIALS LIST

| ITEM | QTY. |
|------|------|
| 4' x 8' x 3/4" plywood | 2 |
| 2" screws | 50 |
| 1-1/4" screws | 10 |
| Wood glue | |
| Paint | |
| Edge banding or wood filler | |

### ADDITIONS FOR THE CRAFTSMAN VERSION

| ITEM | QTY. |
|------|------|
| 1x2 x 8' paint or stain grade board | 4 |
| 1x3 x 9' paint or stain grade board | 1 |
| 1x4 x 9' paint or stain grade board | 1 |
| 1" brads | |
| 1-1/4" brads | |

### ADDITIONS FOR THE CLASSIC VERSION

| ITEM | QTY. |
|------|------|
| 6' base cap molding | 2 |
| 6' base molding | 2 |

**5** **Add the bottom.** Set the bottom in place and drill pilot holes for the screws. Attach the bottom to the toe space frame with 2-in. screws.

**6** **Attach the top.** Set the top in place. Drill pilot holes and drive screws through the top into the sides and back.

**TIP:**
Tack plywood panels together with finish nails to hold them in place while you drill pilot holes and drive the screws.

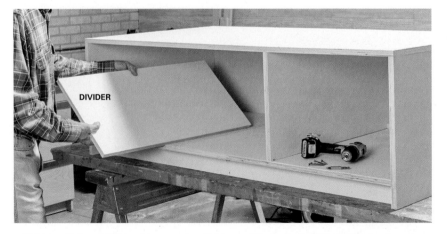

**7** **Install the dividers.** Line up the dividers with the pencil lines (**Photo 4**) and secure them by driving screws through the top and bottom into the dividers.

## Get started by cutting the parts

The first step is cutting the plywood parts to the right size. Follow the **Cutting List** on p. 37 and the **Cutting Diagram** on p. 39. You can get great results with nothing more than a circular saw and a straight-edge guide. With a guide like this, you just make two marks on the plywood for the size of the part you're cutting. Then line up the guide with the marks and clamp it (**Photo 1**). The only trick is to make sure the guide is on the side you want to keep. Then run the saw along the guide's fence to make the cut.

It's quicker and simpler to paint or finish the plywood parts before you assemble them. If you're building the contemporary version, you'll need to cover or fill the raw plywood edges that are exposed. You could apply veneer edge banding to the edges. But if you're going to paint the pedestal, it's easier to simply fill the edge grain with Zinsser Ready Patch or a similar product before painting. Use a small flexible putty knife to trowel the filler onto the edge of the plywood. Let the filler dry. If there are still recessed spots or holes, add a second coat. After the second coat dries, sand the filler smooth. Now you're ready to brush or roll on two coats of paint.

After the paint dries, you can assemble the carcass. Start by screwing the sides to the back (**Photo 2**). Next, build the toe space frame from the four strips of 2-3/4-in.-wide plywood. The frame is sized to allow a 2-in. toe space at the front of the pedestal (contemporary version). Set the frame between the sides and snug it up to the back (**Photo 3**). Drive 1-1/4-in. screws from the inside into the back and sides. Before you install the top and bottom, draw faint pencil lines on the inside faces to indicate the positions of the interior dividers (**Photo 4**).

Since the divider locations are slightly different for the contemporary version, make sure to use the correct dimensions (**Figure D**). On the outside face of the top and bottom, make faint center lines to indicate where screws should be driven. Set the bottom on the toe space frame and attach it with screws (**Photo 5**). Then align the top and drive screws through the top into the sides and back (**Photo 6**). Finish the carcass by lining up the two dividers with your light pencil lines and securing them with screws (**Photo 7**). If you're building the contemporary version, you're done.

**8** **Nail on the trim boards.** Install the trim on the ends of the carcass, starting with the end stiles. Make sure that all of the trim is 3/8 in. below the top surface of the pedestal. Finish by gluing and nailing the trim to the front.

**9** **Glue and nail the nosing.** Cut and fit the 1x2 nosing that runs along the two sides and front of the pedestal. Miter the ends at the corners. Then glue and nail the nosing to the top of the trim.

## Figure E
## Plywood Cutting Diagram

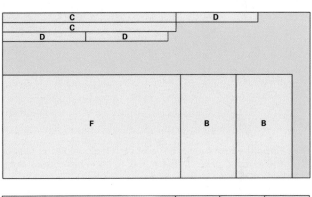

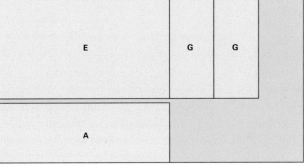

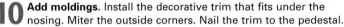

UPSIDE-DOWN
BASE CAP

**10** **Add moldings.** Install the decorative trim that fits under the nosing. Miter the outside corners. Nail the trim to the pedestal.

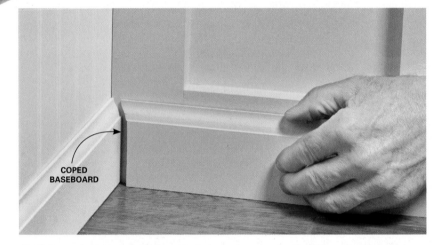

COPED
BASEBOARD

**11** **Cope the baseboard.** For a built-in look, cope the baseboard to fit against the existing base. To learn how to cope baseboard like a pro, search for "coping" at familyhandyman.com.

## DEALING WITH THE DRYER DUCT

Raising your dryer also raises the position of the dryer's exhaust. And that may mean reworking the dryer's exhaust duct. If the current duct enters the wall at least 20 in. from the floor, there's no problem. But if the duct is lower than that, you'll have to raise it. Also, if you want to snug the dryer up to the wall as we did here, you'll need to recess the vent in a dryer vent box. For help with dryer ducting, go to familyhandyman.com and search for "dryer vent install."

Also take a look at the gas and/or electrical lines serving the dryer to make sure they'll accommodate a raised dryer.

## Add a face frame and decorative end panels

Adding 3/4-in.-thick trim boards to the front and sides is all that's required to build the Craftsman version. Set all the trim boards 3/8 in. below the top surface to create a 3/8-in. lip when the top nosing is applied. This lip will help ensure that your washer and dryer don't vibrate off the edge. Use glue and 1-1/4-in. brads to secure the 3/4-in.-thick trim.

Start by installing the end stiles (vertical boards) on the sides. Add the rails (horizontal boards) next, and finish the sides with the two interior stiles. Follow the same sequence to install the front trim (**Photo 8**). Finish this version by gluing and nailing on the 1-1/2-in.-wide nosing (**Photo 9**). We mitered the ends of the nosing, but you could also use square joints and simply fill and paint the exposed end grain.

## Add moldings for a classic look

We chose a base cap molding for under the nosing, and matched the existing baseboard molding for the bottom trim. But you can choose any moldings to fit the style of your room. Miter the ends of the moldings and use 1-in. brads to attach them (**Photo 10**). We wrapped the bottom of the pedestal with standard Princeton-style baseboard to match the baseboard in the room.

**Photo 11** shows how you can cope your new molding to create a tight fit with an existing base molding. For more information on how to cope moldings, go to familyhandyman.com and search for "coping." If your baseboard isn't compatible or you don't care about creating a built-in look, then skip the coping step and just cut a square end on the baseboard.

When you're finished installing the trim and moldings, fill the nail holes. Let the filler dry and sand it smooth. Then brush another coat of paint on the trim and moldings to finish the project.

# NO **CUTTING CORNERS**

## Tips for tight miters and coped joints

**M**iters rarely fit on the first try. More often than not, you'll encounter out-of-square corners, walls that aren't plumb and drywall that has bumps. The secret to making tight-fitting miters is knowing how to adjust your cuts for these real-world conditions. We'll show you tricks you can use to cut door and window casing and baseboard joints to fit perfectly, even when you have less-than-perfect walls and jambs.

## Shim and shave miters

How many times have you set your miter saw exactly on 45 degrees and cut miters on a pair of moldings, only to discover they don't fit? Well, don't worry. There's nothing wrong with your saw or your technique. Miters almost always have to be shaved to fit perfectly.

One method is to simply adjust the angle slightly on your miter saw and recut both moldings. The trouble is that making tiny adjustments to the cutting angle is difficult on many saws. A quicker and easier method is to place a shim against the miter saw fence to slightly change the angle. Move the shim away from the blade for smaller adjustments and closer for larger ones, or vary the thickness of the shim. Remember, both pieces need the exact same cut to fit precisely.

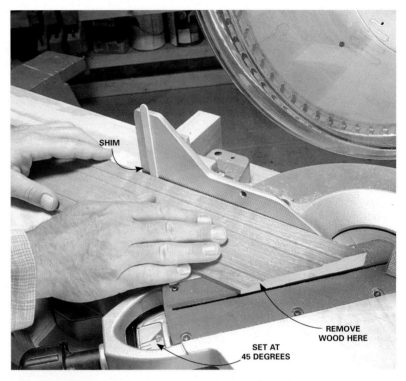

SHIM

REMOVE WOOD HERE

SET AT 45 DEGREES

**1** **Micro-adjust a miter.** Close a gap on the top of a miter by placing a skinny shim (1/16 in. or less) against the portion of the fence farthest from the blade. Slide the molding tight to the shim and against the fence near the blade. Hold it in this position while you make the cut. To close a gap at the bottom of the miter, place the shim near the blade.
**Caution:** Keep your fingers at least 6 in. from the path of the blade.

**2** **Treat both sides the same.** Trim the other half of the miter using the same technique. Use the same shim and place it the same distance from the blade. Drop the blade slowly through the wood to shave thin slices.

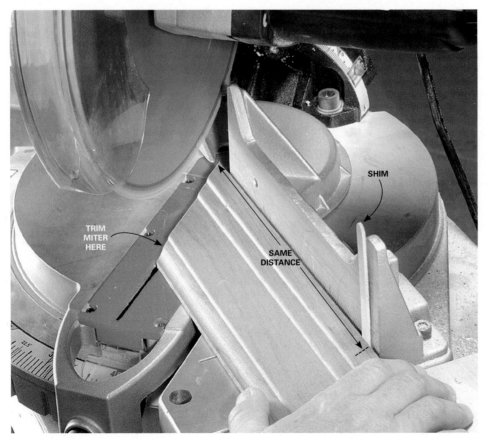

TRIM MITER HERE

SHIM

SAME DISTANCE

## Tilt trim on inset jambs

Occasionally you'll run into a door or window jamb that isn't quite flush with the wall. On a protruding jamb, you can nail the trim to the jamb, slip a shim between the trim and the drywall, and then nail the trim to the wall. Caulk and paint will hide the gap.

An inset jamb demands a different approach. First remove enough drywall so the trim can span the jamb and wall without rocking (**Photo 2**). This solves half the problem. But even now a regular 45-degree miter won't fit because the molding has to tilt down to meet the jamb. Correct this problem by tilting the trim on the bed of the miter box to match the angle at which it rests against the wall. Then make standard 45-degree miter cuts. **Photo 1** shows how to determine the correct thickness for the shim used in **Photo 3** to tilt the molding.

**1** **Custom-cut a shim**. Cut a shim just thick enough to slip under a straightedge spanning the drywall corner. Use this shim to elevate the outside edge of your molding (**Photo 3**) before cutting it.

**2** **Slice the drywall**. Trim back the drywall with a sharp utility knife until the molding no longer rocks when it's set in place against the jamb and drywall. Use a hammer to mash and flatten the drywall if necessary.

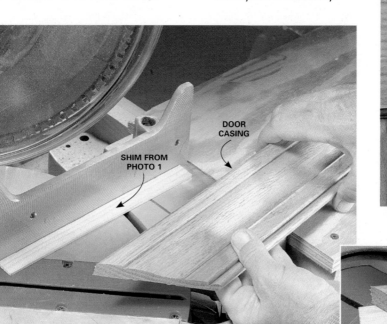

**3** **Tilt the trim with a shim**. Raise the outside edge of the molding with the shim (right) and cut the 45-degree miter. Repeat the process for the opposite miter. If other small adjustments to the angle are needed, follow the tip in **Photo 1**.

## Cope baseboard faster

Coping is better than mitering at inside corners. But on tall baseboards, cutting the long, straight section of the cope with a coping saw is difficult, and the cut is usually wavy. Instead, start the cope as usual (**Photo 1**). Then tip the molding upside down in the miter saw and saw straight down to the profiled section. Finally, complete the cope by sawing out the profile (**Photo 3**).

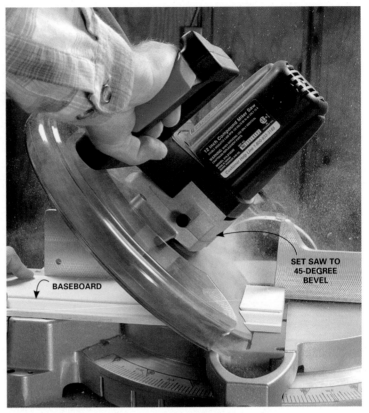

SET SAW TO 45-DEGREE BEVEL

BASEBOARD

**1** **Start with a miter cut.** As with any coped joint, begin by cutting a 45-degree miter on the baseboard. The miter cut provides a profile to guide your cope cut.

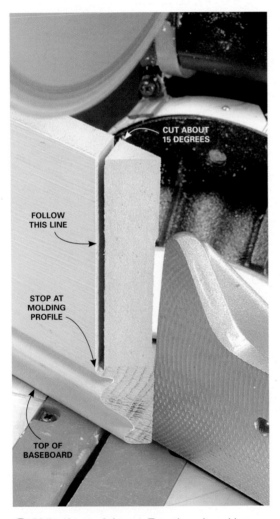

CUT ABOUT 15 DEGREES

FOLLOW THIS LINE

STOP AT MOLDING PROFILE

TOP OF BASEBOARD

**2** **Make the straight cut.** Turn the mitered baseboard upside down. Adjust the angle to about 15 degrees and saw down along the straight section of the beveled cut. Keep the blade slightly to the outside of the line. Let the blade stop before lifting it from the cut.

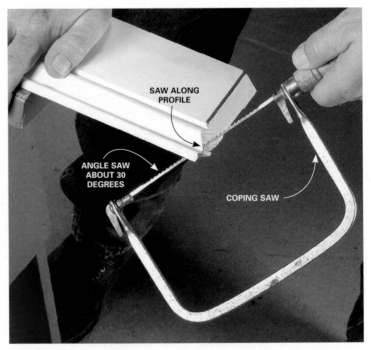

SAW ALONG PROFILE

ANGLE SAW ABOUT 30 DEGREES

COPING SAW

**3** **Cut the curves.** Saw out the remaining profiled section with a coping saw. Tilt the saw to at least a 30-degree angle to create a back bevel for easier fitting.

## Overcut outside corners

Getting outside corners to fit tight is trickier than it looks. The key is to make accurate marks with the baseboard in place rather than relying on measurements. And then cut the piece a little long so you still have the option to shave a little from the angle if it doesn't fit. Since gaps on the back of the corner are barely noticeable, while gaps on the front are glaring, it's a good idea to start by cutting slightly steeper 45-1/2-degree angles first. Then if there's still a gap in the front, cut a slightly steeper angle on both pieces. You'll need a compound miter saw or sliding compound miter saw to easily cut tight-fitting miters on wide baseboard.

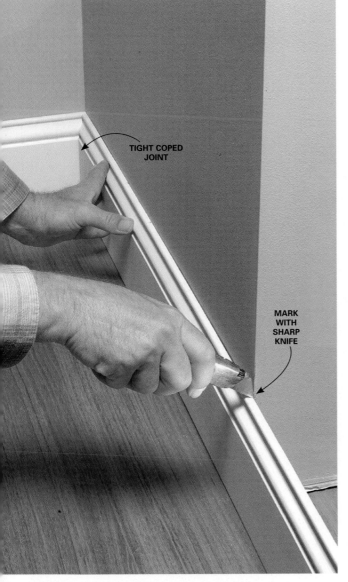

TIGHT COPED JOINT

MARK WITH SHARP KNIFE

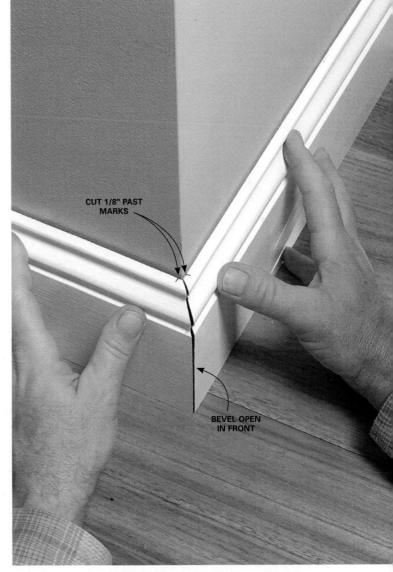

CUT 1/8" PAST MARKS

BEVEL OPEN IN FRONT

**1 Mark with a knife.** Mark outside corners with a sharp utility knife. It's far more precise than a pencil mark. Repeat the marking process on the opposite baseboard. Cut 45-1/2-degree angles on both boards, leaving each an extra 1/8 in. long.

**2 Check the fit.** If the miter is open on the front, increase the cutting angle to about 46 degrees and recut both sides. Be careful to remove only a hair's width from each board. Reduce the angle if the cut is open at the back. When the angle is correct, recut each board just to the outside of the marks before nailing them into place.

## Close gaps at inside corners

Uneven walls or floors that are out of level can cause even perfectly coped inside corners to look lousy. Check the fit of your cope before you nail in either base molding. That way you'll still have the option to shim out the bottom of the square-cut (uncoped) piece to close a gap at the bottom of the cope (**Photo 2**). **Photo 3** shows marking a cope that's open at the top. You then file or plane to the line.

**Gap at bottom**

1-1/4" DRYWALL SCREW

SQUARE-CUT BASE

**2** **Add a screw.** Close a gap at the bottom by removing the square-cut base and driving a drywall screw into the wall about 1/2 in. from the floor. Test the cope and adjust the screw in or out until the cope fits tight.

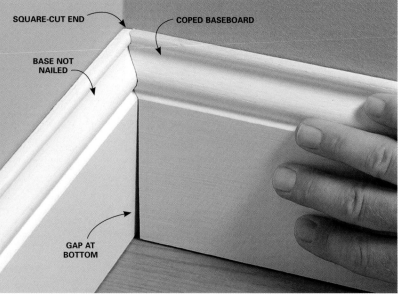

SQUARE-CUT END

COPED BASEBOARD

BASE NOT NAILED

GAP AT BOTTOM

**1** **Check the fit.** Check the fit against the square-cut piece of base before nailing either of the two baseboards. The straight sections rarely fit perfectly.

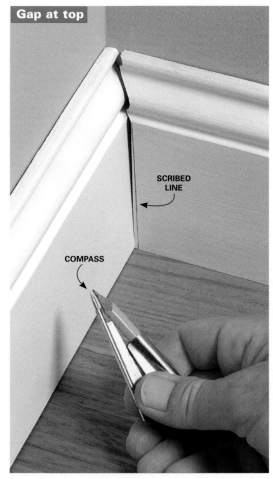

**Gap at top**

SCRIBED LINE

COMPASS

**3** **Scribe and trim.** Close a gap at the top by scribing the gap with a small compass to mark the wood to be removed. Then file to the line.

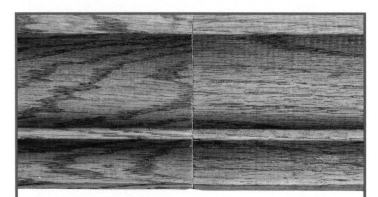

### Avoid Trim Collisions
Here's one of the easiest ways to make your work look better: When sections of trim meet at joints or corners, match the wood tone and grain pattern. It only takes a few seconds, and you'll avoid ugly mismatches like this.

# PLASTER & LATH
## TEAR-OFF

### Do it faster, safer and better

Removing plaster and lath is always an ugly ordeal, but my first try, 25 years ago, was the worst. I made every mistake in the book—mistakes that cost me time, frustration and blood. Since then, I've gotten smarter. Here's what I've learned.

### Prepare for a dust storm

Demolishing plaster and lath is a dusty, filthy job. Wear a dust mask, cover doorways with painter's plastic, turn off the furnace or central air conditioning, and cover HVAC grates.

### MEET AN EXPERT

**Gary Wentz is a carpenter and the editor-in-chief of** *Family Handyman.* **He claims to have torn out more than 2 acres of plaster and lath.**

## Turn off the power!

Old walls hold hazardous surprises like wires without insulation and devices without junction boxes. In one wall I tore out, the wiring was embedded in the plaster! So turn off the circuits inside the wall and check any outlets or switches with a non-contact voltage tester before starting the tear-out.

DIAMOND BLADE

GRINDER

## Cut the plaster

As you break up plaster, cracks can spread to adjoining walls and ceilings. To prevent that, cut the plaster where you want the demolition to stop. I make perimeter cuts with a grinder and a diamond blade. A diamond blade can also cut through metal lath, which was sometimes added over wood lath at corners and archways.

Cutting with a grinder whips up tons of dust. You can also use an oscillating tool equipped with a diamond or carbide-grit blade, which will cut slower but with less mess.

## Cut the lath

After cutting the perimeter of the plaster, cut the wood lath to prevent cracking the adjoining walls and ceilings. An oscillating tool with a round blade is perfect for this.

OSCILLATING TOOL

ROUND BLADE

## Protect the floors

Lath nails and plaster chunks really tear up flooring. The best protection is 1/8-in. hardboard taped together at seams. With wood floors, I use hardboard even if I plan to refinish the floor later. Lath nails can leave deep gouges that are hard to sand out.

## Scrape off the plaster

Chip away a small starter hole with your hammer claw. Then get to scraping. My tool of choice is a bent pole scraper that screws onto a broom handle (mine is a Hyde No. 12070; $15). Some home wreckers prefer an ice scraper or a square shovel. Whatever you use, scrape parallel or diagonal to the lath. If you scrape perpendicular to the lath, your scraper will break through.

POLE SCRAPER

## Scoop up the plaster

Shovel the plaster into buckets or heavy-duty trash bags. If you choose bags, don't fill them too full; plaster is heavy!

## Don't mix plaster and lath

You could tear off plaster and lath at the same time—that's actually a little faster than attacking them separately. But cleaning up a mountain of mixed debris is painfully slow. You can't shovel up the plaster until you fish out all the buried lath, one stick at a time. So tear off the plaster, clean up, and then strip off the lath.

## Yank off the lath

Lath nails come out easily, so you can often pull off two or three rows at a time. I like to use the hook of a wrecking bar. Try to remove full lengths of lath; they're easier to pick up and haul out than a million splintered sticks.

### Does plaster contain asbestos?

Adding fiber to plaster, for extra strength and crack resistance, was standard practice for centuries. The wall shown here contained horsehair. But at least one major plaster manufacturer used asbestos instead, and did so from the 1920s until the '70s. So you can't be sure unless you test. Just search online to find a testing service and send in a sample. You'll get the results in about a week and pay about $60. If the plaster does contain asbestos, check with your local inspector for demolition regulations.

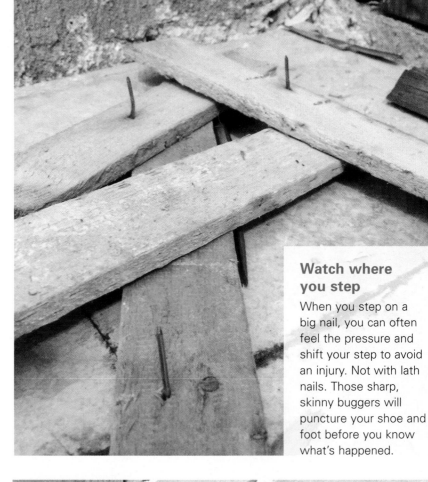

## Watch where you step

When you step on a big nail, you can often feel the pressure and shift your step to avoid an injury. Not with lath nails. Those sharp, skinny buggers will puncture your shoe and foot before you know what's happened.

**Watch the video!**
Go to **familyhandyman.com** and search for "plaster and lath."

## Hit the other side from behind

If you're removing plaster and lath from both sides of a wall, do this: Completely strip one side of the wall, then attack the other side from behind. I like to stab at the lath with a square shovel, right next to studs. As the lath loosens, the plaster breaks away and falls off. After that, the lath is already loosened and pops off with a few more shovel whacks. Karate kicks work too!

**FROM OUR READERS**

### TRASH-BAG DISPENSER

You can build a simple dispenser for your trash bags using 1/2-in. pipe and a few fittings. Screw a floor flange to the cabinet, thread in a 3-in.-long pipe nipple, and then thread a 90-degree elbow onto the nipple. Cut the vertical pipe so it's a bit longer than the width of the roll of bags. Thread the vertical piece into the elbow and slip on the roll.

—Travis Larson

### FLEXIBLE PAPER TOWEL STORAGE

I needed out-of-the-way storage for paper towel rolls. My simple solution uses four eye hooks and two bungee cords. Attach two eye hooks low and two higher up. Stretch the bungee cords from the lower hooks to the upper hooks.

—Mike Davenport

# Handy Hints®

1" BRADS

2" BRADS

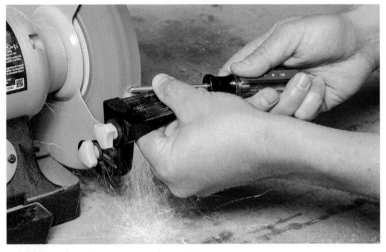

## MAKE YOUR OWN AWL

I like to use an awl to punch small holes in drywall for plastic screw anchors. An awl pushes through easily, resulting in much less dust than drilling. Store-bought awls are usually too small for this task, so I make my own by grinding a sharp tip onto the end of an old, worn-out screwdriver using a disc sander or bench grinder.

—Josh Risberg

## TWO NAIL LENGTHS IN ONE GUN

Small carpentry projects, such as trimming a door, often require a couple different lengths of brad nails. To save time, load the different lengths you'll need into the magazine. When you need to switch, just open up the magazine and put the strip with the correct length of brads first in line. You'll also break fewer strips by loading them all at once. Nail strips tend to break when they're shoved into a pocket or dropped on a hard floor.

—Travis Larson

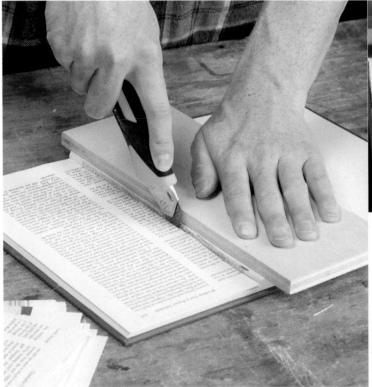

## FIX FOR SAGGING SHELVES

Here's a clever way to keep shelves from sagging. Cut a piece of plywood the height of the space between the shelves and just wide enough to provide support for the shelf. Cut enough pages out of an unwanted book to accommodate the plywood brace. Glue the plywood into the book and tuck it in with your other books, near the center of the shelf.

—Walt Morrison

## SOFA STOPS

Felt pads for furniture feet do a good job of protecting my wood floors, but they turned out to be hard on my walls. After I put the protective pads on my sofa's feet, the sofa slid into the wall every time I sat down, leaving ugly scuff marks. To solve that problem, I screwed two door-stops on the back of the sofa legs at a height that hits the baseboard.

—Dwight Hallock

## EASY-TO-MAKE WINE RACK

If you need more space for wine storage, make this wine rack using pantry shelves and 1x2s. Cut the 1x2s to length to fit the shelf depth and use a router to round over their top edges. Then space the 1x2s about 2 in. apart and screw them to the shelf. Adjust the shelf spacing so there's about 5 in. of clearance for the bottles.

—Robert Lackey

# Handy Hints®

DISC MAGNET

## MEDICINE CABINET MAGNETS

Nail clippers and tweezers tend to get buried in the medicine cabi-net. So I hot-glued a few magnets to the back of the cabinet door to hang these small items in plain sight. I use cheap disc magnets from the hobby store; the more expensive rare-earth magnets are too strong.

—David Farrand

## WRAP TEFLON TAPE IN TIGHT PLACES

Sometimes there's just not enough room to roll Teflon tape around a thread-ed fitting in a wall cavity, under sinks or along the ceiling. So I apply several wraps of tape around a pencil and tear it from the roll. Then I position the pen-cil next to the fitting and start the wind. I hold the starting edge with my fingers and rotate the pencil so it unrolls the tape through the narrow clearance on the other side of the fitting. This tech-nique allows me to keep the tape taut so it applies smoothly.

—Ken Rewinkel

## EASY STORAGE FOR HAIR APPLIANCES

This PVC wye fitting looks like it was designed to store hair appliances! The 4-in. opening is perfect for a hair dryer, and the 2-in. one is just the right size to hold a curling iron or straightener. The fitting is sta-ble enough to sit on a vanity top without tipping. If you don't like the look, either spray-paint it or mount it inside a cabinet with a couple of screws.

—Julie Oellrich

# COLORFUL **KEY STATION**

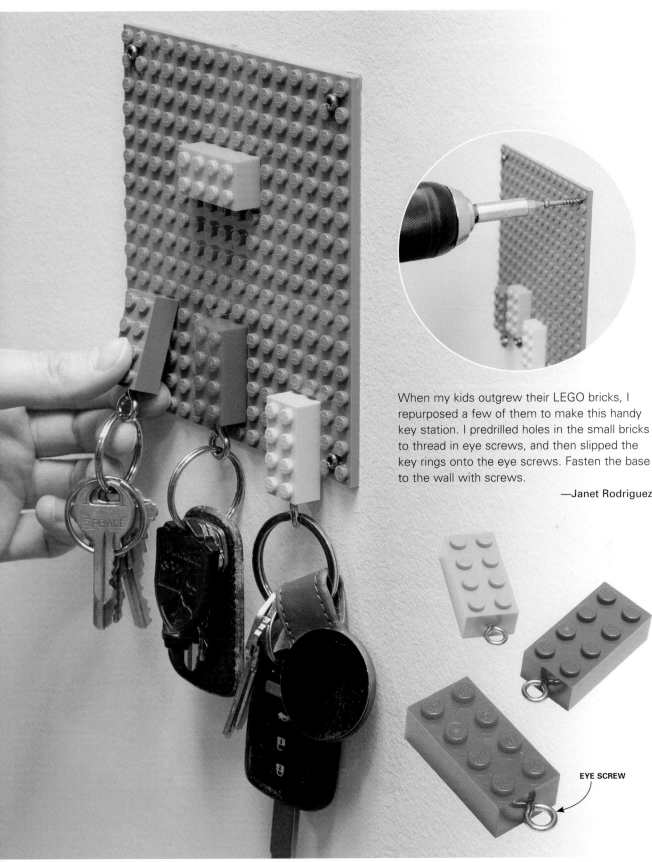

When my kids outgrew their LEGO bricks, I repurposed a few of them to make this handy key station. I predrilled holes in the small bricks to thread in eye screws, and then slipped the key rings onto the eye screws. Fasten the base to the wall with screws.

—Janet Rodriguez

**EYE SCREW**

# HandyHints®

## GUTTER CLEANER

An old plastic spatula makes a great tool for cleaning debris from gutters. It doesn't scratch up the gutter, and you can cut it with snips to fit gutter contours. Grime wipes right off the spatula too, making cleanup a breeze.

## GROCERY BAG SHOE COVERS

When I'm working outside, it never fails that I need to go back into the house for something I've forgotten. But I'm too lazy to take my dirty shoes off, so I keep a stash of plastic grocery bags in the mudroom. I just step into the bags to cover my dirty shoes and tie the handle loops around my ankles. I can go into the house without leaving a trace.

—Lance Wiist

## QUICK FIX FOR MARKER MISTAKES

Who hasn't accidentally written on a white board with a permanent marker? Luckily, it's a snap to remove. Simply write over the permanent marker ink with a dry-erase marker and then wipe with an eraser or a dry cloth. Your dry-erase board will be as good as new!

—Elizabeth Flaherty

PERMANENT MARKER

DRY-ERASE MARKER

## KEEP SHOWER DOORS CLEAN

After a shower, when the beads of water left on your glass door dry, they leave unsightly mineral spots. This dried residue can be tough as nails to remove. You can avoid water beads altogether by coating the glass with an auto-glass treatment. Aquapel and Rain-X are two brands that you'll find at auto parts stores and some discount stores.

## MINI BLIND CLEANING TONGS

Dusting mini blinds is a pain. It's difficult to thoroughly wipe both sides of the slats without bending them in the process. A pair of kitchen tongs makes it a lot easier.

First, cut a rag into two small pieces. Then use twist ties or rubber bands to secure the rags around the tongs. You can close the tongs around each slat and wipe away the dust.

—E. Regaldo

## NO-MESS REFILLS FOR SINK SOAP

Crawling under a kitchen sink to refill the soap dispenser was a hassle, so I tried filling it from above. But when I did, the soap formed an air-lock bubble and overflowed, creating a mess. That's when I came up with the idea of inserting a drinking straw in the bottle to relieve "bubble block." Now when I refill the dispenser, the air escapes through the straw and the soap stays where it belongs.

—Paul Snyder

DRINKING STRAW

## SIMPLIFY BATH CLEANING

Stop using four to six products to clean your bathroom. The pros use one multipurpose cleaner that does it all. Our pros recommend Mr. Clean Multi-Surface Cleaner with Febreze.

# Paint & Stain

## MAKE PAINT LAST

**Painting the exterior of a house takes a lot of time—you won't want to do it again soon! The key to a long-lasting paint job is solid prep work, and here are 17 tips that get the job done.**

**1** **Clean siding and trim**

Dirty surfaces won't hold paint. Remove dirt, mildew, cobwebs and anything else that isn't meant to be there. Do the cleaning in stages. Start by applying a solution of bleach, water and a cleaner such as JOMAX (a bleach activator), using a garden sprayer. Next, remove weathered paint and dirt using a pressure washer. Be careful, as you can easily damage siding and trim with a pressure washer. If you don't feel confident using a pressure washer, a siding cleaner and scrub brush will do the job. Thoroughly rinse to remove any cleaner residue and let the surfaces dry.

## 2 Scrape

After the surfaces have dried completely, scrape off any remaining loose or flaking paint. Applying new paint over flaking paint will cause it to peel far sooner than it should. Before scraping, pound in any nail heads that could nick your scraper blade. You can buy a hardened steel scraper ($5 to $10), or for about twice the price, you can buy a carbide scraper. Carbide holds an edge far longer than hardened steel. With either option, buy a couple replacement blades so you don't have to sharpen as often. You can sharpen a carbide blade using a diamond stone.

**FOUR-SIDED HARDENED STEEL SCRAPER BLADE**

**TWO-SIDED CARBIDE SCRAPER BLADE**

## 3 Remove old caulk

While you're scraping, check the caulking around windows, doors and trim. If the caulk is in good shape and still adhering, leave it in place. If not, dig it out with a 5-in-1 tool (shown), utility knife or putty knife.

## 4 Sand off ridges

After scraping, sand any sharp paint edges, blending them with the surrounding surface. If you don't blend them in, the sharp edges will create thin, weak areas in the new paint. Brush away any dust created by sanding, and then rinse the siding and trim thoroughly.

## 5 Ease sharp edges

Sharp wood edges won't hold paint; there just isn't enough surface area. If you install any new wood, be sure to give any sharp edges a slight round-over. It doesn't take much; a single pass with a sanding block is usually sufficient.

EXTERIOR PUTTY

## 6 Repair damaged surfaces

Don't paint over rotten or insect-damaged wood. Even if it covers, the paint won't last. Replace or repair any damaged wood. Fill nail holes and other small imperfections with exterior wood putty. Sand off excess putty after it's dry.

# Paint & Stain

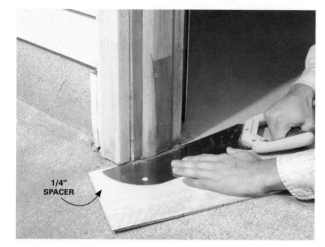

**7** Create a gap between trim and concrete

Boards that abut concrete won't hold paint for long. Water on the concrete wicks up into the wood, loosening the bond between the wood and the paint. To remedy this, trim any wood so that it's about 1/4 in. above concrete.

**9** Keep vegetation trimmed

Plants that come into contact with your exterior walls hold moisture against the paint, which can lead to compromised paint and rotting wood. That means more repair work, more money and more frequent painting.

**8** Keep space between trim & shingles

If trim or siding contacts the shingles, water will wick into the wood and the paint won't last. Lay a 3/4-in.-thick spacer on the shingles and cut any trim or siding to create a gap between the wood and the shingles.

**10** Caulk all cracks & gaps

Caulk around windows, doors, trim and anywhere else water could get behind a painted surface. Use interior/exterior paintable latex caulk. Be sure to prime first; primer adheres to bare or slightly dirty surfaces much better than caulk.

**11** Don't forget the threshold

The bottom of a wood doorjamb will rot prematurely if you don't caulk the line where the threshold meets the jamb.

## 12 Seal end grain

When you install or expose new wood, seal any end grain with a paintable water repellent, such as Woodlife Classic clear wood preservative. Allow the repellent to dry according to the directions, then prime and paint.

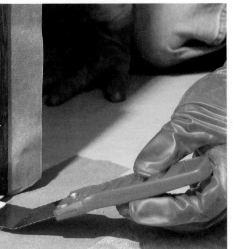

## 13 Don't stall on painting

Primer loses its bonding properties with prolonged exposure to UV light. After priming, you have a window of time to apply paint. Check the label on your can, as the amount of time can vary among manufacturers. We checked with two major companies. One said that paint must be applied within one week; the other said anywhere from four to six weeks.

## 14 Wait for good painting weather

Avoid painting on hot days, in direct sun and in windy weather. Ideal temperatures for painting are between 50 and 90 degrees F. Temperatures below 50 degrees can prevent the paint from adhering to the surface properly. Hot weather, wind and direct sun all

cause paint to dry too quickly, preventing adequate penetration of the primer and/or paint. It can also cause oil paint to blister. When possible, work in the shade, following the path of the sun throughout the day. Never paint when rain is imminent or right after it rains. Painting a damp surface can cause paint to bubble.

## 16 Keep an eye on your paint job

Whenever you're out doing yard work, check in on your paint. Look closely for areas of cracked or peeling paint, or wood that might be rotting. With a little spot maintenance, you can extend the life of your paint job by a few years.

## 15 Spot-prime

Prime nail heads, putty and knots before priming the whole surface. These areas are more difficult to cover, so they need a little extra attention.

## 17 Prime all bare wood

You can get good results with oil or latex primer. For bare woods with a high tannin (a dark, natural pigment) content, such as cedar and redwood, use a stain-blocking exterior primer. Stain-blocking primers prevent "bleedthrough" of tannin as well as stains from old, rusty nails.

SPECIAL SECTION
PAINT & STAIN

# Paint & Stain

## HAVE STAINS MATCHED AT THE PAINT STORE

I've refinished a number of furniture pieces and wood trim when matching an existing stain was important. I've had far better luck getting stains matched by the staff at the paint store than I've had trying to mix colors off the shelf myself. Just bring in a sample piece to be matched. Keep in mind that stain can look different on different pieces of wood. So if you're doing trim, for example, don't just bring in the piece that's easiest to remove; choose a sample piece that has the color and tone you want. You'll also need to bring in an unfinished test board of the same species and with the same grain characteristics as those of the piece you're trying to match.

—Brad Holden

TEST BOARD

SAMPLE

## STRAIN OUT THE GOOBERS

A half-full can of paint that sits around for a few days will develop gooey chunks and strands of partially dried paint that can ruin your results. To filter them out, buy a pack of paint strainers. These cheap mesh bags catch the goobers and purify the paint. Fussy painters use them even on paint that's fresh off the store shelf.

WATERPROOF COATING

STRAINER

## DO WATERPROOF COATINGS WORK?

The short answer is yes. We've used waterproof coatings in basements with great results. But careful prep work is critical; the coating can't stop water unless it can bond solidly to masonry. And we always recommend that you first regrade the landscape and add or upgrade downspouts and gutters. For more info, search for "wet basement" at familyhandyman.com.

C-CLAMP

## C-CLAMP HANDLES

Quart-size paint cans don't have handles, but they'd be so much easier to use if they did. Here's my solution: Attach a C-clamp to the can. It actually works better than a bail because it's out of the way for dipping the brush, and it keeps the can from swinging. Your clamp will get paint on it, but cleaning it up is easy.

—Mike Watt

# Paint & Stain

## DON'T OPEN PAINT CANS WITH A SCREWDRIVER

Sure, a screwdriver works, but it leaves dents in the seal. And that leads to gooey chunks in the paint. Pick up a paint can opener when you buy the paint.

## PAINTBRUSH PROTECTORS

After thoroughly washing and air-drying my brushes, I wrap them with the same painter's plastic that I use to mask off trim and protect the floors. The tape on the edge sticks to the metal ferrule, and the plastic is the perfect length to cover the bristles and help maintain their shape.

—Joe Martin

ScotchBlue
Brand/Marque/Marca

MULTI-SURFACE | SUPERFICIES MULTIPLES |

with/con/avec
Edge-Lock™
Paint Line Protector
Protector de líneas de pintura
Système de protection des bordures

PRE-TAPED PAINTER'S PLASTIC WITH DISPENSER
Unfolds to 24 in/po to protect against paint splatters and drips
Clean removal for up to 14 days

PLÁSTICO PRE-ENCINTADO PARA PINTORES CON DISPENSADOR
Se extiende a 24", 60 cm para proteger

24 in/po
60.9 cm

## ROLLER SPINNER

To spin-dry a mini roller, chuck a 1/4-in. bit into your drill. Slip the roller onto the bit and pull the trigger. Centrifugal force whips the water right out. I recommend doing this in a bucket, utility sink or outdoors.

—Spike Carlsen

# Paint & Stain

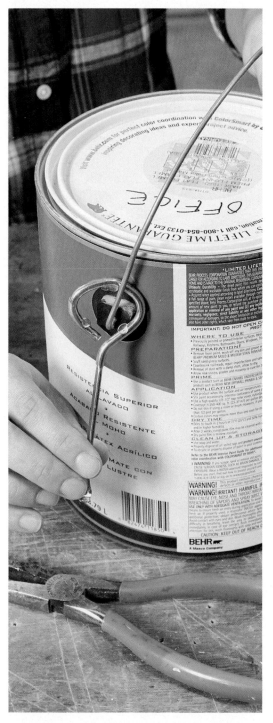

## TIDY PAINT-CAN CLOSING

After you pour paint from a can, some paint always ends up in the can's rim. When you tap the lid back on, paint splatters everywhere. To avoid this, throw a rag over the lid before tapping it shut. Also, use a block of wood that spans the lid so you don't deform the can or lid with the hammer. Just tap the block a couple of times, give it a quarter turn and tap again.

—Jerome Coffel

## LET IT REST IN PEACE

My son and I painted our rowboat perfectly. For faster drying, I turned on a fan—and blew dust all over it, creating thousands of tiny "dust whiskers." There are lots of ways to destroy a finish with dust before it dries: opening the garage door, running a shop vacuum, sweeping the floor… I'm sure you can invent your own method. Or you could just walk away and let it dry in peace.

—Mark Hawley, *Family Handyman* Field Editor

## HANDY PAINT-CAN OPENER

Every time I bought paint, I got a free paint-can opener, but I still could never find one when I needed it. Now, I grab a pair of pliers and open the loop on the handle just enough to slip it around the bail. No more hunting for openers—all my paint cans have one attached.

—Ray Alvarez

# 2 Electrical and High-Tech

BIEHLER MICHAEL/SHUTTERSTOCK

## IN THIS CHAPTER

**Home Care & Repair** ..................................68
*9 Simple Tips for Faster Wi-Fi,*
*Add Solar Power to Your Shed,*
*An Electrical Panel Myth and more*

**Electrical Cable Basics** .............................77

# HomeCare&Repair

**TIPS, FIXES & GEAR FOR A TROUBLE-FREE HOME**

## ADD SOLAR POWER
## TO YOUR SHED

**Do** you have a shed or other outbuilding that could use light and/or power? In many cases, running an underground cable from your house to the building is the most economical way to go. But if the building is a fair distance from the house, so that wiring it would be a hassle or a large expense, consider a solar-powered system.

If you just need some light for putting away yard tools, you can get by with a simple system costing $100 or less. But if you want AC power for tools or charging batteries, you'll need to spend more than $3,000 for a high-end system.

**MEET AN EXPERT**

Chris Pesce is a solar systems designer for earthtechproducts.com, a large online solar kit component seller.

## Solar kits eliminate guesswork

You can cobble together your own system with individual parts, but that can be dicey. Matching the right collectors, charge controller and battery takes some know-how. If you want AC power, you'll also need an inverter that converts DC voltage to AC for outlets. All those components must be compatible and work together flawlessly or you'll have big issues. Plus, the components have to be suited to the climate you live in. Some can handle extreme heat, cold or dampness while others can't. So unless you just want occasional short-term lighting, we recommend buying a kit.

You can find local or online companies by searching for "solar kits." Most companies will help you pick a kit or design one for you to exactly suit your needs. Shopping locally can save you big on shipping; this stuff is bulky and heavy. The kits listed below are from earth-techproducts.com.

You'll find many low-priced solar shed kits, and most of them work fine—for a while. But cheap kits often fail in about a year. So check the manufacturer's warranty and replacement terms before you buy, and try to find online reviews from long-term owners.

### WHAT YOU GET IN A KIT

If you need brighter or longer-lasting light, you'll have to spend upwards of $2,000. That will give you a 4-ft., 1,600-lumen light that will work for up to two days without recharging.

Want an outlet? For about $3,000, you can purchase a kit that has greater battery storage capacity and an inverter that will provide AC power suitable for recharging tool batteries and powering small electric tools.

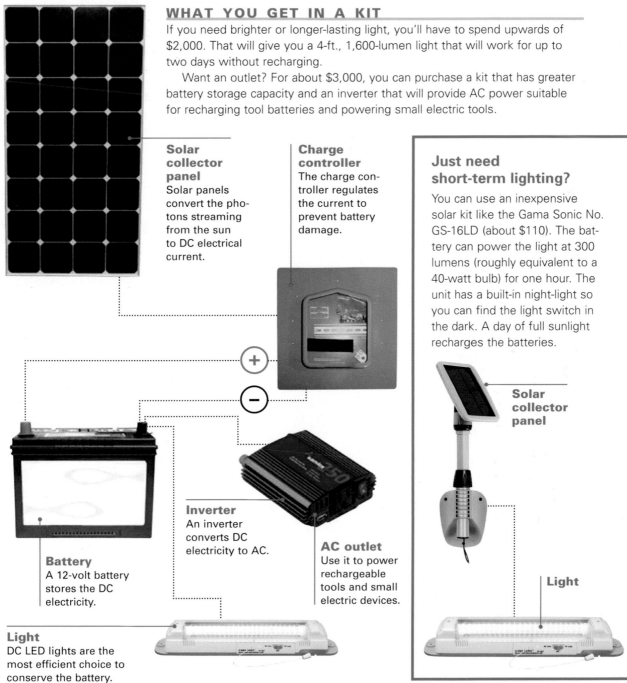

**Solar collector panel**
Solar panels convert the photons streaming from the sun to DC electrical current.

**Charge controller**
The charge controller regulates the current to prevent battery damage.

**Battery**
A 12-volt battery stores the DC electricity.

**Inverter**
An inverter converts DC electricity to AC.

**AC outlet**
Use it to power rechargeable tools and small electric devices.

**Light**
DC LED lights are the most efficient choice to conserve the battery.

### Just need short-term lighting?

You can use an inexpensive solar kit like the Gama Sonic No. GS-16LD (about $110). The battery can power the light at 300 lumens (roughly equivalent to a 40-watt bulb) for one hour. The unit has a built-in night-light so you can find the light switch in the dark. A day of full sunlight recharges the batteries.

**Solar collector panel**

**Light**

# HomeCare&Repair

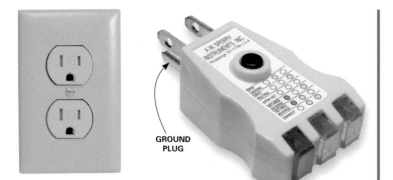

GROUND
PLUG

## GROUND PLUG UP OR DOWN?

Whether to install an outlet with the ground plug on the top or bottom is an age-old debate, but it doesn't matter either way. However, one reader had this to say: "Receptacle testers are meant to be used with the ground prong on the bottom. You can see the lights either way, but you can only read the printed information with the ground plug on the bottom. So if for no other reason than making receptacle testers easier to read, outlets should be installed ground down."

With that settled, let's get to the more serious controversy. Should toilet paper rolls dispense from over the top or underneath?

## GET THE RIGHT LED
## FOR YOUR FIXTURE

Most LED bulbs need good airflow around them because heat buildup can greatly shorten their life span. That's why most LEDs aren't rated for enclosed fixtures. Any fixture with less than 1/2 in. of clearance around the bulb's circumference is considered an enclosed fixture, even if it has an opening. So be sure you buy LED bulbs rated for use in an enclosed fixture. You'll find the rating on the package. Available at home centers, these bulbs cost about the same as other LED bulbs.

ENCLOSED-
FIXTURE
SYMBOL

## ALUMINUM WIRING
## CAN BE HAZARDOUS

If you have aluminum wiring in your house, you might have a fire waiting to happen. Many houses built between 1965 and 1972 were wired with aluminum instead of copper. The wiring itself isn't a problem; aluminum conducts electricity safely. The trouble is at the connections. The U.S. Consumer Product Safety Commission (CPSC) reports that homes with aluminum wiring are 55 times more likely to have "fire hazard conditions" than homes wired with copper.

ALUMINUM
WIRING

## Fix the problem

Completely rewiring your home isn't practical in most situations—it means tearing into walls and ceilings. But an electrician can make the connections safe by adding a short section of copper wire to the end of each aluminum wire. That way, copper rather than aluminum will be connected to each switch, outlet or other device.

COPALUM connectors are preferred by the CPSC, but they require a trained contractor and a special tool. AlumiConn is another brand that can be purchased from online suppliers. These connectors can be installed by any trained electrician but may require that existing junction boxes be replaced with larger ones to make room for the connectors.

ALUMICONN
CONNECTOR

ALUMICONN

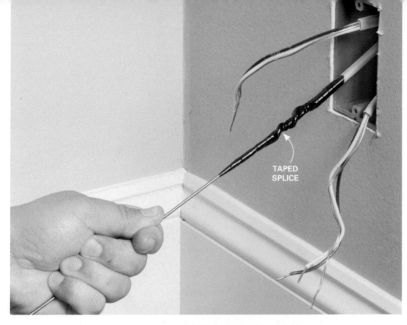

TAPED SPLICE

## TWO WIRE-SPLICING METHODS

I use a coat hanger to fish electrical cable through walls, and for longer runs, bare copper wire.

Cut your cable at an angle so its end is tapered instead of blunt. Leave the wire nearest the point of the angle cut about 3 in. longer than the other two wires. Straighten the coat hanger and make a small loop at the end.

Feed the wire through the loop and wrap it around the coat hanger. Start your tape wrap on the cable, above the splice. Tightly wrap the tape spirally until you've wrapped down onto the coat hanger. Each consecutive wrap overlaps the previous one, reducing the possibility that a tape edge will snag on something when you're pulling it past obstructions.

Copper wire isn't as stiff as a coat hanger, so it's likely to pull free of the coat hanger–style splice. If you're using a bare copper wire as your fishing tool, use a Western Union splice. Start with two L's, then wrap each wire around the other without looping them back on themselves. The taping step is the same for both methods.

—Al Hildenbrand, Master Electrician

### ① Coat Hanger Splice

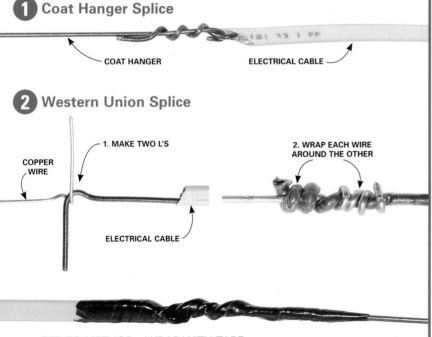

COAT HANGER

ELECTRICAL CABLE

### ② Western Union Splice

COPPER WIRE

1. MAKE TWO L'S

2. WRAP EACH WIRE AROUND THE OTHER

ELECTRICAL CABLE

EITHER METHOD—WRAP WITH TAPE

## WHAT SIZE IS THAT WIRING, ANYWAY?

If you're adding an outlet, you need to use wire the same gauge as the existing wiring. How do you tell if your old wiring is 12-gauge or 14-gauge?

Here's a simple visual. Twelve-gauge is about the thickness of a nickel, and 14-gauge is about the thickness of a dime. Also, look at the breaker for the circuit in question to see if it's a 15-amp or a 20-amp breaker. A 20-amp circuit requires wire that's 12-gauge or larger.

14-GAUGE

12-GAUGE

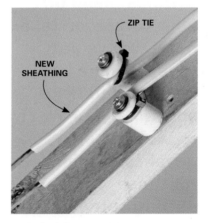

ZIP TIE

NEW SHEATHING

## KNOB-AND-TUBE INSULATION FIX

The insulation on knob-and-tube wiring gets brittle with age. When you're working with it, the insulation may just crumble in your hands. You can easily reinsulate a section using a length of the plastic jacket from a piece of nonmetallic sheathed cable (often referred to as Romex).

## 9 SIMPLE TIPS FOR FASTER WI-FI

Spinning pinwheels and slow status bars got you down? Keeping current with the latest technology is usually the fix, but if you're the kind of person who'd rather change a set of brake pads than open the settings menu on your computer, take heart. We've put together nine low-tech fixes to help speed up your Wi-Fi, as well as some advanced options for those who enjoy getting software dirt under their fingernails.

**1** **Move your router**
- **Place your router in a central location.** As you consider a central location, think top to bottom as well as side to side.
- **Put your router up high in the room.** That way, it's above obstructions.

- **Keep your router away from other appliances.** For example, an inexpensive, poorly shielded microwave can cause a lot of Wi-Fi interference.
- **Don't enclose your router.** A Wi-Fi router isn't a thing of beauty, but tucking it in an enclosed space will degrade the signal and possibly cause it to overheat.
- **Imagine the physical barriers that can block the signal.** Hidden chimneys, brick walls and utility rooms with lots of metal between you and the router can greatly affect signal strength.

## Restart your router regularly

Some router firmware is a little buggy, and over time it gets slow. A simple restart often brings it right back up to speed. Unplug your router, wait 30 seconds and then plug it back in.

Some routers can be configured to restart at regular intervals. Look in your owner's manual to see if your router has this feature and how to access it. Alternatively, you can just make a note to restart your router once a week.

**WIRELESS ADAPTER**

ELECTRICAL & HIGH-TECH

## Get a new router

Check your router's WLAN (Wireless Local Area Network) standard. It will consist of the number 802.11 followed by a letter or letters. You'll find this information in the owner's manual. If you don't have the owner's manual, download it by searching your router's make and model online.

- **802.11b and 802.11g.** These are the oldest and slowest versions, with a maximum speed of 54 Mbps (megabits per second).
- **802.11n.** This is a newer version with a maximum speed of 300 Mbps.
- **802.11ac.** This is the latest version, offering speeds of up to 1 Gbps (gigabits per second).
- **802.11ac MU-MIMO** (Multi-User Multiple Input Multiple Output) router. MU-MIMO routers send and receive multiple data streams simultaneously to multiple devices without speed drop-off.

If you have an older version, consider an upgrade. If you're renting your router and modem, it makes sense financially to purchase a router. You can get a good one for about $100. Plus, the firmware on rental units is often inferior.

## Give your computer a boost

If you upgrade your router but your computer is more than two or three years old, its wireless adapter may not be compatible with your speedy new router.

To reap the benefits of an 802.11ac router on an old computer, look into a USB 802.11ac wireless adapter. Just slip the adapter into a USB port on your computer and enter your router's password when prompted. These adapters are available at big box stores and online for $20 to $100.

## Buy a wireless range extender

Routers broadcast pretty well up to about 150 ft., beyond which the signal gets weak. But this depends on your walls and other obstructions. For a large area, or if you have thick walls, you can buy a wireless range extender to boost your signal. Range extenders pick up the signal from your router and rebroadcast it.

Like your router, a range extender should be elevated and in the open. Be sure the extender you purchase is compatible with your router's WLAN standard.

A range extender has the advantage of being able to connect to your current system. The downside is that the rebroadcast signal is only about half the bandwidth of your router. Range extenders cost anywhere from $20 to $125.

**INTERNET**

### How it works
A wireless range extender picks up the signal from the router and rebroadcasts it, giving you better coverage for your whole house.

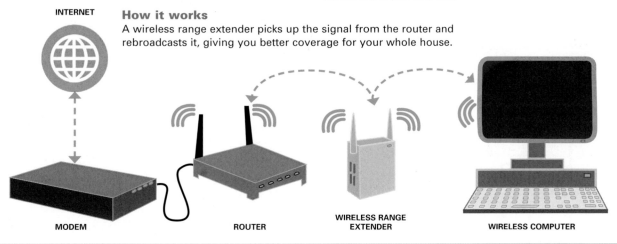

MODEM    ROUTER    WIRELESS RANGE EXTENDER    WIRELESS COMPUTER

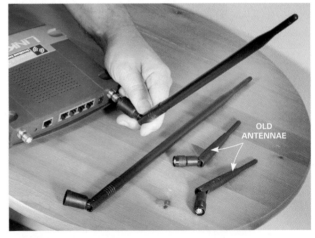

# HomeCare&Repair

Enter http://linksysSmartWiFi.com in a web br...
to complete your router setup.
You also can type 192.168.1.1 in a browser to start setup.

...SmartWiFi.c...
...outer setup.
...ype 192.168.1.1 in...

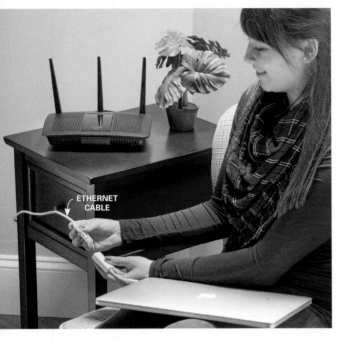

ETHERNET CABLE

## 6 Plug in when you can

A router can only handle so many devices and their competing Wi-Fi signals. If you treat your Wi-Fi as a resource and connect to it sparingly, you'll have plenty of bandwidth available for when you do use it. Whenever you're working near your router, plug into it using an ethernet cable. This frees up more bandwidth for other Wi-Fi devices.

## 7 Switch to 5GHz, maybe

If you have a dual-band router, try switching from the more common 2.4GHz band to the 5GHz band. 5GHz is faster and less congested, but it doesn't have the same range and wall penetration as 2.4GHz.

To make this switch, you'll need to find your router's IP address. It'll be a long number starting with 192, 172 or 10, located either on your router or in your owner's manual. Enter this IP address into your browser's address bar and hit return. That'll take you to your router admin page. Click on the wireless settings tab, and you'll see where to switch from one band to the other.

## 8 Buy a "mesh" Wi-Fi system

A "mesh" or "whole-home" Wi-Fi system is designed to provide coverage to your entire house. These systems come with a main router that connects to your modem, and several hubs that you place throughout your house. A Wi-Fi system is similar to a range extender in giving coverage to hard-to-reach areas. Unlike a range extender, however, a Wi-Fi system gives full Wi-Fi signal at each hub. Also, you can't add the system to your current router. Expect to pay $130 to $500 for a system.

### How it works
C=COMPUTER
H=HUB
M=MODEM
R=ROUTER

The signal is picked up from the router, giving full Wi-Fi signal at each hub.

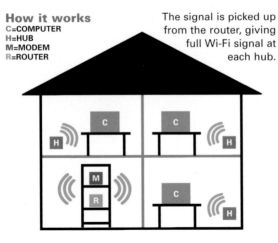

OLD ANTENNAE

## 9 Add a stronger antenna

The antennae that come with your router might not be strong enough to cover your house, leaving some rooms with a weak signal. Add a "high-gain" external antenna to boost your signal and better cover your whole house. You can purchase one online for less than $20.

To find out if your house has weak signal areas, turn on your phone's Wi-Fi and walk around the house, watching the Wi-Fi signal. There are also mobile apps, such as Netgear's WiFi Analytics, to help you find where your coverage is weak or strong. HeatMapper and inSSIDer Office are two other tools used to map your signal.

## FASTER WI-FI: ADVANCED OPTIONS

Here are a few tips that'll likely require you to do a bit of research online and in your owner's manual to figure out how to make them work for your setup.

### Update router firmware
Router manufacturers regularly update their software to improve performance and speed. Update your firmware even if your Wi-Fi speed is fine, as you'll get updated security and features.

### Update computer software
A computer has a Wi-Fi network adapter, which runs on driver software. Be sure your computer is up to date and has all the latest drivers from the manufacturer installed.

### Dual frequency routers
Some routers can operate in 2.4GHz and 5GHz at the same time. Some of these routers automatically choose which frequency is best for a given situation. For example, when you're far away from your router, it'll choose 2.4GHz, but when you're closer, it'll opt for the faster 5GHz.

### Find a clear channel
Most people use their router's default channel, but if nearby wireless networks are on the same channel, you'll get signal congestion. Go into your wireless settings and switch your router to broadcast on a less congested channel. Some routers do this automatically.

### Set Priorities
Most modern routers have Quality of Service (QoS) tools to limit the amount of bandwidth that apps use. Enter your router's IP address into your browser address bar to access your wireless settings. You can prioritize which apps and devices get the highest speed.

### Use a VPN (Virtual Private Network)
If some websites are faster than others, try a VPN. VPN is an online service offered by several providers for a small monthly fee, allowing you to create a secure connection to another network over the Internet. With a VPN, all your traffic is encrypted and appears as if it's originating from another location.

### Dual WAN (Wide Area Network)
Many midrange to high-end routers offer a "Dual WAN" option, which allows you to connect multiple ISPs and configure them for use in different scenarios. You can set up your router to operate in one of two modes:
- **Failover mode.** Your router automatically switches to the second ISP only when the primary connection goes down. It's typically used when the second connection charges for data usage (like cell adapters).
- **Load Balance mode.** This uses both ISPs at once, sharing the load. Single large-file downloads won't be faster, but this mode improves overall when many people are using the internet at once.

### Create another access point
Run an ethernet wire to a different location in your house and set up another router with the same SSID and password. Devices will automatically connect to the stronger signal.

### Install DD-WRT
DD-WRT is an open-source custom wireless firmware, created and maintained by people other than the router manufacturer. Many manufacturers now offer routers with DD-WRT already installed, but you can download it and install it yourself on a wide variety of routers. DD-WRT can improve performance and provide access to more advanced networking features.

## MEET AN EXPERT

Andy LeTourneau is a senior software engineer at Clockwork Active Media Systems in Minneapolis.

ELECTRICAL & HIGH-TECH

## AN ELECTRICAL PANEL MYTH
We stumbled onto an online discussion in which a homeowner claimed his monthly electric bill dropped 30 percent after he installed a new circuit breaker panel. This seemed unlikely, so we contacted master electrician and inspector John Williamson to get his take.

"In theory, simply installing a new electrical panel wouldn't result in any energy savings because an electrical panel doesn't normally impose a load on the electrical system," says John. "The panel itself doesn't consume power. That said, I suppose an old panel could be in bad condition, with many loose or corroded connections, which may cause a resistance to current flow and create wasted power in the form of heat. But a 30 percent reduction in one's electrical bill doesn't seem plausible."

# HomeCare&Repair

BIEHLER MICHAEL/SHUTTERSTOCK

DAVID CARILLET/SHUTTERSTOCK

## RECYCLING YOUR COMPUTER?
## DESTROY YOUR HARD DRIVE

Before you scrap your old computer, it's smart to phys-
ically damage the hard drive. It probably holds recover-
able personal information, even if it has been "erased."
You can obliterate the drive with an angle grinder as
shown above, but all you really need to do is scratch,
dent and batter the disk. A screwdriver and hammer
will do the job. Removing the drive from the computer
is a bit trickier and varies by model. For help with that,
search online by typing in your computer model together
with "remove hard drive."

—Elizabeth Flaherty

# ELECTRICAL CABLE BASICS

## Home wiring demystified

By **Brad Holden**

ELECTRICAL &
HIGH-TECH

**B**efore you take on your next home wiring project, arm yourself with basic information about the electrical cable or wiring you're likely to see. The wire and cable aisle at your home center can be a pretty confusing place. In this article, you'll learn how to identify different cable types and their use, and how to determine the size of individual wires and their purpose. You'll be able to cut through the confusion, get exactly what you need and ensure that your wiring is safe.

## Cable vs. Wire

People often use these terms interchangeably, but there's a difference: Cable is an assembly of two or more wires in a single jacket. Wires are the individual insulated or bare conductors inside the jacket.

## Wire Gauge

Wires come in different sizes/gauges to work with the amperage of the circuit in which they're used. It's counterintuitive, but the larger the number, the smaller the wire. The most common sizes you'll find in residential work are 14-gauge and 12-gauge. Larger appliances such as electric stoves, electric water heaters, electric dryers and central air units will often use 10-, 8- or even 6-gauge wire.

## Cable by the Numbers

An electrical cable is classified by two numbers separated by a hyphen, such as 14-2. The first number denotes the conductor's gauge; the second denotes the number of conductors inside the cable. For instance, 14-2 has two 14-gauge conductors: a hot and a neutral. This cable also contains a bare copper wire as the ground. Individual conductors are also color-coded, which tells you their purpose in the circuit.

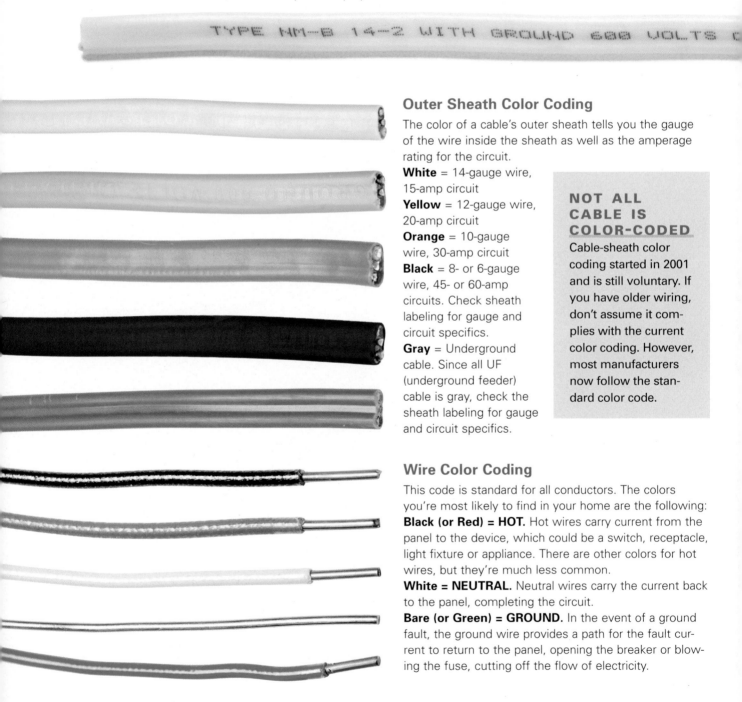

TYPE NM-B 14-2 WITH GROUND 600 VOLTS

## Outer Sheath Color Coding

The color of a cable's outer sheath tells you the gauge of the wire inside the sheath as well as the amperage rating for the circuit.

**White** = 14-gauge wire, 15-amp circuit

**Yellow** = 12-gauge wire, 20-amp circuit

**Orange** = 10-gauge wire, 30-amp circuit

**Black** = 8- or 6-gauge wire, 45- or 60-amp circuits. Check sheath labeling for gauge and circuit specifics.

**Gray** = Underground cable. Since all UF (underground feeder) cable is gray, check the sheath labeling for gauge and circuit specifics.

### NOT ALL CABLE IS COLOR-CODED

Cable-sheath color coding started in 2001 and is still voluntary. If you have older wiring, don't assume it complies with the current color coding. However, most manufacturers now follow the standard color code.

## Wire Color Coding

This code is standard for all conductors. The colors you're most likely to find in your home are the following:

**Black (or Red) = HOT.** Hot wires carry current from the panel to the device, which could be a switch, receptacle, light fixture or appliance. There are other colors for hot wires, but they're much less common.

**White = NEUTRAL.** Neutral wires carry the current back to the panel, completing the circuit.

**Bare (or Green) = GROUND.** In the event of a ground fault, the ground wire provides a path for the fault current to return to the panel, opening the breaker or blowing the fuse, cutting off the flow of electricity.

## NM-B — Nonmetallic Cable

This is the most common type of electrical cable in homes
built since the mid-'60s. "Nonmetallic" simply means
that the outer jacket is not metal. It's often referred to as
Romex, which is a brand name. Typically, NM-B cable has
either two conductors and a ground, or three conductors
and a ground. The conductors are individually insulated,
wrapped in paper and sheathed in plastic. Ground wires
are either bare copper or insulated in green.

**14-2** Used for general lighting and receptacle circuits.
15-amp circuit maximum.

**14-3** Used for three-way switches and split receptacle
circuits. 15-amp circuit maximum.

**12-2** Used for 20-amp kitchen, bathroom, laundry and garage
receptacles; 230-volt heating circuits up to 3,700 watts; and
115-volt circuits up to 1,800 watts. Can be used anywhere
in place of 14-2.

**12-3** Same uses as 12-2, with the addition of three-way
switches and split receptacle circuits.

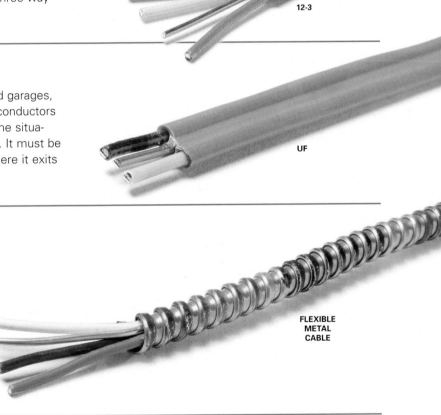

14-2

14-3

12-2

12-3

ELECTRICAL &
HIGH-TECH

## UF — Underground Feeder Cable

UF is used primarily to bring power to detached garages,
outbuildings or outdoor lighting. The insulated conductors
are molded into the sheathing. Depending on the situation, UF is either direct-buried or run in conduit. It must be
protected from physical damage by conduit where it exits
the ground and is exposed.

UF

## Flexible Metal Cable

Flexible metal cable is common in
unfinished areas where the cable would
otherwise be exposed and subject to
physical damage. It's also sometimes
used inside walls. A bare aluminum
wire is in continuous contact within the
metal sheathing. The combination of
aluminum wire, sheathing and metal
boxes grounds the circuit.

FLEXIBLE
METAL
CABLE

## Stranded Wire vs. Solid

STRANDED

Stranded wire is more flexible than solid.
If you're pulling wire through conduit,
stranded wire makes it easier to get
around corners and bends in the conduit.
However, if the situation requires pushing
wires through conduit, you'll want to use
solid wire.

SOLID

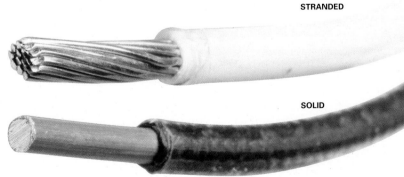

# Welding

## GETTING STARTED IN **WELDING**

**W**hether you'd like to build custom cars or just fix a cracked lawn mower deck, learning to weld gives your DIY game a serious boost. To help you choose a machine that meets your needs, we'll outline the three basic welding systems. Ideally, you'll pick one that can handle both your first effort and more advanced projects as your skills grow.

### Welding basics

All of these welding systems work essentially the same: An electric arc generates enough heat between the electrode (stick or wire) and the metal being joined to melt both together and create the bond. To ensure a strong bond, the super-hot area around the weld is surrounded by a cloud of inert gas to prevent oxygen and contaminants in the air from weakening the weld. That gas is provided either by the flux inside or around the electrode, or by a bottle of gas that feeds the joint as you weld.

### Choosing your first welder

To get started, you'll likely spend $200 to $400 for a quality welding machine. Check online to see the range of what's available because most home centers carry only one or two models. A 120-volt welder, powered by a conventional outlet, can weld metal up to 5/16 in. thick. You'll need at least a 20-amp (preferably a 30-amp) circuit.

The higher your machine's amp output, the thicker the material it can weld. Most people work with angle iron and tube steel no thicker than 1/4 in. Any 120-volt machine will suffice for this.

If you're really serious about welding and want more flexibility for future projects, get a 240-volt machine powered by a 50-amp circuit. A 240-volt machine makes welding thick material much easier and faster. Most welding machines have a chart inside a flip-up hood detailing the exact setup you'll need (amps, electrode size, etc.) for a given thickness of material. You can buy a single machine capable of MIG, TIG and stick, but it'll cost about $1,200.

Besides the welding machine, set aside about $200 for basic accessories.

## MEET AN EXPERT

**Jordan Dickinson is a professional welder and the owner/operator of Union Speed & Style, a custom auto, motorcycle and fabrication shop in Monticello, Minnesota.**

## MIG Welding

### Whom it's for:

A MIG welder is the most user-friendly type of welder. If you're looking for a general welding system that's easy to learn and good for most welding needs, this is it. MIG welders have an automatic wire feed system.

### Cost

- $250 and up.

### Pros

- Welds steel, aluminum and stainless.
- Can weld materials as thin as 26 gauge.
- Good for materials up to 5/16 in. thick.
- Relatively easy to learn.
- Nice-looking welds (with practice).
- Fast to lay down a finished weld.
- Doesn't produce lots of spatter.
- Little need to clean up the bead after welding.

### Cons

- Materials must be very clean.
- The wire feed mechanism on cheap machines can be troublesome.

### Flux-Core Setup

A MIG machine can also run flux-core wire. Flux inside the wire creates the protective gas shield, so you don't need bottled gas. Flux core works well outdoors, where bottled gas can blow away. It's the fastest and deepest penetrating process, perfect for production and thick material. Dual-shield flux-core wire, used mainly for very thick material, does require bottled gas.

**Buy quality. The wire feed mechanisms on a cheap MIG welder will frustrate you forever.**

### MIG SETUP

A MIG machine has an automatic wire feed with a bottle of inert gas to shield the weld. With MIG welding, the wire is the electrode as well as the filler material.

### Wire Feed Mig Welder

The wire spool is inside the machine or in a separate wire feed box. This feeds the wire through the gun when the trigger is pressed.

### Bottled Gas

For a MIG setup, you'll need a bottle of gas, typically $CO_2$ or a $CO_2$/argon mix. Straight $CO_2$ is the cheapest option. Adding argon creates a better-looking weld. A filled tank costs $80 to $160 depending on the tank size and the gas mixture.

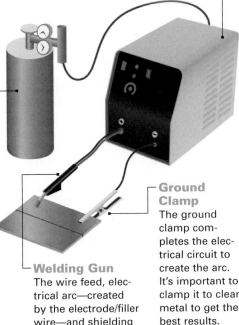

FILLER WIRE/ELECTRODE

SHIELDING GAS

ARC

WELD BEAD

### Welding Gun

The wire feed, electrical arc—created by the electrode/filler wire—and shielding gas are activated by pressing the trigger.

### Ground Clamp

The ground clamp completes the electrical circuit to create the arc. It's important to clamp it to clean metal to get the best results.

# Welding

## TIG Welding

**Whom it's for:**

If you want to do projects that require attractive finished welds, such as sculpture or motorcycle exhaust systems, TIG welding is for you.

TIG welding takes lots of practice, as it requires both hands as well as one foot. Compared with MIG or stick welding, it's a bit like going from driving an automatic to driving a stick shift. TIG welding is well suited for auto bodies, chassis/frame, aluminum oil pans, stainless exhaust, metal art, sheet metal, piping systems, motorcycles and bikes.

**Cost**

- $250 and up.

**Pros**

- Capable of greater precision than the other processes.
- Strong, high-quality welds.
- Nice-looking weld beads.
- Welds a large range of alloys.

**Cons**

- Parts must be very clean.
- High-quality machines are expensive.
- Requires lots of practice to become proficient.
- Much slower than MIG.

If you haven't welded in a while, practice on scraps before welding actual parts.

## TIG SETUP

With a TIG setup, the electrode is a tungsten wire. The electrode is not the filler material, as it is with the other processes. The filler is typically a long handheld rod instead of a wire feed spool, and you control the amperage using a foot pedal.

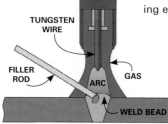

**Bottled Gas**

For a TIG setup, you'll use either pure argon or an argon/helium mix. A filled tank costs $80 to $200 depending on the tank size and mixture.

**Foot Pedal**

The foot pedal controls the amperage going to the gun. Some alloys are sensitive to thermal shock, which causes materials to expand at different rates, causing stress and even cracking. The variable amperage allows for a soft start and stop, helping eliminate thermal shock.

**Filler Rod**

In TIG welding, the filler material is fed by hand. Filler rods are available in different sizes and alloys to suit the job.

**Ground Clamp**

The ground clamp completes the electrical circuit to create the arc. Clamp it to clean metal for the best results.

**Welding Gun**

The electrical arc in TIG welding is created by a tungsten electrode in the gun. The arc and shielding gas are activated by pressing the trigger. If you don't want a foot pedal to control amperage, you can get a TIG gun with amperage control on the gun.

## Stick Welding

**Whom it's for:**

If you mostly want to do down-and-dirty welding where appearance isn't an issue, stick welding is for you. It's a simple, cheap way to repair dirty or rusty trailers and equipment (especially outdoors).

**Cost**

- $100 to $1,000.

**Pros**

- Economical.
- Best for welds that don't need to look nice.
- Works well on dirty and rusty parts.
- No bottled gas required.

**Cons**

- Best used outdoors—there's lots of splatter and smoke.
- Can't be used on metals thinner than 18 gauge.
- A bit difficult to learn, and it does require some practice.
- Slag must be removed after welding using a chipping hammer followed by wire brushing, because slag absorbs moisture and won't accept paint.

You won't be laying down perfect beads right off the bat, but you can get strong, serviceable welds with a few hours of practice.

## STICK SETUP

The flux on the outside of the electrode/filler rod provides the shielding gas, so no bottle is required. This is the machine you want for ultimate portability, as a stick welder is often integrated into a generator and works well outdoors.

**Filler Rod**
With stick welding, the filler rod is also the electrode. It's coated with flux, which creates the shielding gas, so no bottled gas is required.

**Electrode Clamp**
This clamp holds the electrode/filler rod.

**Welding Machine**
A stick-welding machine offers ultimate portability. No bottled gas is required, and the machine is often integrated into a gasoline generator.

**Ground Clamp**
The ground clamp completes the electrical circuit to create the arc. Clamp it to clean metal for the best results.

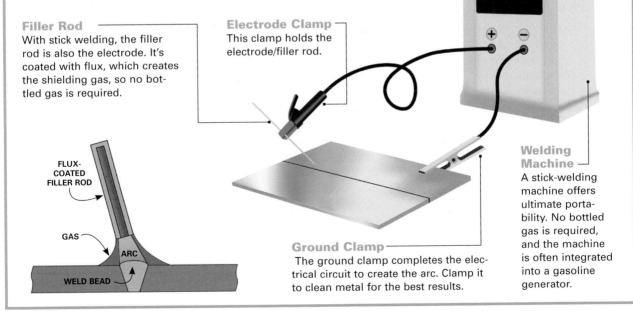

FLUX-COATED FILLER ROD

GAS

ARC

WELD BEAD

# Welding

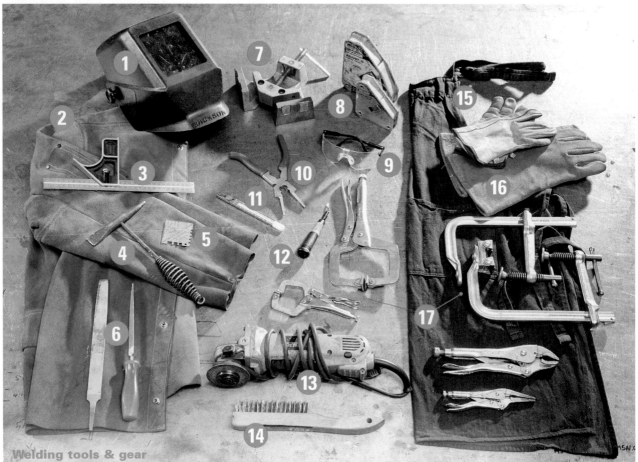

**Welding tools & gear**
You don't need all of this to get started. Get the basic safety gear first, and the rest as you need it.

**1.** Auto-darkening helmet ($40 to $100). These helmets let you see normally through the face shield until the gun sparks. As soon as the spark is detected, the face shield darkens to protect your eyes.

**2.** Welding jacket ($20 to $80). Made from thick leather, a jacket prevents sparks and molten metal from burning your clothes or skin.

**3.** Square. This tool lets you make square and angled lines on steel.

**4.** Chipping hammer. You'll use this to remove slag from the weld bead after stick welding.

**5.** Sheet metal gauge. You have to know the thickness of your material. This is the perfect quick reference.

**6.** Metal file. You'll need a few files for shaping parts that you can't get at with an angle grinder.

**7.** Framing jig ($50). A framing jig is indispensable for holding parts at a 90-degree angle for tack welding.

**8.** Welding magnets ($10 to $50). Welding magnets are used to hold parts together at precise angles while they're being tack-welded.

**9.** Safety glasses. Eye protection is a must for all power tool use, but it's especially critical anytime metal particles are likely to go airborne.

**10.** MIG pliers ($30). A welder's multi-tool, it's used for nozzle and tip installation, wire cutting, nozzle cleaning and slag removal.

**11.** Soapstone. Used to mark metal for cutting and welding, soapstone remains visible under extreme heat and has low electrical conductivity.

**12.** Deburring tool. This is used to remove the wire edge left on a piece of steel after it's been cut.

**13.** Angle grinder ($30 to $100). You'll use an angle grinder to shape parts before welding, and to grind and refine the bead after welding.

**14.** Metal brush. This is the go-to tool to clean parts before welding.

**15.** Apron ($40). An apron protects your clothes for non-welding tasks, such as grinding or cutting.

**16.** Welding gloves. These thick leather gloves with a long cuff protect your hands and forearms from sparks and molten metal.

**17.** Welding clamps and C-clamps. Welders use all kinds of clamps to hold materials in place for tack welding. You can't have too many.

# BUILD A
# WELDING TABLE

### Admit it: You've always wanted to learn how to weld. This pro will show you how.

## MEET AN EXPERT

**Heidi Olson, a certified welder, has experience making cooling parts for walk-in freezers and cold-storage rooms.**

**W**elding intimidates a lot of people, even some of us hard-core DIYers. And that's a shame because welding opens up a whole new world of household repairs and cool projects. We asked a pro welder to demonstrate some basic techniques by building a welding table. She'll walk you through each step and provide helpful tips along the way.

A metal welding table is the perfect project to start with because you can build all your future welding projects on it. The materials will cost about $160.

This table was built using a Lincoln 210MP. This machine can function as a MIG (metal inert gas/wire feed) welder, a TIG (tungsten inert gas) welder and a stick welder, but we used the MIG wire-feed function.

## MATERIALS LIST

| ITEM | QTY. |
|------|------|
| 1-1/4" x 1-1/4" x 1/8" x 10' angle iron | 3 |
| 32" x 20" x 1/8" sheet metal | 2 |
| 1-1/2' x 1/8" x 4" round tube | 1 |
| 4" x 130-lb.-rated caster with brake | 4 |
| 7/16" non-zinc or galv. nuts (fit to casters) | 4 |

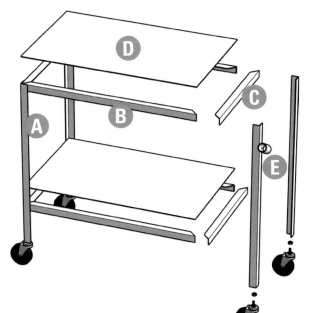

## CUTTING LIST

| ITEM | QTY. | DIMENSIONS | NAME |
|------|------|------------|------|
| A | 4 | 1-1/4" x 1-1/4" x 1/8" x 31" | Legs |
| B | 4 | 1-1/4" x 1-1/4" x 1/8" x 32" | Table/shelf side brace |
| C | 4 | 1-1/4" x 1-1/4" x 1/8" x 20" | Table/shelf end brace |
| D | 2 | 32" x 20" x 1/8" * | Table/shelf |
| E | 1 | 1-1/2" x 1/8" x 4" * | Steel pipe |

\* Have it cut by supplier

# Welding

**1** **Cut metal with a chop saw.** Fourteen-inch metal-cutting saws like this, outfitted with an abrasive blade, cost $100 to $200. These saws can cut bricks and pavers as well. A large metal-cutting saw with carbide teeth cuts metal like butter and with less burrs, but it will set you back more than $250. Never put a carbide-tooth blade on an abrasive saw because this saw runs at twice the rpm, a speed that could destroy the blade or worse. Miter saws designed to cut wood also spin too fast for metal-cutting blades, and since their motors aren't sealed, the metal chips and shavings can destroy the motor.

**2** **Grind the edges.** Smooth rough edges with an angle grinder. It's also important to grind away any paint or rust. Wire-feed welders work best on clean metal.

GAP

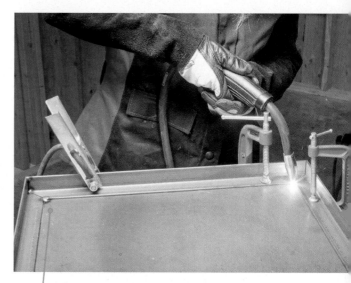

**4** **Ground the metal.** Workpieces need to be grounded in order to complete the circuit and create an arc. If your workspace is a metal table, the ground clamp can be attached to the table, but if it's a wood table, the clamp needs to be attached directly to the workpiece. **Note:** You may want to build your table on the ground to avoid burn marks in your workbench top. We didn't mind the marks.

TACK

**3** **Leave a gap.** Metal from the wire is being added to the weld and will mound up a bit. If you're welding a butt joint that you want to look good, leave a small gap, at least the thickness of the wire, to minimize the buildup. Grinding right angles into the abutting surfaces will also create room for the wire and lower the profile of the bead. This wasn't a crucial step on this project because these welds are on the bottom of the shelves and won't be seen.

**5** **Tack first.** Line up the shelf braces on the surface of the table and clamp them together. Tack each brace corner to the table and to each other before welding the whole joint. This will allow you to make corrections if something gets out of alignment.

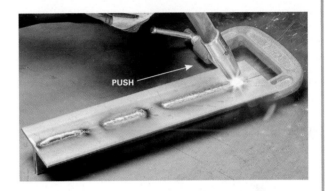

VOLTAGE TOO LOW, WIRE SPEED TOO FAST     WIRE SPEED TOO SLOW     PERFECT!

### Practice first

Each type of welder is different, so read your operator's manual. Achieving a good weld comes down to combining the right voltage with the proper wire speed, and this requires practice. Fine-tune the settings on the welder by practicing on the same material you plan to work with.

The wire should protrude about 1/2 in. from the gun, and the gun should be about 3/8 in. away from the surface before you pull the trigger. When you're working on horizontal surfaces with wire-feed welders, you want to push the gun forward. The gas creates a contaminant-free environment, which improves the welding process. If you pull the gun, it could outpace the gas.

The speed at which you move the gun will also affect how hot the metal gets and how much wire you lay down. One popular welding technique is to move the tip slightly forward and back as you go. Called "whipping," it helps control your speed, creates good penetration, and results in a narrower bead than you'd get by making tiny circles as you moved along.

The welding process shouldn't produce snapping or popping noises. If a welder is adjusted properly, you should hear a consistent buzzing or sizzle, like the sound of bacon frying. This all may seem complicated, but in just a few minutes you'll be creating solid welds (maybe not pretty ones—that comes later).

PUSH

FUME EXTRACTOR

**6 Disperse the heat.** Welding too long in any one area creates excessive heat, which will expand the metal so much that the whole project could warp when it cools. Weld a few inches on one side, rotate the assembly, weld a few inches on another side, and so on. There is no reason to weld the whole joint between the table/shelf surface and the braces. Note: Fume extractors start at about $1,200 but are unnecessary if you're welding in a well-ventilated area.

### BUYING METAL

Home centers and hardware stores carry a small variety of sheet metal and common steel stock. The selection and prices are fine for smaller welding jobs, but for larger projects like this table, shop at a metal supplier. Metal suppliers charge up to 50 percent less, and most will be able to cut your sheet metal to exact dimensions.

MAGNET SQUARE

**7 Square, clamp, tack and then weld.** Follow the same procedure you used to assemble the table and shelf: Be sure everything is square and fitting together properly before welding all the joints. Tackle one leg at a time. Square the leg to the shelf horizontally and vertically before tacking it into place, and then square, clamp and tack the leg to the tabletop. Follow the same procedure for the other three legs. There are magnets available to help hold pieces in place, but a framing square and C-clamps will also do the job.

# Welding

## BUILD A WELDING TABLE continued

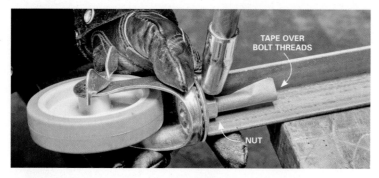

TAPE OVER BOLT THREADS

NUT

**8** **Protect threads from splatter.** Buy casters that have threaded stems (bolts) so you can replace one if it gets damaged. Weld the nut in place while it's attached to the caster. That way, the caster will line up perfectly with the bottom of the leg. Whenever you weld near nuts and bolts, always protect the threads with tape.

GUN HOLDER

**9** **Accessorize.** You'll always be looking for a safe place to set down your welding gun, so a gun holder is a must-have accessory on every welding table. A simple pipe works great. You could also add a box at the end to hold your hand tools.

### WELD SMART—STAY SAFE
- Wear thick leather gloves.
- Wear a welding cap under your helmet. (Yes, we know our expert didn't wear one.)
- Wear a long-sleeve shirt and pants made from cotton or leather. (These will also protect you from the arc rays, which can burn your skin like rays from the sun.)
- Wear hearing protection and safety glasses when cutting.
- Wear a welding helmet when welding to protect your face from sparks and your eyeballs from welder's flash (sunburn on your eyes).
- Keep flying sparks away from flammable or explosive materials.
- Don't touch the electrode (wire) with bare skin, and keep yourself and your clothing dry.
- Remove loose jewelry.
- Always maintain a proper ground.
- Always weld in a ventilated area, even if you use a fume extractor.
- Only weld on bare metal. Breathing in the fumes from zinc and other galvanized coatings can be extremely hazardous to your health.

**10** **Weld "vertical down."** Welding from the top down works best, so whenever possible, try to keep your welding surface in a vertical position. The arcing process turns the metal into a liquid, and gravity pulls it down, resulting in a smoother bead.

**11** **Grind sharp edges.** Grind down the sharp edges of the table and any ugly beads you want to smooth out. Clean the surface of the metal before you paint. Start with a household degreaser/cleaner and then wipe down with acetone. Don't paint the tabletop or top rail; you won't be able to ground your next welding project through the table with the ground clamp.

**12** **Keep the gun clean.** The nozzle and the tip on the gun will get covered in splatter, so it's important to clean them off periodically. Welding pliers are the perfect tool for the job. They're also designed for cutting wire and removing bushings, tips and nozzles, and they can work as a hammer in a pinch.

# 3 Plumbing, HVAC & Appliances

## IN THIS CHAPTER

Home Care & Repair .................................90
   *No-Wiggle Toilet, Mini-Split Systems
   and more*

Toilet Tune-Ups .......................................97

Stay Warm When the Power's Out ........101

No Water? Now What? ...........................104

Prevent Frozen Pipes ............................109

Handy Hints ...........................................113
   *Self-Draining Dehumidifier and more*

Great Goofs .............................................114

# MINI-SPLIT SYSTEMS

### What is a mini-split?

Mini-split systems are A/C and heating units that are increasingly popular, mainly because most installations don't require ductwork. Similar to conventional HVAC systems, mini-splits have an outdoor condenser and one or more air handlers inside. They're somewhat like a window A/C unit split in half—hence the name.

### How does a mini-split work?

Like a conventional A/C unit, a mini-split uses copper tubing to carry the refrigerant from the outdoor unit, which contains the compressor and condenser, to the indoor air handler. But with a mini-split, the conditioned air blows directly out of the indoor air handler into the room, rather than being routed through ductwork. A typical compressor can run four or five air handlers, which are mounted in different zones (or rooms) throughout the house. Indoor units can be mounted on the wall, floor or ceiling.

In the winter, the refrigerant absorbs heat from the outside (because the refrigerant is far colder than the air) and carries it to the air handlers. In the summer, the refrigerant absorbs heat from inside the house, carrying it out to cool the house.

### Will a mini-split work for you?

A mini-split is a viable option for a house with no existing ductwork, such as one with a boiler and radiators. You won't have to install ductwork, which can be both expensive and difficult to accommodate. A mini-split can also be a good choice for a large house with rooms that don't get used often. Rooms that aren't served well by existing forced-air systems also make good candidates.

Manufacturers claim that a mini-split system can cut your heating and cooling costs by up to 50 percent. However, the savings vary according to the square footage of the conditioned space and the efficiency of the equipment you're replacing.

### Are mini-splits DIY friendly?

Most mini-splits are installed by professional HVAC companies, but you can buy do-it-yourself kits with prices starting at about $1,500. (Pros will charge at least double that.) If you go online and search for "DIY mini-splits," you'll find many companies that can provide you with products and advice.

Installing a mini-split yourself, however, is advanced DIY. You'll have to run electrical service to the unit and route refrigerant lines through the walls from outside. These units come with precharged refrigerant lines, a big benefit because charging the lines requires special know-how and tools.

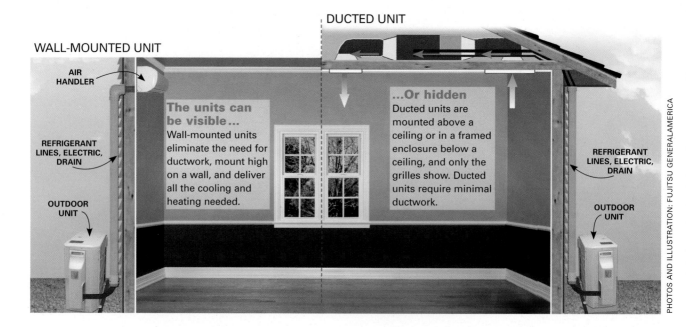

**DUCTED UNIT**

**WALL-MOUNTED UNIT**

AIR HANDLER

REFRIGERANT LINES, ELECTRIC, DRAIN

OUTDOOR UNIT

**The units can be visible...**
Wall-mounted units eliminate the need for ductwork, mount high on a wall, and deliver all the cooling and heating needed.

**...Or hidden**
Ducted units are mounted above a ceiling or in a framed enclosure below a ceiling, and only the grilles show. Ducted units require minimal ductwork.

REFRIGERANT LINES, ELECTRIC, DRAIN

OUTDOOR UNIT

PHOTOS AND ILLUSTRATION: FUJITSU GENERALAMERICA

## Choose your style

Indoor air handlers come in a variety of styles including wall mount, floor mount or ceiling mount. Choose the one that you find most suited for the room where the unit will be installed.

CEILING UNIT

FLOOR UNIT

WALL UNIT

TORN RUBBER
LOOSE NAIL
NAIL MISSING

## INSPECT PLUMBING VENTS

Next time you're up on the roof, take a look at the rubber gaskets around plumbing vent pipes. Those gaskets sometimes crack, tear and let in rainwater. If you have all-metal vent flashing, you're in luck. It's much less likely to leak and often outlasts the shingles.

## PLASTIC PEX FITTINGS ARE OK

If you're concerned about using plastic fittings instead of metal for PEX, worry no more. Professional plumbers are buying three times more plastic than brass. Brass fittings cost about five times as much, which likely has something to do with it. And pros don't want a callback to fix their own work on their dime. So obviously, pros trust the plastic fittings. Manufacturers trust them as well; the warranties for plastic fittings are similar if not identical to those for their metal counterparts.

Metal fittings are required, however, where the fitting is exposed to UV light. Also, no plastic pipe or fittings can be used within 18 in. of water heating devices. Check your local building code in case there are other requirements where you live.

# HomeCare&Repair

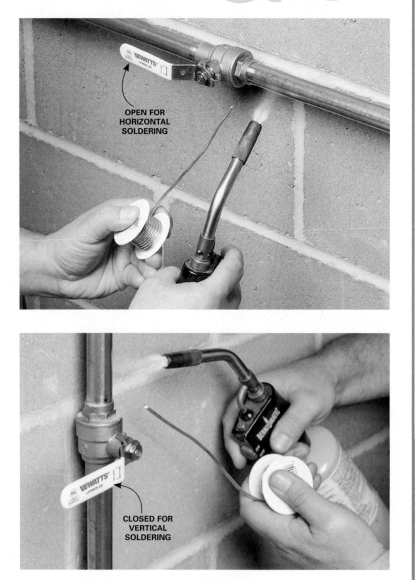

OPEN FOR HORIZONTAL SOLDERING

CLOSED FOR VERTICAL SOLDERING

## SOLDERING BALL VALVES

Many ball valve manufacturers recommend soldering with the valve in the closed position. But if the ball valve contains water and is sealed closed, heating the valve on both ends can turn the trapped water to steam and rupture the ball valve seal. For that reason, our pro plumber, Les Zell, prefers to have horizontal valves open while he's sweating the joints. It allows expanding gas or air to exit and reduces the chance of blowing bubbles through the solder joint. But if the ball valve is in a vertical position, it's best to close it so no solder can run into the ball and prevent the valve from opening or closing properly.

**MEET AN EXPERT**

Les Zell is a master plumber with more than four decades of experience in the field.

## PEX CAN LIMIT WATER FLOW

We love PEX. But most PEX tubing has a smaller inside diameter than its copper counterpart. More important, PEX connectors are much smaller. Some nominal 1/2-in. plastic connectors have an interior diameter as small as 5/16 in. This can make a difference in your water flow.

**Easy solution:** If you're concerned about water flow, step up the size of the PEX. If you're replacing a 1/2-in. copper pipe with PEX, for example, use 3/4-in. PEX instead of 1/2-in.

1/2" COPPER PIPE

1/2" PEX

## FREEZING PIPES ... ON PURPOSE!

Sometimes, turning off the water at a shutoff valve isn't the best option. I needed to replace two valves on a boiler for a three-story building. I could either wait for heating season to end and drain the system, or I could isolate the valves with ice plugs and avoid the hassle of draining and refilling the system. So I decided to go for the latter. I rented the Ridgid SF-2500 SuperFreeze, which circulates refrigerant through two freeze heads, forming a pair of ice plugs. The unit cost $60 for a day at my local rental center. It can't be used on plastic pipes, just copper up to 2-1/2 in. or steel up to 2 in.

—Kurt Meyers, Contributing Editor

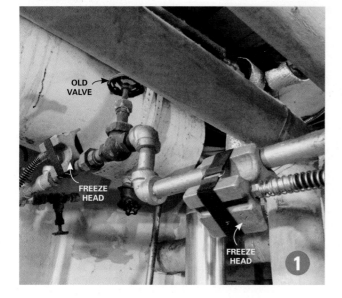

OLD VALVE

FREEZE HEAD

FREEZE HEAD

①

③

NEW VALVE

②

**1 Attach the freeze heads.** Strap the freeze heads into position on both sides of the repair using the included hook-and-loop straps or a quick clamp. Think through the placement because once freezing begins, you can't move the heads until the repair is complete. Be sure you have the clearance you need to turn wrenches and make any necessary cuts. If you need to solder, keep the freeze heads at least 3 ft. away from the heat source for each inch of pipe diameter.

**2 Spray water to form an ice bridge.** With the heads in place, switch on the machine. After five or 10 minutes, spray water on the heads to form an ice bridge for more efficient freezing. It took about 45 minutes for plugs to form in this 3/4-in. steel pipe.

**3 Repair the pipes.** Once the plugs form, make the repair and turn off the machine. The plugs will melt in about 15 minutes.

# HomeCare&Repair

## THE ROOT OF THE PROBLEM

Your sewer line is a particularly attractive water source to tree roots, especially if you live in an arid climate. Roots can bore right through the tiniest cracks and holes in any pipe.

Once inside the pipe, roots will eventually fill or even break a pipe. If you suspect you have roots in your drain, the best starting point is to hire a professional to run a camera down the drain to see the extent of the problem. Depending on the situation, you have four options.

**1 Line replacement**

This costs $1,500 to $5,000, determined by the length of the line. If you're on a city sewer system, it could easily be more than that; hand-digging may be required if there are other utility lines nearby.

**2 Spot repair**

With the use of a camera, an isolated damaged area can be located, cut out and replaced for $500 to $600.

**3 Lining or pipe-bursting**

These options cost $5,500 to $10,000. A pipe, either MDPE (medium-density polyethylene) or HDPE (high-density polyethylene), is forced through the old pipe, breaking the old pipe as it progresses. The upside of this method is that you only need a hole at each end of the pipe, instead of having to dig a trench to replace the old pipe with a new one.

MR. ROOTER

**MONSTER ROOT REMOVED FROM SEWER LINE**

### MEET AN EXPERT

**Michael Kura has more than 30 years of plumbing experience in the residential, commercial and biotechnical fields. He is a franchise owner with Mr. Rooter Plumbing of Mendocino and Lake Counties in California.**

CLAY PIPE

## 4 Cabling

This method uses a spinning steel cable with cutters on the end, which snakes through the line, cutting out the roots. It's a temporary solution that is done regularly for about $200. You can rent or buy a machine, but it can be dangerous to do cabling yourself. The cable can whip and backlash, causing cuts or even lost fingers. Cuts from dirty cable can cause serious infections.

### Search and removal
A pro can use a cable with a camera attached to determine the exact location and extent of the problem. The cable can also be used to cut out roots.

DRAIN CAMERA

## SLOW-FILLING WASHER?
## CLEAN THE INLET SCREENS

If your washing machine fills at a slow trickle, your inlet screens are likely plugged. These screens catch debris in the water supply and protect a washer's internal parts. To get at them, turn off the water supply valves behind the washer, pull the machine out and disconnect the hoses. Remove the screens with needle-nose pliers. Be gentle; they're easy to damage. Clean the screens or buy new ones at a home center or an appliance parts store. Carefully press them into place with a screwdriver. Before you reconnect the hoses, check them, too. Some contain screens that can be removed and cleaned just like inlet screens.

SCREEN

# HomeCare&Repair

## NO-WIGGLE TOILET

**If** your toilet leaks because of a faulty wax ring, you might not know it until the floor is already damaged. Some say to skip the caulk around the toilet so you get an early warning of a leaking wax ring. But the most common cause of wax ring failure is movement. If you don't caulk, you're relying on two bolts to prevent that movement. Think about it. You've got a 60-lb. toilet, 40 lbs. of water and maybe a 200-lb. person. That's a lot of strain on two bolts. Plus, according to code, a toilet must be caulked to the floor. But don't just caulk around the base after installing the toilet and hope for the best. Here's one method.

**Note:** It's often the case that two wax rings are needed. Calculate the distance from the top of the toilet's underside to the top of the floor flange, and then double that dimension. If that number is more than the thickness of one wax ring, use two. The flange is supposed to be flush with the finished floor. If it's not, one solution is to use an extension flange and/or replace the collar or flange so the flange is flush with the floor. Make sure the floor flange is securely attached to the floor and that the floor itself isn't in need of repair.

PLASTIC SHIMS

**1 Level the toilet.** Set the new toilet in place, with a level on the rim to see where you need to shim under the base. Mark the shim locations on the floor with tape. Use only plastic shims.

PAINT STICK SPACERS

**2 Set the toilet on spacers.** Install the new wax ring on the floor flange. Fasten the flange bolts to the flange using nuts. Set spacers on the floor to keep the toilet off the floor.

SHIM

**3 Caulk the base.** Apply a bead of caulk right under the base's rim. Make sure the shims are in position.

CAULK

**4 Seat the toilet.** Press the toilet down to the floor, apply caulk where the spacers were, snug up the bolts and tool the caulking.

# TOILET
## TUNE-UPS

### 9 super-simple ways to optimize your flush

By **Brad Holden**

The toilet is arguably the most important seat in the house. If your toilet isn't flushing well, don't just live with it! You can probably fix the problem in less than 30 minutes. We've put together nine simple tips to help you get the best possible flush every time.

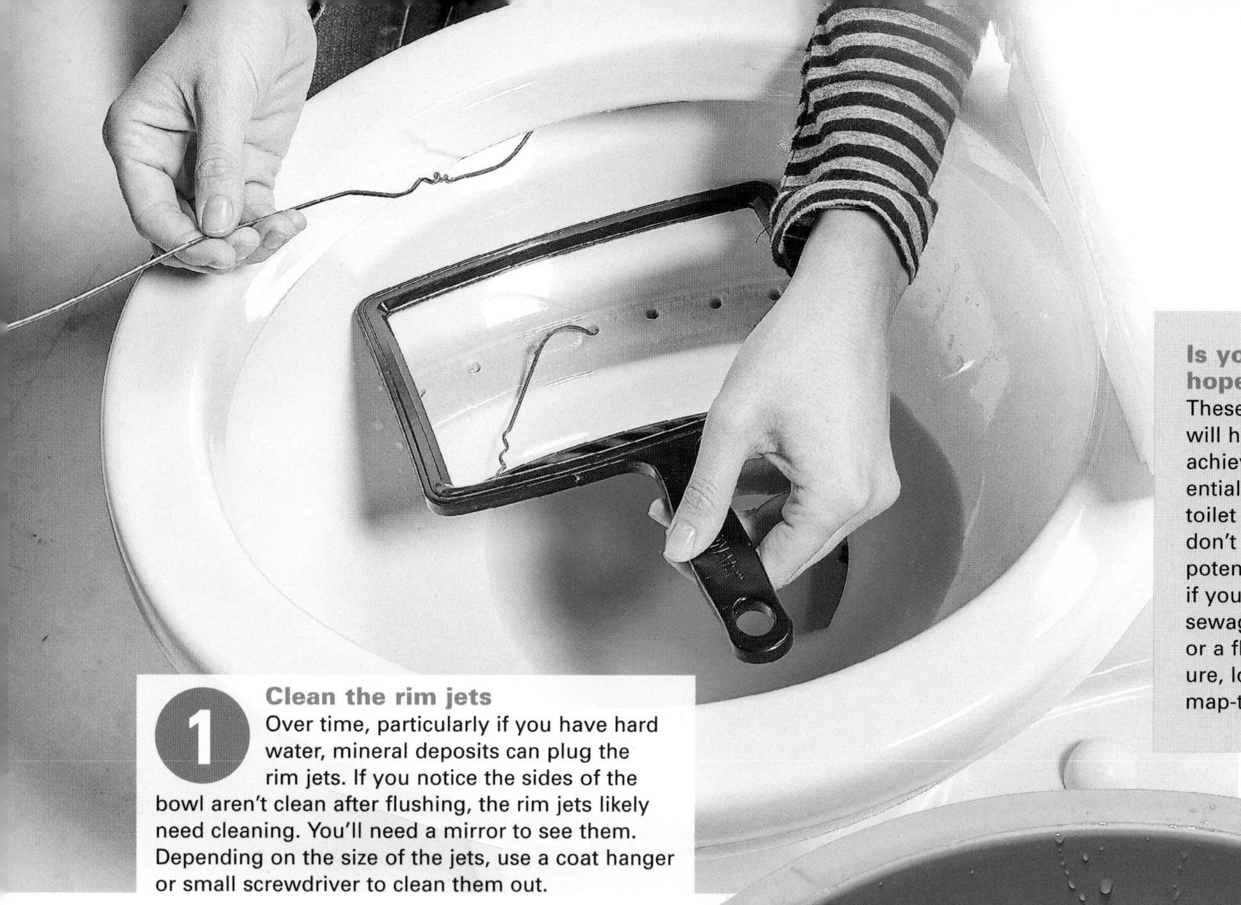

**1 Clean the rim jets**

Over time, particularly if you have hard water, mineral deposits can plug the rim jets. If you notice the sides of the bowl aren't clean after flushing, the rim jets likely need cleaning. You'll need a mirror to see them. Depending on the size of the jets, use a coat hanger or small screwdriver to clean them out.

CHAIN FLOAT

FLAPPER

SINGLE-PLY    TWO-PLY

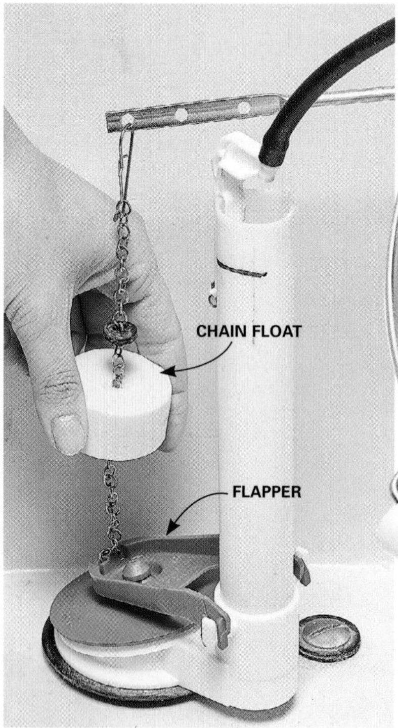

**2 Get a flapper with a chain float**

A chain float helps the flapper stay open a bit longer, allowing more water to enter the bowl for a better flush. You can adjust the float up or down on the chain to fine-tune how long the flapper remains open.

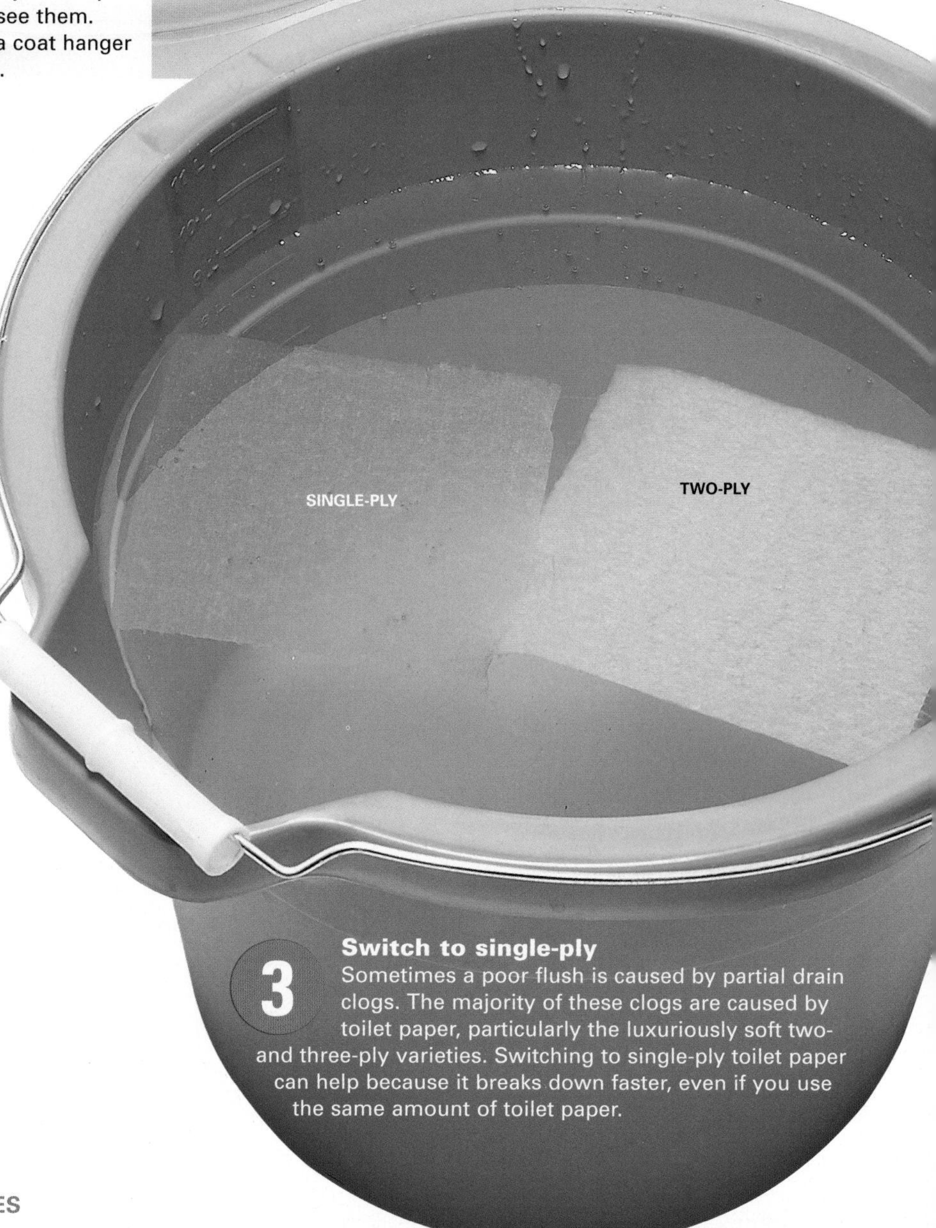

**3 Switch to single-ply**

Sometimes a poor flush is caused by partial drain clogs. The majority of these clogs are caused by toilet paper, particularly the luxuriously soft two- and three-ply varieties. Switching to single-ply toilet paper can help because it breaks down faster, even if you use the same amount of toilet paper.

**4** **Try a different flapper**
The flapper is the part inside the tank that goes up when you press the flush handle. There are hundreds of flapper styles, including some that allow you to adjust the amount of water per flush—but not all are compatible with every toilet. Plumbers often carry a variety in their truck and, through trial and error, choose the one that works best. If you've tried everything else, buy a few different flappers and see which one works the best on your toilet. Check map-testing.com to find flappers compatible with your specific toilet. Flappers cost $3 to $20 each.

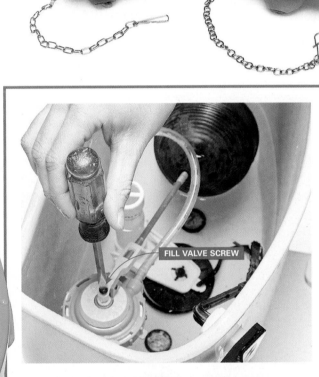

FILL VALVE SCREW

**5** **Adjust the water level**
Most toilets have an indicator line showing the proper water level. If yours doesn't, set the fill level 1 in. below the top of the overflow pipe. Closer than that might be asking for trouble. In the evening, the demand on your municipal water supply drops, which can increase water pressure. This can cause the water level in your tank to rise a bit.

If water is continuously flowing into the overflow pipe, you're flushing money as well as water down the toilet. There are many different mechanisms for adjusting your tank's water level. The most common methods are an adjustment screw on the fill valve, an adjustment screw connected to the float, or a spring clip connected to the float.

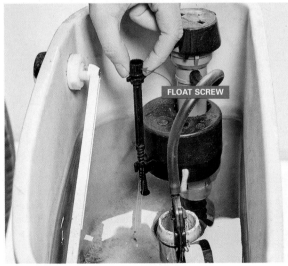

FLOAT SCREW

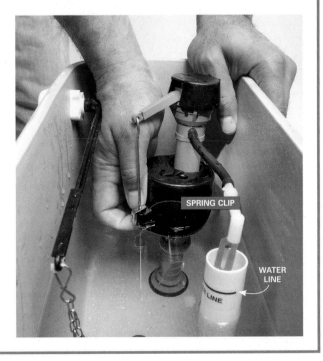

SPRING CLIP

WATER LINE

LINE

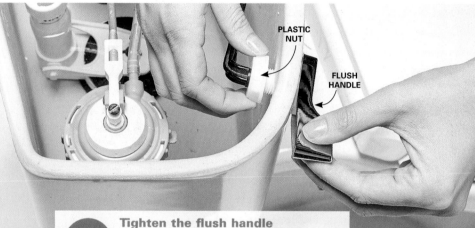

PLASTIC NUT

FLUSH HANDLE

**6** **Tighten the flush handle**
A nut inside the tank holds the flush handle in place. If it's loose, it can throw off the chain adjustment. Tighten the nut, being careful not to overtighten; it just needs to be snug.

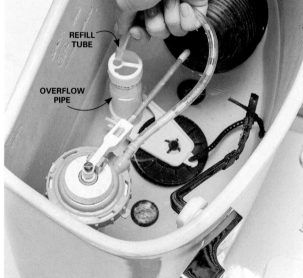

**7** **Open the water supply all the way**
When you flush, it's not just the water from the tank that's making the flush. The fill valve also opens, allowing more water to immediately enter the tank. The more water flowing in, the better your flush will be.

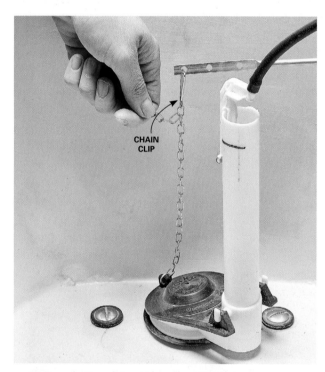

CHAIN CLIP

REFILL TUBE

OVERFLOW PIPE

**8** **Adjust the flapper chain**
Adjust the chain so that it just allows the flapper to seat. If the chain is too long, the flapper will close too soon for a good flush. If the chain is too short, the flapper won't seal. To adjust the length, move the clip to a different chain link. Be sure there are no kinks in the chain, squeeze the clip closed and cut off the excess chain.

**9** **Aim the refill tube**
Make sure the refill tube is aimed directly into the overflow pipe; you don't want any water spraying outside it. That little tube refills the bowl with water from the tank after flushing. A low water level in the bowl contributes to a weak flush, and fails to clean the sides of the bowl.

# STAY WARM WHEN THE POWER'S OUT

## 10 tips to keep your house from turning into a deep freeze

By **Brad Holden**

PLUMBING, HVAC & APPLIANCES

**H**eating systems need power. Even natural gas, propane and oil furnaces often use electricity for ignition, power dampers, fans or pumps. A power outage is always inconvenient. But in low temperatures it can be catastrophic. Frozen pipes can burst, causing thousands of dollars of damage in just a few minutes, and within a few hours, the damage costs can easily reach six figures. But there are ways to keep your home habitable and above freezing without power, even in the coldest weather.

**Caution:**
When using any fuel-powered heat source, it's imperative to have operating battery-powered carbon monoxide and smoke detectors.

# Furnace Backup Tips

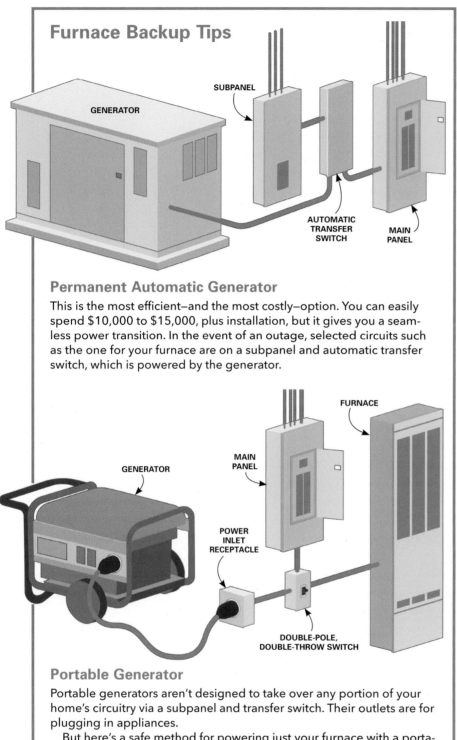

## Permanent Automatic Generator

This is the most efficient—and the most costly—option. You can easily spend $10,000 to $15,000, plus installation, but it gives you a seamless power transition. In the event of an outage, selected circuits such as the one for your furnace are on a subpanel and automatic transfer switch, which is powered by the generator.

## Portable Generator

Portable generators aren't designed to take over any portion of your home's circuitry via a subpanel and transfer switch. Their outlets are for plugging in appliances.

But here's a safe method for powering just your furnace with a portable generator. Connect a heavy-duty double-pole, double-throw switch (such as Leviton No. 1262; $40 at home centers) to the furnace, along with a power inlet receptacle (such as Leviton No. 5278-CWP; $40 at home centers). If the utility power goes out, flip the double-pole switch to disconnect the permanent furnace circuit, and then run a cord from the portable generator to the inlet. The double-pole, double-throw switch prevents the portable generator from back-feeding the entire house or, worse, the utility's system. To be extra safe, turn off the main circuit breaker at the main service, disconnecting the house, to eliminate any chance of back-feeding the utility.

## Other options to keep your house warm

If the generator methods aren't an option for you, there are other, less costly measures you can take.

### Don't panic

If your home is well insulated, it's typically a matter of days, not hours, before pipes will freeze, even in subzero temps.

### Move to one room

It's far easier to keep one room in the house comfortable than to heat the whole house. If you have a basement, that's a good choice, because it's usually easier to maintain a constant temperature underground.

### Use your blinds

Keep the blinds closed except to let in direct sunlight.

## Use your fireplace

Fireplaces are notoriously inefficient heat sources, as lots of heat goes up the chimney. But in an emergency, you can keep warm by a fire if you have enough wood to burn. A gas fireplace works too, and is more efficient than a wood-burning fireplace.

## Block drafts

Little drafts around doors and windows go unnoticed when the furnace is operating. But when the power's out, these drafts really bring on the chill. Block drafts with towels. **Note:** Don't block drafts if you're running a fuel-powered heater. These small air intrusions help the heaters burn efficiently and provide ventilation.

## Preheat your home

If you have advance warning, set the thermostat higher than usual and heat typically unused spaces to boost thermal mass.

## Keep doors closed

Opening a door to the cold lets out a lot of heat. Limit trips in and out of the house, opening doors only when necessary.

**Caution:**
Propane and kerosene heaters produce carbon monoxide just as gas stoves, ovens and fireplaces do. When running any fuel-powered heat appliance during a power outage, it's imperative to have operating battery-powered carbon monoxide and smoke detectors. Read and adhere to all of the heater manufacturer's warnings.

MR. HEATER

## Indoor-safe propane or kerosene heater

Propane or kerosene heaters are safe for indoor use only if they're labeled "indoor-safe" and you follow the manufacturer's instructions. They come in different sizes to suit the area to be heated. These portable heaters are available at home centers and online, ranging in price from $80 to $500. Manufacturers recommend opening a window an inch or so when using these heaters, particularly in a super-insulated home. If you're using a fuel-powered heater in a very small room, open a door to an adjoining room.

# NO WATER? NOW WHAT?

## 27 tips to prepare for a water outage

By **Brad Holden**

**W**hen disaster strikes and there's no water coming out of the tap, don't get left high and dry. Instead, follow our advice on storing water so you'll always have an immediate reserve. You'll also need to be prepared to purify water that may be unsafe, and to conserve the water you've stored.

*STORE YOUR WATER SUPPLY IN A COOL, DARK PLACE. HEAT & SUNLIGHT CAN DEGRADE WATER QUALITY.*

 **Store water in a food-safe container.** Water doesn't have an expiration date, but it can become unsafe to drink if it's not stored properly. For long-term storage of large quantities of water, food-grade plastic is the gold standard. In a last-minute stock-up for short-term storage, the gold standard changes to anything that's clean. In this case, use a method of purification if there's any suspicion that your water may be unsafe to drink.

**2** **Consider specialized water storage containers,** such as the WaterBrick ($35 each). Made for potable water or food, these food-grade containers have a tight seal and stack like blocks for easy storage.

 **Don't store plastic water containers directly on a concrete floor.** The chemicals used in concrete—not to mention oil spills on a garage floor— can leach nasty chemicals into your water supply, giving it a bad taste or making it unsafe to drink. Store your plastic containers on cardboard or on a wooden pallet.

**4** **Buy a water bladder** to put in your tub. The WaterBOB ($35) holds 100 gallons of water for drinking. Just set it in your tub, wrap the spout around the faucet and fill it up.

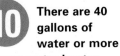

**5** **Store 1 gallon per day per person.** The length of time you want to plan for is up to you. The Federal Emergency Management Agency (FEMA) recommends a two-week supply for each person. When you consider all water use—flushing, showers, handwashing, dishes, laundry, teeth brushing and outdoor watering—that's a LOT less water than we typically use daily. The U.S. Geological Survey estimates that we use an average of 80 to 100 gallons of water per day per person.

**7** For serious water storage, **consider investing in a cistern.** It's very costly, but you'll be able to store anywhere from 200 gallons to thousands of gallons of potable water.

**8** **Food-grade stainless steel drums** are excellent for water storage because they don't let in UV light. On the downside, a 55-gallon stainless steel drum will set you back about $500.

**9** **Install a rainwater collection system.** You'll still need to purify the water, but it's a good way to take advantage of a natural resource.

**10** **There are 40 gallons of water or more in your water heater.** To extract this water, turn off your water at the house's main shutoff, and turn off the gas/power to your water heater. Open a couple faucets above the water heater, if possible, to break the vacuum effect. Hook up a hose and drain the water from the tank. If there are solids in the water, filter them out before using it.

**6** **Stock up on hand sanitizer.** By using hand sanitizer instead of soap and water, you can stretch your water supply further.

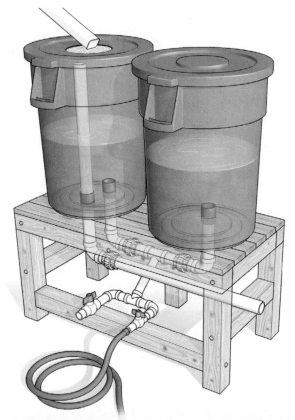

**11** **Don't store water in a container that can't be sealed.** If a container doesn't have a tight seal, all sorts of contaminants can enter.

IF YOU HAVE A WELL, BE SURE YOU HAVE BACKUP POWER TO OPERATE IT.

**12** **If stored water tastes flat, oxygenate it** by pouring it back and forth between two clean containers.

**13** **Decrease your activity** and keep cool to minimize the amount of water you need to stay hydrated.

**14** **Fill up your pool.** Even a wading pool works. This water will need filtration and purification before you can drink it.

**15** **Do laundry ahead of time.** If you know you'll likely be without water, be sure you have enough clean clothes to get you through.

**16** **Fill bathtubs and sinks with water.** You won't be able to drink this water without purification, but you'll be able to use it as is for washing and flushing the toilet.

**17** **If you have power, use the water from your dehumidifier.** Yes, it's distilled water, but you shouldn't drink it, as it's not purified or filtered. Use this water for washing, toilet flushing or watering plants.

**18** **Camp showers** ($10 to $100) are available in a wide variety for those who require a bit more luxury than a sponge bath. This might be a good option if you have a plentiful supply of water.

**19** **Flush the toilet with a bucket of water,** but pour it into the tank instead of the bowl. This method uses less water than pouring it directly into the bowl. Unpurified water, such as water stored in the tub without a container, is perfect for toilet flushing.

**20** **Dispose of toilet paper in a wastebasket.** Yes, you'll still be flushing your toilet, but there won't be the typical amount of water going through the drain from other sources, so it's more likely that toilet paper could cause a backup.

**21** If you're storing plastic bottles of water for an emergency, **you should use/rotate your supply once a year or so.**

**22** **Avoid contact with floodwater,** which can be extremely toxic. It likely contains all sorts of chemicals as well as raw sewage.

**23** **Stock up on Clorox wipes** and hand wipes. Use these for general cleaning instead of soap and water.

JUST BECAUSE WATER IS CLEAR DOESN'T MEAN IT'S SAFE. BACTERIA, VIRUSES, CYSTS & POTENTIAL TOXINS ARE NOT VISIBLE TO THE NAKED EYE.

**24** **Glass containers** are good, if properly sanitized. But they're heavy to transport and they break easily.

**25** **Freeze jugs of water.** If the power is out, they'll help keep your frozen food safe a bit longer. When the ice melts, you can use it for drinking.

**26** **Filter out solids** through a coffee filter before purifying water.

**27** **Stock up on disposable plates and utensils.** Conserve your supply of water by minimizing the number of dishes you have to wash.

## Have a way to purify your water

- **Boiling** kills parasites, bacteria and other pathogens in water. It does not, however, eliminate all forms of chemical pollution. Also, you'll still need to filter out any solids. A camp stove ($10 to $150) is a good item to have on hand for boiling because your power might be out as well. Any camp stove will do, but a portable stove that burns wood is nice in case there's a shortage of other fuel to purchase. Don't use camp stoves indoors—they generate carbon monoxide.

IF THERE'S A FLOOD, DON'T ASSUME YOUR WELL WATER IS SAFE. TEST IT.

- **Water purification devices** ($15 to $450) are available at camping supply stores. They come in sizes suitable for one person or large groups. Some of these devices are capable of purification as well as filtration.

- **Iodine** is another household chemical that can disinfect water. It is, however, a harsher chemical than bleach. On the upside, you can also use it to treat wounds. Using 10 percent povidone-iodine, add 8 to 16 drops per quart of water, depending on the water's cloudiness.

- **Water purification tablets** are available at camping supply stores. They fit neatly in an emergency kit, are easy to use and usually have a shelf life of up to five years.

- **Bleach** is a readily available household item that can be used to purify water. Use only regular, unscented chlorine bleach with either 6 or 8.25 percent sodium hypochlorite as the active ingredient. Using a clean eyedropper and 6 percent hypochlorite bleach, add eight drops per gallon. For 8.25 percent, use six drops per gallon. Stir the water and let it stand for half an hour. If the water doesn't have a slight chlorine odor, repeat the dosage and let it stand for 15 more minutes. In general, you'll need more bleach if the water is cold or murky. Bleach has only a six-month shelf life, so be sure to keep a fresh supply.

# PREVENT FROZEN PIPES

## 13 tips to prepare your plumbing for winter

**We** all know that water expands when it freezes. That's not a problem with the ice cubes in your freezer, but if that ice forms in your plumbing, it's a potential disaster. A frozen pipe can crack, spewing hundreds of gallons of water into your home. Fortunately, you can take steps to help prevent a catastrophe and put your mind at ease.

**SHUTOFF VALVE**

**BLEEDER CAP**

**1** **Shut off outdoor faucets.** Turn off outdoor faucets at their shutoff valves. Open the faucet and then open the bleeder cap on the shutoff valve to drain any water out of the pipe. If you don't drain the pipe, it can still freeze and crack. Leave the bleeder cap open with a bucket underneath to catch any drips. If the dripping continues, your shutoff valve needs to be replaced.

**4** **Cover hose bibs.** Insulated covers slow the heat loss from a pipe as it travels through the wall out into the cold. They provide some protection for very little cost (about $3 at home centers).

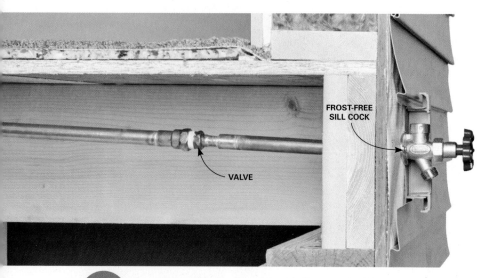

**FROST-FREE SILL COCK**

**VALVE**

**2** **Install frost-free sill cocks.** Unlike a typical faucet, the working parts of a frost-free sill cock— valve, seat and washer—are located up to 18 in. inside the wall instead of right at the faucet. When the sill cock is properly installed, with a slight downward pitch, water drains from the pipe every time you turn off the knob at the faucet. Frost-free sill cocks are available at home centers for $15 to $55.

**3** **Disconnect hoses.** A water-filled hose left out in cold weather will freeze. If the hose is still connected to the faucet, ice can back up into the pipe inside your house, causing the pipe to crack. Disconnect all hoses from their faucets, drain them and store them for the winter.

**5** **Get an early warning.** A Wi-Fi thermostat lets you control and monitor your home's temperature using your smartphone. If the temperature in your house drops, you'll get an email or text alert. Other types of alert systems are also available. Some send alerts to your cell phone via a phone jack in your house. Others send an alert to a landline or cell phone. For more on these devices, see our Winter '17 issue or visit familyhandyman.com. Wi-Fi thermostats are available at home centers for $100 to $500.

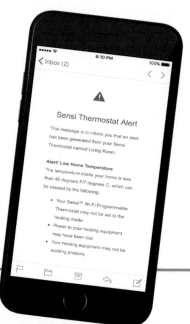

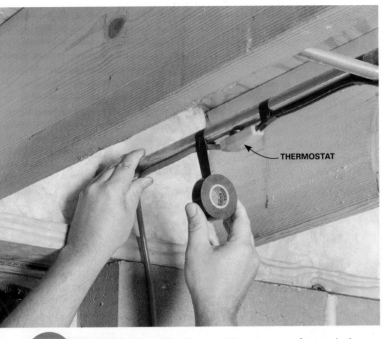

THERMOSTAT

RIM JOIST INSULATION

**6** **Install heat cable.** Heat cables are a perfect solution for vulnerable pipes. They have an integral thermostat that senses pipe temperature, turning the heat on and off as needed to keep the pipe from freezing. You'll need an accessible outlet to plug in the cable. Heat cables are available at home centers for $15 to $40, depending on the length.

**8** **Seal around rim joists.** The rim joist is a likely area for cold air intrusion. Seal cracks or holes using expandable foam and then insulate between the floor joists. Be sure that you don't insulate a pipe from the heat in the rest of the house. Also, inspect around holes where cables, wires or pipes pass through an exterior wall. Insulate where you can, and seal drafts with caulk or expandable foam. After insulating, be sure you have combustion air for the furnace coming in through a makeup air pipe.

MAIN SHUTOFF

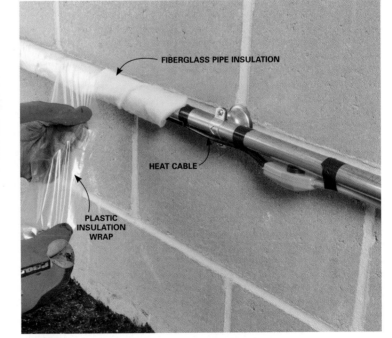

FIBERGLASS PIPE INSULATION

HEAT CABLE

PLASTIC INSULATION WRAP

**7** **If you leave town, shut off the water.** If you're leaving town for a few days or more, turn the water off at the main shutoff. That way, if a pipe does freeze and crack, you'll have far less damage. Shut off your automatic icemaker so it doesn't continually try to make ice, burning out the motor. Even if the ice bin is full, the ice will evaporate and the icemaker will try to make more.

**9** **Insulate pipes.** If you have pipes in an unheated area, such as a crawl space, an attic or a garage, use heat cable and cover it with pipe insulation. Pipe insulation alone does little, as it's only a matter of time before cold air can reach the pipe. In fact, insulating pipes without also using heat cable can prevent warm air from getting to them. Various types of pipe insulation are available from home centers for about $2 to $6.

**10** **Insulate your garage door.** If you have water lines in the garage, insulate the garage door, if not the whole garage. Consider a combination of heat cable and insulation as well. If it's really cold, put a portable heater in the garage.

**INSULATION RETAINER PIN**

## During a cold snap:

What constitutes a cold snap depends on your climate and your home's insulation. A temperature of 32 degrees F isn't cause for alarm in Minnesota, but it might be in Mississippi.

**11** **Keep the temperature steady.** During extreme cold, bypass your thermostat's program and leave the temperature steady. You may even want to turn it up a couple of degrees.

**12** **Open kitchen cabinet doors.** Being behind closed doors, kitchen plumbing pipes are vulnerable, as the heat from the rest of the house can't reach them. Open the cabinet doors to allow heat to circulate into the cabinets. A fan or portable heater pointed inside the cabinet also helps circulate warm air.

**13** **Leave faucets running.** A trickling faucet acts as a relief valve for the pressure that builds up if a pipe does freeze. That pressure relief can prevent a frozen pipe from cracking. A slow trickle is all you need. It'll bump up your next water bill a bit, but compared with major home repairs, that's an easy price to pay. Don't leave a faucet running if the drain is on an exterior wall, though; the drain can freeze, causing the sink to overflow.

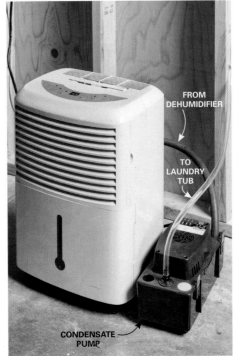

FROM DEHUMIDIFIER

TO LAUNDRY TUB

CONDENSATE PUMP

## SQUIRT-GUN TOILET DRAINER

When you're repairing or replacing a toilet, you need to remove all the water. Simply shutting off the water supply and flushing won't do it. A sponge works, but it's kind of slow. So I use an old squirt gun to suck the water out and squirt it into a bucket, leaving just the last few drops to sponge out.

—Dale Conklin

## SELF-DRAINING DEHUMIDIFIER

If you forget to empty the tank on your dehumidifier, it'll either overflow or shut off. That defeats the whole purpose of running a dehumidifier in damp areas. I didn't have a floor drain in that part of the basement, so I bought a condensate pump ($40 to $100 at home centers) and tubing and rigged it to my dehumidifier. Then I ran the tubing up to the ceiling, through the joist areas and down to the laundry tub. Now the dehumidifier runs full time, and I never need to empty the tank or worry about it shutting off.

—Doug Baltzer

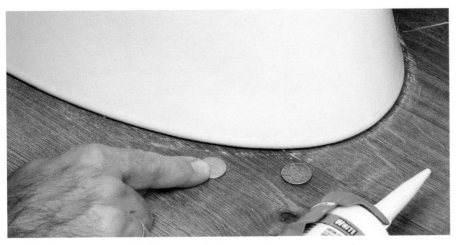

## A PENNY FOR YOUR TOILET SHIMS

I often use spare change as shims to level a toilet. Coins provide a firm seat, and each denomination is a different thickness. Simply slide as many coins as necessary under the toilet until it's completely level. Then tighten the flange bolts and caulk along the floor as usual. The caulk will hide the coins. Washers work well too.

—Les Zell, Master Plumber

# GreatGoofs®

## PASSING THE MUCK

When I was a youngster, we lived in an apartment complex. One day after work, my father was greeted with the news that the kitchen sink was full of standing water. After studying the situation, my father cleverly reversed the hose on the vacuum so it blew instead of sucked and blasted the clog past the sink trap.

It wasn't long before there was a knock at the door. The next-door neighbor lady was there—covered with soapy water and disgusting goo. She explained that she had been cleaning vegetables in the kitchen sink when there was a sudden, loud—and drenching!—eruption from her kitchen drain. She wanted to know if my father knew what could have caused this disaster. (Apparently the apartment units shared a drain line.) My father looked her right in her mucky face and said he had "no idea" what happened. He enjoyed many years of retelling the story of how his bright idea had led to a bald-faced lie.

—Jim Naperala

## OLD FATEFUL

The sewage ejection pump in our basement died. I had no trouble installing the new one, and finished in 20 minutes. It worked great…but the next day we found the carpet soaked with raw sewage and laundry water. I figured the float switch had gotten snagged on the electrical line.

Here comes the stupid part. I loosened the discharge line with the unit still plugged in! The jiggling of the pipe caused the float switch to work itself free, and the pump kicked in. The pressure blew the coupling apart and then the fun really began. Picture an open fire hydrant but with cold, stinky sewer water, drenching me and everything else within 10 ft.

—Travis Fowler

## 'F' IS FOR FLUB— AND FLOOD

I couldn't get the valves that feed my washing machine to stop leaking, so I replaced the entire faucet assembly. The installation went fine. I reconnected the washer hoses and double-checked for leaks. Satisfied with my leak-free connections, I started a load of clothes and went upstairs.

Everything seemed fine—until I returned to the laundry room and found myself standing in a pool of soapy water. Unfortunately, I'd forgotten to put the drain line back into the laundry tub, and an entire washer's worth of dirty water had poured onto my floor. Talk about washed up!

—William C. Sinclair

# 4 Woodworking & Workshop Projects & Tips

## IN THIS CHAPTER

Get the Best Plywood for Your Buck .....116

Flip-Top Bench ................................122

Quick & Easy Cabinet Doors ...............130

Easy Crate Shelf ..............................136

Viking Long Table..............................140

Cedar Bath Mat.................................148

French Cleat Tool Wall .......................150

Floating Shelf (with a Secret Drawer) ...156

Make Your Own Barn Wood...................160

Backyard Cantina ..............................165

Bottle Caddy ....................................169

Wipe-On Poly ...................................173

Compressor Cart ...............................179

Handy Hints .....................................180
*Quick Mixing Surface, No-Wait Glue,
Convenient Bench Clamps and more*

# GET THE
# **BEST PLYWOOD**
# FOR YOUR BUCK

**15 tips for better cabinets
and furniture**

**B**uilding furniture and cabinets is an investment of both time and money. So when you're buying plywood for these projects, shop wisely. Your choices will have a huge impact on the building process and the results. This article will help you decide exactly what you need and help you avoid common plywood pitfalls.

## MEET AN EXPERT

Brad Holden, an associate editor at *Family Handyman*, has been building cabinets and furniture for 30 years. In that time, he has absorbed so many slivers and ingested so much sawdust that he's practically made of wood.

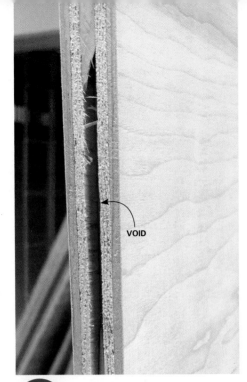

VOID

**1** **Inspect the edges.** Look closely at the core veneers on the edge of the sheet. They should be straight and of uniform thickness and have few, if any, voids. If you see a lot of voids and overlapping core veneers along the edge, there will be more throughout the sheet that won't be visible until you cut it. Overlapping veneers cause undulations that aren't visible until after you've applied a finish.

**2** **Bring a friend.** Plywood in 4 x 8-ft. sheets is heavy and unwieldy. Unstacking, inspecting, restacking, loading and unloading are much easier with an extra set of hands.

**3** **Check for flatness.** Don't expect perfection—you probably won't find it. Just try to find the best of the pile. Sight down all the edges just like you'd do if you were buying 2x4 studs. Sometimes, sheets are warped in multiple directions, resembling a potato chip. Leave these for some unlucky, less-informed buyer. If you're buying 1/4-in. plywood, don't worry about flat and straight; it won't be either. But you'll likely fasten it to structural parts, which will keep it flat.

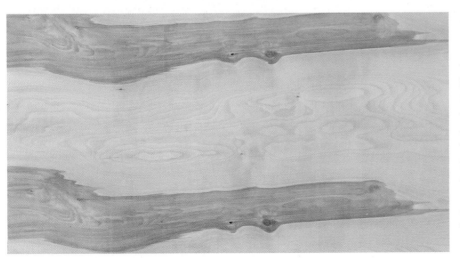

**4** **Watch for buried treasure.** The most beautifully figured face veneers will be at the lumberyard. But when I'm at the home center, I like to check out the back faces of the plywood or even plywood that's meant for underlayment. Because most people look for consistency of color and grain, there are some striking veneers that get written off as ugly. Quite often, something catches my eye that could be a really cool design element.

Special Order Product

**5** **Special-order from the home center.** Some home centers will special-order many different species, core options and veneer cuts. But beware: You won't be able to look at the actual sheets before buying, and you probably won't be able to return or reject them unless they're damaged or otherwise unusable. If it's just that you don't like the grain pattern, you're probably stuck with it.

**6** **Using stain? Beware of birch.** Any species accepts a clear finish such as polyurethane just fine. But if you're planning to stain your piece, beware of birch, pine and maple. These species take stain very unevenly and can end up looking blotchy. If you're set on one of these species, use prestain conditioner, which helps them take stain much more evenly. Even better, look at samples of different species with a clear finish and see if there's one that has the color you like without stain.

**7** **Know the grading system.** Hardwood veneer plywood has a front and a back face and is graded by the quality of each face. The front face is graded using a letter (A – D), with A being the best. The back face is graded using a number (1 – 4), with 1 being the best.

Front face – A

Back face – 2

**8** **Shop the home center for convenience and savings.** Baltic birch is a premium plywood found at lumberyards. A 3/4-in., 5 x 5-ft. sheet has 13 core veneers and costs about $70. Some home centers carry a similar product, called "classic birch." A 3/4-in., 4 x 8-ft. sheet has 10 core veneers and costs $50 to $60. It's strong with good screw-holding capability, making it a good, affordable alternative. It's perfect for less visible cabinet parts, drawers and shelving. As for other plywood, home centers have a more limited selection, carrying mostly veneer core (maybe MDF core), grade B2 and lower. Face veneer cuts are typically rotary cut or plain sliced, and in-stock species will usually be red oak, birch and maple. But the home center is a good option to save a little money.

**9** **Don't have plywood delivered.** If you have a way to haul sheets of plywood yourself, do it. The person pulling sheets for delivery isn't going to hand-select the nicest sheets for you. If delivery is your only option, inspect the sheets before the delivery truck leaves and reject any that are damaged or unusable. You may not have the option of rejecting a sheet because you don't like the grain pattern.

VENEER ADHESIVE SHOWING THROUGH

**10** **Sand at your own risk.** All plywood needs at least light sanding before finishing. Sometimes, the face veneer on home center plywood is so thin that the pink veneer adhesive shows through. On several occasions, I've had birch veneer turn translucent after light sanding with 220-grit paper. If you suspect that the veneer is ultra thin, don't use a power sander. Just sand by hand.

**11** **Shop lumberyards for quality and selection.** For a large selection of the best-quality hardwood veneer plywood, visit a lumberyard. A lumberyard that caters to cabinetmakers will give you enough options to make you dizzy. A 4 x 8-ft. sheet will cost anywhere from $80 to $120 or more depending on the species and the cut of the face veneer. Some lumberyards also stock 10-ft. sheets.

**12** **Using paint? Choose MDF or birch.** For projects I'm going to paint, I like MDF (medium-density fiberboard) or birch. B-grade birch or lower is fine. Sometimes, you'll even see plywood classified as "paint grade." Birch is close-grained with a smooth texture that doesn't show through paint. With an open-grained species like oak, the grain is visible under paint. MDF, of course, has no grain pattern, making it a good choice for painted projects. But for structural parts, I like birch veneer. For tips on building with MDF, search for "MDF" at familyhandyman.com.

## CAN YOU GET THE BOW OUT?

Admit it: You've tried flattening sheets of plywood. I have too. I've tried weights, clamps, wetting down the concave side, sun-drying the convex side and gluing opposing bowed sheets together. Nothing seems to work with any reliability. If the core veneers weren't in a perfect state of equilibrium and all in harmony when they were bonded together, the sheet has little chance of flattening out. The only recourse is to save the flattest sheets for the largest parts and use the worst sheets in smaller components, minimizing any curvature.

**13** **Don't just grab the top sheet.** Be picky and dig through the pile for the best sheets. Spending extra time to find the flattest undamaged sheets with appealing grain pattern is well worth the effort. But be kind and restack! And take heart; the bottom sheet is usually a bad choice anyway because it's most prone to forklift damage.

**14** **Watch out for damage.** You can often cut around minor damage in an otherwise good sheet (if you can, you might even be able to get a discount). But sanding out deep dents (above) isn't an option. You may not be able to sand out stains either. The purple stains shown result from a reaction between oak tannin and steel.

**15** **Look at the face veneers.** If only one side of your project will be visible, like a closed cabinet, don't worry about the back face. If you're building an open bookcase where both faces are visible, make sure you like the look of both faces.

## HOW VENEER IS CUT

The way the veneer was sliced from the log determines its look. The more common cuts—rotary and plain—are also the least expensive. Quarter-sawn and rift-sawn are more labor intensive to cut and are considered more attractive by most people.

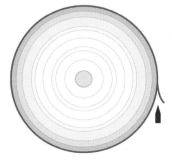

**Rotary-cut** veneer is peeled from the log like paper towels from a roll. It produces a wide, "loud" grain pattern.

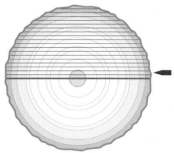

**Plain-slicing** produces a repeating pattern, typically showing large "cathedrals" in the grain.

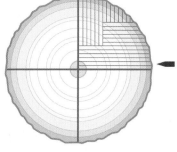

**Rift-sawing** produces veneer with tight, straight lines.

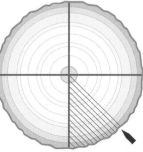

**Quarter-sawing** produces veneer with the same tight, straight lines as rift-sawing but includes the signature "ray flecks."

## CORE OPTIONS AND OPINIONS

The materials used to make plywood's inner core affect several important characteristics: weight, strength, rigidity, stability, flatness, screw-holding capability, consistency of thickness, and evenness of the veneer.

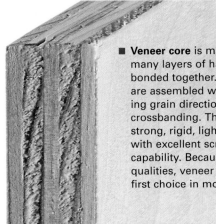

- **Veneer core** is made up of many layers of hardwood bonded together. The layers are assembled with alternating grain direction, called crossbanding. This makes a strong, rigid, lightweight sheet with excellent screw-holding capability. Because of these qualities, veneer core is my first choice in most cases.

- **Particleboard core** is the least expensive option. Like MDF core, it's flat and stable with consistent thickness. But particleboard core is a bit worse in the screw-holding category. Also, it's a special-order product, at least from my lumberyard, whereas MDF core is readily available.

- **MDF core** has a few advantages over veneer core. The thickness is more consistent, and MDF gives a smooth, even surface for the face veneer. It's also more stable and it's typically flatter. However, MDF core isn't as strong as veneer core, it doesn't hold fasteners as well and it's heavy. But if I'm making one-piece doors, I'll choose MDF core every time because of its flatness and stability.

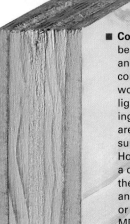

- **Combination core** weds the best attributes of MDF core and veneer core. The center cores are crossbanded hardwood, providing strength, light weight and screw-holding capability. The outer cores are MDF, giving a flat, uniform surface for the face veneers. However, combination core is a compromise: It doesn't have the screw-holding capability and rigidity of veneer core, or the flatness and stability of MDF core.

- **Lumber core** consists of edge-glued strips of wood, usually basswood. On both sides of the core, there's a crossbanded veneer, then the face veneer. Like veneer core, it has excellent screw-holding capability, strength and rigidity. But it's considerably more expensive and harder to find than veneer core, so I almost never use it. However, it's a good choice for long shelves.

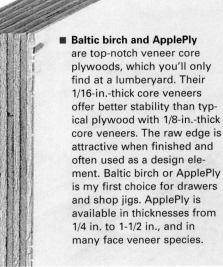

- **Baltic birch and ApplePly** are top-notch veneer core plywoods, which you'll only find at a lumberyard. Their 1/16-in.-thick core veneers offer better stability than typical plywood with 1/8-in.-thick core veneers. The raw edge is attractive when finished and often used as a design element. Baltic birch or ApplePly is my first choice for drawers and shop jigs. ApplePly is available in thicknesses from 1/4 in. to 1-1/2 in., and in many face veneer species.

# FLIP-TOP BENCH

## A space-saving workshop on wheels!

By **Spike Carlsen**

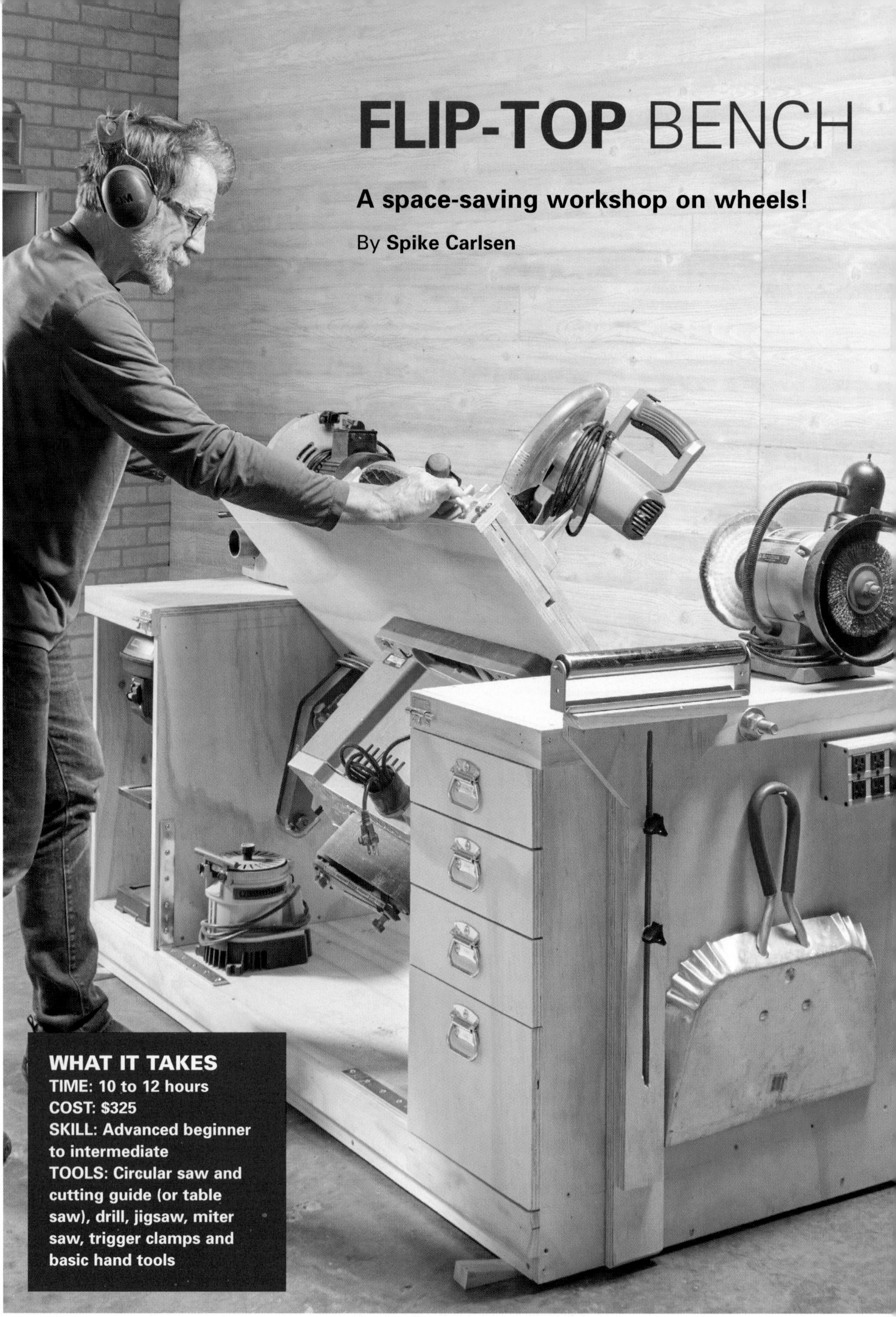

**WHAT IT TAKES**
TIME: 10 to 12 hours
COST: $325
SKILL: Advanced beginner to intermediate
TOOLS: Circular saw and cutting guide (or table saw), drill, jigsaw, miter saw, trigger clamps and basic hand tools

IT FLIPS! DOUBLE YOUR WORK SURFACE

O ver the years I've had a variety of workshops and workbenches. When I was a young apartment dweller, my workshop was a 3 x 3-ft. broom closet (for real!). Today, I'm lucky enough to have a shop with plenty of elbow room. But in between, most of my workshops consisted of a workbench loaded with tools, tucked into the corner of a garage or basement. If this sounds like you, check out this flip-top workbench. The revolving center section gives you a double platform for your benchtop tools.

## LOADED WITH FEATURES

**1.** The **wheels** make it mobile (and the simple lock wedges make it immobile).

**2.** The **drawers** and recessed **pegboard cabinet backs** give you convenient places to stash tools, supplies and accessories.

**3.** The **open side cabinet** gives you space to store a small drill press or other slim benchtop tool.

**4.** The **outfeed roller** lends a helping hand for handling long materials.

**5.** The **power strip** allows you to plug in multiple tools.

Of course, you could configure the workbench so one side holds benchtop tools while the other serves as a wide-open work surface.

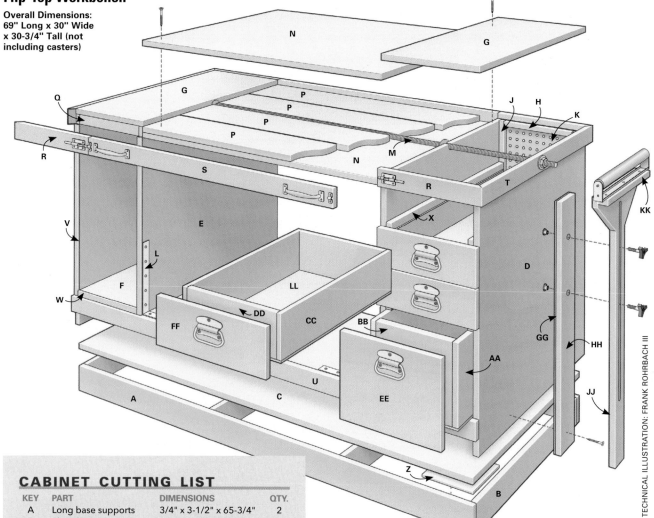

## Figure A
## Flip-Top Workbench

**Overall Dimensions:**
69" Long x 30" Wide
x 30-3/4" Tall (not
including casters)

1-1/4" SCREW

## CABINET CUTTING LIST

| KEY | PART | DIMENSIONS | QTY. |
|---|---|---|---|
| A | Long base supports | 3/4" x 3-1/2" x 65-3/4" | 2 |
| B | Short base supports | 3/4" x 3-1/2" x 27" | 4 |
| C | Base plywood | 3/4" x 28-1/2" x 65-3/4" | 1 |
| D | Long cabinet sides | 3/4" x 28-1/2" x 30" | 2 |
| E | Short cabinet sides | 3/4" x 28-1/2" x 25-3/4" | 2 |
| F | Cabinet bottom | 3/4" x 28-1/2" x 12" | 2 |
| G | Cabinet top | 3/4" x 28-1/2" x 13-1/2" | 2 |
| H | Short panel cleats | 3/4" x 3/4" x 10-1/2" | 4 |
| J | Long panel cleats | 3/4" x 3/4" x 25" | 4 |
| K | Pegboard back | 1/4" x 12" x 25" | 2 |
| L | L-brackets | 1" x 10" x 10" | 2 |
| M | Threaded rod | 3/4" x 72" * | 1 |
| N | Top & bottom platforms | 3/4" x 28-1/2" x 40" | 2 |
| P | Middle platform strips | 3/4" x 6-3/4" x 40" | 4 |
| Q | Cabinet backer boards | 3/4" x 1-1/2" x 12" | 4 |
| R | Front cabinet banding | 3/4" x 2-1/8" x 14-1/4" ** | 4 |
| S | Platform banding | 3/4" x 2-1/8" x 40" | 2 |
| T | Top side banding | 3/4" x 2-1/8" x 30" *** | 2 |
| U | Bottom banding | 3/4" x 2-1/2" x 67-1/4" | 2 |
| V | Side cabinet edging | 1/4" x 3/4" x 24-1/2" | 6 |
| W | Bottom cabinet edging | 1/4" x 3/4" x 12" | 3 |
| X | Drawer runner | 3/4" x 3/4" x 24" | 6 |
| Y | Platform lock wedges | 1-1/2" x 3/4" x 6" **** | 2 |
| Z | Caster shims | 1/4" x 8" x 8" plywood | 4 |

*Cut to length once cabinet is fully assembled (optional)
**Flat to long end (45-degree angle)
***Long end to long end (45-degree angles)
****Tapered from 3/8" to 3/4"

## DRAWERS AND ROLLER STAND CUTTING LIST

| KEY | PART | DIMENSIONS | QTY. |
|---|---|---|---|
| AA | Large drawer sides | 3/4" x 8" x 22" | 2 |
| BB | Large drawer ends | 3/4" x 8" x 10-1/4" | 2 |
| CC | Small drawer sides | 3/4" x 3-1/2" x 22" | 6 |
| DD | Small drawer ends | 3/4" x 3-1/2" x 10-1/4" | 6 |
| EE | Large drawer front | 3/4" x 10" x 13-3/8" | 1 |
| FF | Small drawer fronts | 3/4" x 4-1/2" x 13-3/8" | 3 |
| GG | Roller stand spacer | 1/4" x 3-1/2" x 28" | 1 |
| HH | Roller stand leg | 3/4" x 3-1/2" x 28" | 1 |
| JJ | Roller stand arm | 3/4" x 11" x 26" * | 1 |
| KK | Roller horizontal support | 3/4" x 1-1/2" x 12" | 1 |
| LL | Drawer bottoms | 1/4" x 11-3/4" x 22" | 4 |

* At wide top section
**Note:** The roller, tee nuts and wing nuts are available online.

**1** **Build the base.** Assemble the base frame from 1x4s, check for square, then install the 3/4-in. plywood sheathing and secure it with 2-in. screws.

## Start level and square

For the flip-top workbench to "flip," the base, side cabinets and revolving work surface must be flat and square. This means starting with flat plywood, making square cuts, installing components square to one another and checking your accuracy along the way.

Start by ripping three sheets of 3/4-in. plywood into 28-1/2-in.-wide panels using either a table saw or a circular saw and guide. To see how to build a guide, search for "circular saw guide" at familyhandyman.com. Set the long cutoffs aside; you'll put them to good use later. Cut parts C, D, E, F, G and N to length.

Build the 1x4 base (A and B) and sheathe it with 3/4-in. plywood (**Photo 1**). Build the two side support cabinets as shown in **Photo 2**. Note that one of the vertical supports is longer than the other so it can extend down alongside the base to add rigidity to the cabinet. Make sure each cabinet box is square. Secure the 3/4-in. x 3/4-in. cleats (H, J), insetting them 3 in. from the back of the box. Cut the pegboard panels (K) to size and glue and nail them into place. These panels help keep the cabinet boxes square and rigid.

Position the cabinets (**Photo 3**) and secure them to the base with a couple drywall screws. Measure to make sure the cabinets are equidistant from each other at the top, bottom, front and back. If you need to adjust the cabinets, remove the screws, adjust them, then resecure them with a couple more screws. Use a square to ensure the front of the cabinet is square to the

**2** **Build the side cabinets.** Assemble the two side cabinets. Make sure the parts are square to one another; cabinets built at an angle tend to stay at an angle.

**3** **Install the cabinets.** Secure the side cabinets to the base with a couple temporary screws. Make sure the distance between the two cabinets is equal at the front, back, top and bottom. Install the L-brackets.

**4** **Drill the pivot holes.** Find the exact center of both sides of both cabinets and drill 3/4-in. holes so the top of the hole is just kissing the bottom of the cabinet top. Use a jigsaw to square off the top edges of the holes so you can insert the threaded rod easily.

**5** **Insert the threaded rod.** Wiggle and slide the threaded rod through the two holes in the first cabinet, slip a pair of washers over the end of the rod, then fit the rod through the holes in the second cabinet. Slide a temporary spacer block over each end of the rod (see Photo 6), then loosely install the outer washers and locknuts.

platform, then secure the 10-in. L-brackets (L) with a few screws. Note: You'll firmly fasten the cabinets and L-brackets in place once the revolving platform is in place.

## Install the tool platform

Measure and mark the exact centers of the cabinets on both sides. Measure down 3/8 in. from the bottom of the top piece of plywood (G) to establish crosshairs. Drill a 3/4-in. hole (**Photo 4**); the top should just kiss the bottom of the cabinet top. Use a jigsaw to square off the top edges of the holes so the hole is U-shaped.

Feed the 6-ft. threaded rod through the holes in the first cabinet, slide two 3/4-in. washers over the rod as shown in **Photo 5**, then finish sliding the rod through the holes in the second cabinet. Let the end protrude about 2 in. past the cabinet on one side, slide a temporary spacer block (seen in **Photo 6**) over the end, then install

**6** **Slide in the first layer of the platform.** Secure temporary cleats to both cabinets, keeping them 3/4 in. below the rod, then slide the first platform layer in place. Even up the front and back edges with those of the cabinets on each side.

a 3/4-in. washer and locknut. Add a spacer block, washer and locknut to the other "long" end too. Leave the nuts a little loose for now.

Install a pair of temporary horizontal cleats 3/4 in. below the threaded rod. Slide one of the platform panels (N) into place so the front and back edges are exactly even with the front and back edges of the cabinets (**Photo 6**). Check to make sure the gaps between the panel and cabinets are equal. If not, adjust the cabinets and L-brackets until the gaps are equal. Now permanently install the L-bracket and cabinet screws.

The center layer of the platform consists of four strips (P). Apply glue to the backs of two of these strips. Position them on each side of the threaded rod, leaving a gap slightly less than the thickness of a credit card, then secure them with 1-1/4-in. drywall screws. Install the two outer strips (**Photo 7**) even with the outside edges of the platforms.

Apply glue to the center strips (**Photo 8**), position the final full platform panel (N) and secure that in place with 2-in. drywall screws. This top panel should be flush with the tops of the side cabinets. Give your top a 180-degree test spin to ensure it aligns with the edges of the cabinets in both positions.

## Install the trim and hardware

Install the backer boards (Q) along the inside top edges of the cabinets. Rip 1x3s to the thickness of your revolving platform (2-1/8 in. to 2-1/4 in. depending on the true thickness of your plywood) and install the banding boards (R, S, T and U). You'll need to drill holes through the side trim boards (T) to accommodate the rod, then remove the nuts, slide the trim boards into place, then secure the washers and locknuts for good. Use locking pliers to prevent the threaded rod from turning as you tighten the nuts; make sure the cabinets are snug to the platform while the platform can still revolve freely.

**7** **Install the middle layer of the platform.** Glue and screw the four middle panels into place, spacing the inner panels a "shy credit card thickness" away from the rod and holding the outer panels flush with the first layer.

**8** **Secure the third layer.** Apply wood glue to the middle panels, position the third layer and secure it in place with 2-in. drywall screws.

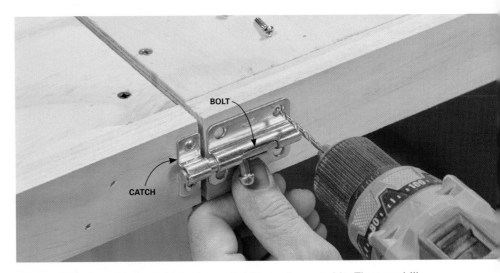

**9** **Install the barrel bolts.** Add the trim using Figure A as a guide. Then predrill holes for the barrel bolts and catches and secure with screws. Positioning the catch farther away from the bolt will provide more "play" when latching.

**10** **Install the drawer runners.** Lay out the positions of your drawers on masking tape, then use a temporary plywood spacer to hold the runners in place while you attach them. Rip the spacer to width as you install the smaller upper drawers.

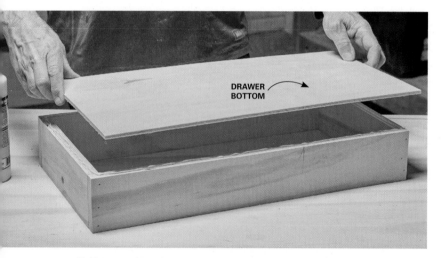

**11** **Install the drawer bottoms.** Use the drawer bottom to square up the drawer box. Attach it with glue and finish nails.

**12** **Install the drawer front.** Using screws as spacers, clamp the drawer front to the drawer box and secure it in place with four screws driven in from the back side.

Install the four barrel bolts—one on each corner of the revolving platform—as shown in **Photo 9**. If the bolts don't slide freely, use a pair of locking pliers to open up the U-shaped part of the catch.

Install the 1/4-in. edging strips (V and W) along the edges of the cabinets (except for the front of the drawer cabinet).

Add the four platform handles. With the help of an assistant, tilt the workbench onto its back and install the four casters. You want a 1/2-in. gap between the floor and bottom of the platform. To create that gap, install 8-in. squares of 1/4-in. to 1/2-in. plywood (Z), as needed, before you install the casters.

Cut a pair of 1-1/2-in. x 6-in. wedges that taper from 3/8 in. on one end to 3/4 in. on the other. To lock your workbench into place, tap them into the space under the platform. To remove them, tap them out with a hammer.

## Build the drawers

Apply masking tape to one side of the cabinet opening and mark out the desired number and size of drawers you want. Each opening should be 1/2 in. taller than the finished drawer; the drawer should be built 1/4 in. narrower than the cabinet opening. We elected to install three shallow drawers for benchtop tool bits and accessories, and one deeper drawer for hand power tools.

Use a scrap piece of plywood as a spacer for installing the lowest drawer runners (**Photo 10**), then rip the scrap to width and use it as a spacer for installing the other runners as you move upward.

Build the drawer boxes from leftover 3/4-in. plywood, then glue and screw the

| MATERIALS LIST | |
|---|---|
| ITEM | QTY |
| 3/4" x 4' x 8' AC plywood | 3 |
| 1x4 x 8' | 3 |
| 1x3 x 8' | 4 |
| 1/4" x 3/4" x 8' | 2 |
| 1/4" x 4' x 4' pegboard | 1 |
| 1/4" x 4' x 4' plywood | 1 |
| 3/4" x 72" threaded rod | 1 |
| 3/4" washers | 4 |
| 3/4" locknuts | 2 |
| Barrel bolts | 4 |
| Fixed handles | 4 |
| Drawer D-handles | 4 |
| Casters | 4 |
| 1-1/4" screws | 1 lb. |
| 2" screws | 1 lb. |

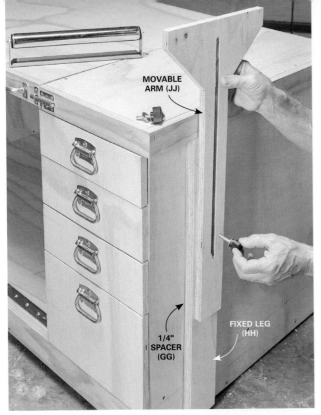

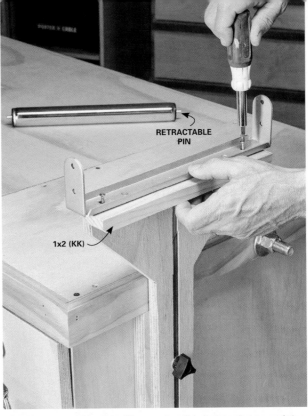

**13** **Mount the movable arm.** Cut the arm to shape and cut the slot down the center. Secure the movable arm to the underlying tee nuts with wing nuts.

**14** **Mount the roller.** Glue and nail a 1x2 to the top of the arm, then screw the roller carrier into place. A retractable pin in the roller allows you to remove and remount the roller.

1/4-in. plywood bottoms into place (**Photo 11**). Determine the heights of the drawer fronts and cut them from leftover plywood. Use a couple of screws as spacers (**Photo 12**), clamp the front to the drawer box, then secure the front in place with four screws driven in from the back.

## Build the roller stand

You can build up to four roller stands to help support material as you work. Drill holes and 1-in. counterbores into the back of the fixed leg (HH), then tap the tee nuts in place. Add a 1/4-in. spacer strip (GG) and secure the fixed arm to the cabinet side. Use a jigsaw to cut the movable arm (JJ) to shape and to cut the slot down the center (**Photo 13**). Secure the movable arm to the tee nuts with wing nuts. Glue and nail a 1x2 to the top of the movable arm, then screw the roller carrier into place (**Photo 14**). Secure the tools to the flip-top (**Photo 15**).

## Using it

The barrel bolts will fit snugly into the U-shaped catches—you want them snug for stability. **Take note:**

- It may be difficult to latch all four barrel bolts at one time; just make sure to always latch at least three of them for stability.
- If you find the barrel bolts difficult to slide in and out by hand, use a couple taps of the hammer to slide the bolt in and out.
- If the bolts fit really tight, use pliers to slightly open up the U-shaped catch of the barrel bolt.

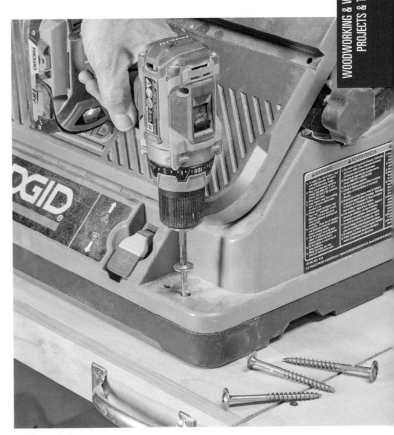

**15** **Secure the tools.** Drive heavy-duty, large-head, coarse-threaded screws through the tool mounting holes into the flip top. Be sure they penetrate 2 in. Keep balance in mind as you select the tools and determine their positions.

# QUICK & EASY
# CABINET DOORS

## A table saw is all you need!

By **Tom Caspar**

**If** you've got a table saw, here's a new way to put it to work: making cabinet doors. You don't need any special jigs—just your saw, large or small, a miter gauge and a sharp blade. And you don't need any specially prepared wood; material from a home center will be fine.

**MEET AN EXPERT**

Tom Caspar has been a professional wood-worker and custom furniture builder for more than 40 years.

## Choosing the wood

Plan to use 1x3 or 1x4 hardwood boards for the door's frame. You'll find this material at most home centers and lumberyards. These are just nominal dimensions, of course. The actual dimensions will be 3/4 x 2-1/2 in. or 3/4 x 3-1/2 in.

Store-bought wood has very straight and square edges. For the best results, use the wood in the widths it comes in. Narrower boards ripped from wider ones have a good chance of warping, a problem you won't be able to fix. Plus, you'll have a hard time making the new ripped edge smooth, square and crisp, which you'll need for tight joints. Be picky when you choose your wood. Sight down each piece to make sure it's flat and straight. If it's not, your door won't be flat or straight either, and it certainly won't close right!

For the panel, look for 1/4-in. plywood that lies flat, but don't worry if it's not exactly 1/4 in. thick. Using

this technique, that won't matter. You'll adjust the width of the grooves to fit the plywood.

## Sizing your doors

It's a good idea to make your doors 1/8 in. extra tall (so you can trim their ends after gluing). Make a list of the parts of your doors before you begin. For each one, you'll

### A mortise-and-tenon joint without all the fuss

Here's a classic way to put together a strong, good-looking door without making any unsightly holes.

TENON

MORTISE

need two stiles (the vertical parts), two rails (the horizontal parts) and one panel. Figuring the length of the stiles is easy. Take the height of the door you want and add 1/8 in. Figuring the length of the rails is more complicated. First, measure the total width of two stiles placed side by side. Subtract this number from the width of the door you

## Figure A
## Frame-and-Panel Door
The panel and tenons both fit into the same groove.

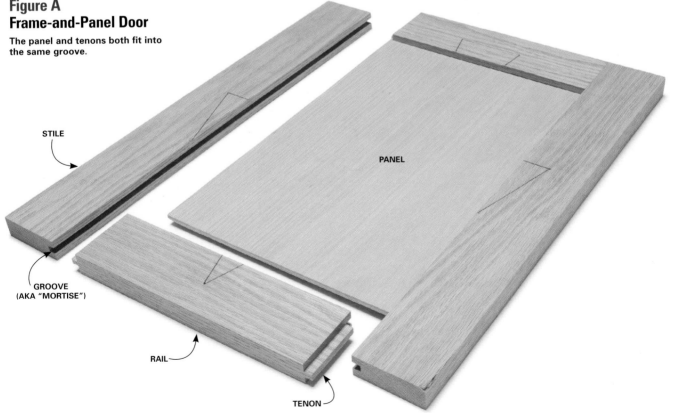

STILE

PANEL

GROOVE
(AKA "MORTISE")

RAIL

TENON

**1 Set up your miter gauges.** Adjust your miter gauge to 90 degrees and fasten a wood fence to it. I use two miter gauges to make sure the fence won't wiggle when slid back and forth.

WOOD FENCE

STOP BLOCK

CLIPPED CORNER

**2 Cut parts to length.** Saw a fresh slot through the fence. Measure from the slot to a block in order to cut the door's parts to length.

**3 Mark the parts.** Assemble the door's stiles and rails. Draw the four sides of a "cabinetmaker's triangle" to identify which part goes where.

want. Then add 1/2 in., the length of two tenons (see **Figure A**).

You'll also need at least two extra "test" pieces the same thickness as your rails and stiles. For your safety, they should be at least 12 in. long.

It's best to cut the plywood panel extra large at first. Rip it 1 in. wider than the length of the rails and 1 in. shorter than the length of the stiles.

## Cut the rails and stiles

To build a square door, the stiles and rails must all be exactly the same length with perfectly square ends. A table saw makes that easy.

The simplest method is to use the miter gauge that came with your table saw. Attach a straight 24-in.-long hardwood 1x3 for more accuracy and to avoid splintering out the end of the cut. This fence also provides a place to clamp stops (**Photo 1**). The fence should be about 2-1/2 in. tall and 24 in. long.

A better method is to use a second miter gauge. When you tie two miter gauges together with a fence, the pair will function as a table saw sled. You'll get perfectly straight, square cuts every time. (You can buy a second miter gauge for less than $20 online. The brand shouldn't matter—most are made to fit 3/4-in. slots.) Use a combination square (**Photo 1**) to set the miter gauges at 90 degrees.

The best way to cut duplicate parts is to use a "stop block" (**Photo 2**). It's just a square block with the corner nipped off to prevent dust buildup. Cut a fresh slot in the fence, then measure from the slot to the block to set up each cut. Clamp the stop block to the fence. A small C-clamp works well because it won't wiggle loose like some other clamps.

Precut your stiles and rails 1 in. extra long so they're easier to handle. To cut them to the exact length, first place the part on the left side of the fence. Cut about 1/4 in. off the part's right end to square it up. Slide the part over until it touches the block, and then cut the left end. Trim both ends of the test pieces now as well. Lay out the parts with the best sides facing up, then mark them (**Photo 3**).

## Cut custom grooves

Next, cut the grooves that receive the plywood panels and tenon tongues along the inside edges of all the pieces. The width of the grooves must match the thickness of your plywood. You'll accomplish this by making multiple passes, widening the groove a little each time until it's just right. It doesn't matter if you have a thin-kerf or standard blade—either will work. Start by drawing a centerline on the end of one of your test pieces. Place this piece on your saw, then adjust the saw's fence so that the blade is positioned slightly off the line. Next, adjust the height of the blade to cut a bit more than 1/4 in. deep. (Halfway between 1/4 in. and 5/16 in. is about right.) Saw a groove (**Photo 4**). Always use a featherboard to hold the wood tight to the fence as you push.

Next, flip the board end for end and make a second cut (**Photo 5**). This widens the groove. Check the groove's depth and adjust your blade up or down if necessary. See if your panel fits. The panel should slide into the groove without requiring any force, but it shouldn't wiggle, either. If the groove is too narrow (and it probably will be on the first try), nudge your saw's fence a tiny bit and repeat both cuts. If the groove is too wide, adjust the fence and start a new groove on the other side of the test piece. When you have the fence setting just right, cut grooves in all the rails and stiles.

## Saw the tenons

This setup also requires some fine-tuning, so begin by using one of your test pieces. Put the miter gauge back on the saw and clamp a block 1/4 in. away from the slot in the saw's fence (**Photo 6**). Place one of the rails or stiles next to the blade, then adjust the blade's height to cut just a bit lower than the groove (about 1/16 in.).

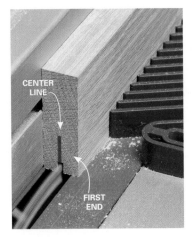

**4** **First pass.** Raise the blade a little over 1/4 in. Move the saw's fence so the groove will be slightly off center. Cut the groove the full length of both stiles.

**5** **Second pass.** Turn each stile end for end and cut a second groove next to the first one. See if your panel fits. If it doesn't, adjust the saw's fence and make both cuts again.

**6** **Set up for cutting tenons.** Clamp a block exactly 1/4 in. from the far side of the fence's slot. This distance is a little less than the depth of the grooves.

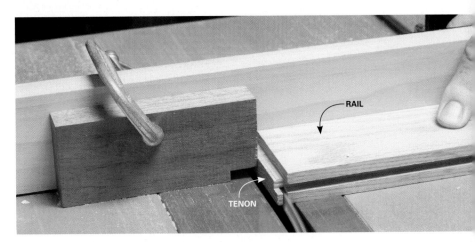

**7** **Cut the tenons.** Adjust the blade even with the groove. Make overlapping cuts, then flip the piece over and repeat. Test the fit of the tenon in a groove. If the fit is too tight, raise the blade and try again.

RAIL

**8** **Set the fence.** Next, set up the saw for cutting the plywood panel to size. Move the saw's fence so the distance from the blade matches the length of the door's rail.

**9** **Cut the panel to width.** Rip the panel good side up to avoid scratches and chips.

**10** **Measure for length.** Partially assemble the door. Measure the distance between the rail's tenons to determine the panel's length.

Make overlapping cuts on one end of the test piece (**Photo 7**). Flip the piece over and make the same cuts. See if the tenon fits into the groove as well as the plywood did. If the tenon is too tight, raise the blade a tiny bit and cut from both sides again. If the tenon is too loose, start over using a different end of a test piece. Once you get the blade set at the correct height, saw tenons on the ends of both rails.

## Cut the panel

Saw the panel to width first. It should be exactly as wide as the rails are long. Use one of the rails to position your saw's fence (**Photo 8**), then cut the panel (**Photo 9**).

To figure out the panel's length, assemble three sides of your door (**Photo 10**). Measure the distance between the tenons and subtract 1/16 in. Set your saw's fence to this dimension, then saw the panel (**Photo 11**). Sand all edges of the panel so it slips into the grooves easily.

## Glue the door

It's essential that you glue the panel into all four sides of the frame. That's what really holds the door together; the tenons alone are too short. To avoid cleaning up lots of excess glue,

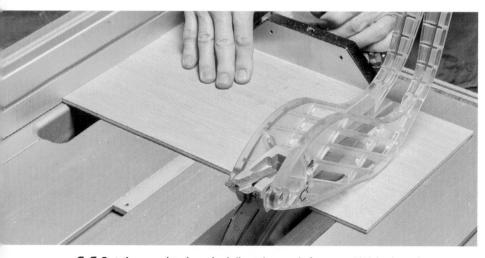

**11** **Cut the panel to length.** Adjust the saw's fence to 1/16 in. less than the distance you measured. Use a miter gauge to steady the wood when you cut it.

### Get help with the hinges
Building doors is only part of the story. You also have to hang them. Euro, or "cup" hinges, are the easiest, most forgiving means of hanging your new cabinet doors. For help sizing your doors to fit your cabinets, along with tips for selecting and installing Euro hinges, go to familyhandyman.com and search for "Euro hinges."

it's best to apply glue to the grooves rather than to the panel (**Photo 12**). I prefer using a small bottle of Elmer's Glue-All because its tip can be finely adjusted to lay down just a tiny amount of glue. But standard wood glue will also work.

Apply glue to both sides of the groove in one stile and one rail. Apply glue to the tenon of that rail. Push the rail into the stile, making sure the top edge of the rail is even with the end of the stile. Slide in the panel (**Photo 13**). Then apply glue to the groove, tenons and shoulders of the second rail. Slide the rail into place, again making sure it's even with the end of the stile. Apply glue to the remaining stile and nudge it into place.

Clamp the door as shown in **Photo 14**. Lay a straightedge across it to make sure it's flat. If one of the rails is tilted, correct this by raising or lowering the clamps. Wipe up the excess glue with a putty knife and a damp rag. Wait at least an hour before removing the clamps. To even up the ends of the door, cut 1/16 in. from each end using the table saw. The result: a perfect door.

**12** **Dribble glue in the grooves.** Apply a thin layer of glue to both sides of the groove in one stile. Apply glue to the tenon of one rail, then assemble. Make sure the rail is even with the end of the stile.

**13** **Slide in the panel.** Push the panel into the assembly. Apply glue to the second rail and slide it into place. Then apply glue to the other stile and push it home.

**14** **Clamp the joints tight.** Place the door on a couple of 2x4s to make room for the clamps. Tighten the clamps, clean off the glue, and that's it!

# EASY CRATE SHELF

## Hang up your crates, take them down— this convenient rack can handle a lot of stuff!

By **Jeff Gorton**

OPENINGS CAN FACE UP OR OUT!

To browse a variety of crates, check out cratesandpallet.com

**1 HOUR PROJECT**

Wooden crates are a staple at flea markets and antiques stores, but now you can also buy them at home centers. The crates shown here cost about $10 each, and are sturdy enough to hold books and record albums. We wanted a quick and convenient way to hang the crates, and easily take them down if needed, so we devised this simple hanging rack.

The rack is just a 1x8 board with hangers every 16 in. We assembled the hangers from machine screws, nuts and aluminum bar stock. The most difficult part of the project is cutting the aluminum and drilling the holes. And even this is simple enough for a beginning DIYer.

### Display or storage for any room
- Crates are available in various shapes and sizes
- Apply a clear finish, stain or paint
- They're easy to hang and take down

## WHAT IT TAKES
**TIME:** 1 hour
**COST:** $15 plus crates ($10 each)
**SKILL:** Beginner
**TOOLS:** Drill, 3/4-in. or larger spade bit, 1/4-in. drill bit, hacksaw, square, adjustable or 7/16-in. wrench

**1** **Cut the aluminum.** Mark the bar at 7-1/4 in., clamp it to your workbench and cut it with a hacksaw, or a miter saw and a carbide blade. Dull the razor-sharp ends with 100-grit sandpaper.

ALUMINUM BAR

HACKSAW

This is a simple project that you'll be able to finish in about an hour. Our crate rack can hold four crates, but you can make yours shorter or taller to fit your needs. It's designed to hold crates with 3/8-in.-thick slats. But you can easily modify it to accommodate crates with thicker slats by adding the right combination of nuts and washers to the machine screws. Remember, if you want to hang crates with slats thicker than 3/8 in., you'll need to increase the length of the machine screws accordingly.

Start by making the aluminum hangers. Use a square and a pencil or fine marker to mark the aluminum bar. Clamp the aluminum bar to a solid surface and use a sharp, 32-tooth hacksaw blade to cut along the line (**Photo 1**). Aluminum is so soft that you can easily clean up and polish the cut end with sandpaper. When you're done cutting and smoothing the aluminum, mark the hole locations using **Figure B** as a guide and drill the holes (**Photo 2**). Finish the hangers by threading on the nuts (see **Photo 4**).

The next step is to drill holes in the 1x8 to accept the hangers. Choose the

Overall dimensions:
72" Tall x 7-1/4" Wide

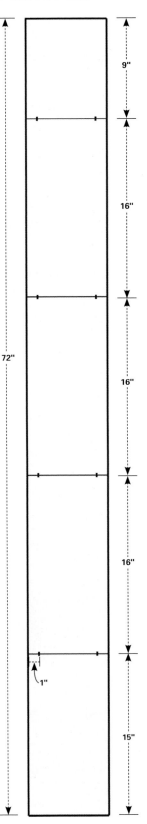

9"

16"

16"

16"

72"

15"

1"

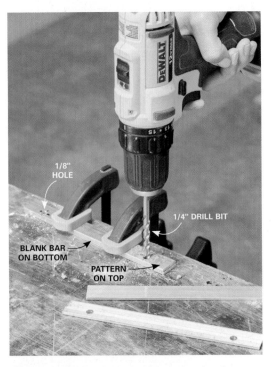

1/8" HOLE

1/4" DRILL BIT

BLANK BAR ON BOTTOM

PATTERN ON TOP

**2** **Drill holes for the bolts.** Mark the aluminum using **Figure B** on p. 139 as a guide. Drill a 1/16-in. hole at each mark. Then enlarge the hole by drilling with a 1/4-in. bit. Clamp the completed aluminum hanger on a blank hanger. Drill 1/4-in. holes using the completed hanger as a guide.

7/8" SPADE BIT

3/8"-DEEP RECESS

**3** **Mark and drill the board.** Mark the hole locations on the back of the board. Drill 3/8-in.-deep recesses with a spade bit. Then drill out the center with a 1/4-in. bit.

## Figure B
## Hanger Holes

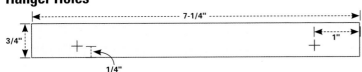

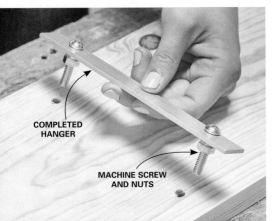

**COMPLETED HANGER**

**MACHINE SCREW AND NUTS**

**4 Mount the hangers.** Slide the machine screws through the holes in the board. If the fit is too tight, enlarge the holes in the 1x8 slightly by wiggling the 1/4-in. bit in the hole while the drill is running. Put a machine screw into each hole and thread two nuts onto each screw. They only need to be finger-tight.

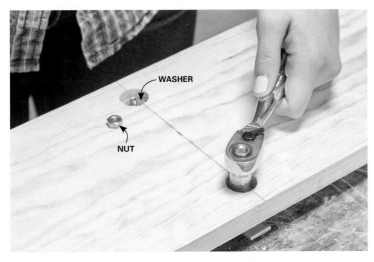

**WASHER**

**NUT**

**5 Tighten the hanger nuts.** Add washers and thread the nuts onto the machine screws. Tighten the nuts with a wrench.

best-looking side of the 1x8 to face out. Then turn the board over and use the dimensions in **Figure A** to draw square lines across the back of the 1x8. Mark the hole locations and drill recesses and mounting holes (**Photo 3**). Mount one of the hangers on the board (**Photos 4** and **5**) and check the fit by sliding one of the crates onto the hanger. The crate slat should slip easily behind the aluminum bar. If the fit is too tight, remove the hanger and add a washer to the bolt. Mount the hangers, along with additional washers if needed, to complete the project.

Because the crate rack with crates could be quite heavy, we recommend that you mount it to a stud or other solid wood (**Photo 6**). If there isn't a stud in your ideal location, use two heavy-duty hollow-wall anchors like the Toggler brand Snaptoggle anchors instead.

**6 Screw the board to a stud.** Locate a stud in the spot where you want to install the rack. Screw the top of the board to the stud. Use a level to plumb the board. Then drive a screw through the bottom.

**STUD MARK**

**2-1/2" SCREW**

**LEVEL**

**ADD SCREW AT BOTTOM**

## MATERIALS LIST

Everything you need to build this crate rack is available at home centers.

**1x8 PINE BOARD:** We used a 6-ft. board, but you can match the length to the number of crates or baskets you want to hang. Choose a straight board that's not twisted or cupped.

**CRATES:** We purchased crates at a home center. To see a variety of crates and find retailers, visit cratesandpallet.com.

**1/8-IN. x 3/4-IN. ALUMINUM BAR:** Allow 8 in. for every crate hanger. This project required a 3-ft. length.

**NUTS AND MACHINE SCREWS:** You'll need two 1/4 x 20 machine screws 1-1/4 in. long and six 1/4-in. nuts for every hanger. That's eight machine screws and 24 nuts for this project.

**SPADE BIT:** The size isn't critical, but it must be at least 3/4 in.

**HACKSAW:** A blade with 32 teeth per inch is ideal. Check the label to find out.

**HANGING HARDWARE:** You'll need two 2-1/2-in. screws or two heavy-duty drywall anchors to hang the crate rack.

# BUILT-TO-LAST
# VIKING LONG TABLE

**Big enough for the whole clan
and costs less than $200!**

by **Spike Carlsen**

## MEET AN EXPERT

Spike Carlsen is a former editor at *Family Handyman*. His sixth book, *Building Unique and Useful Kids' Furniture*, is now available. When he's not making sawdust, you can find him—and his ever-expanding family—feasting around his original Viking table creation in Stillwater, Minnesota.

When the Vikings of yore built something—a longboat, a lodge, even a drinking horn—it was sturdy and simple, functional yet attractive. This table fits that mold. It's big, rock-solid and buildable with basic tools, yet it has a certain elegance to it.

This style of table is known as a draw-bore trestle. The "trestle" is the stretcher that connects the legs, and "drawbore" refers to the "bored" mortises and tenons that "draw" the legs and trestle tightly together to create a stable base.

You can easily shorten (and lighten) your table by modifying the dimensions given. The benches that accompany this table are built using the same template and same basic procedures. To find out how to build them, search for "Viking benches" at familyhandyman.com.

## WHAT IT TAKES
**TIME: 25 to 30 hours**
**COST: $180**
**SKILL: Intermediate**
**TOOLS: Circular saw, jigsaw, router, belt sander, drill, clamps and basic hand tools**

## It's "knockdownable"!

The table, built as shown, is enormous—long, wide and weighty. But by removing two wedges and eight screws, you can separate the legs, tabletop and trestle so you can store the table for the winter or move it to a different location.

## Pick the right wood

If you're building this table for inside use, you can use everyday dimensional lumber or more expensive hardwoods. But if it will be used outside, consider one of the following weather-resistant options:

**CEDAR, REDWOOD OR CYPRESS.** One of these "premium" exterior woods is most likely available in your area. Select boards with the most heartwood—the darker inside part of the tree, which is more durable than the lighter-colored sapwood. The downside? These woods can be wickedly expensive and, in some cases, soft.

**TREATED LUMBER.** It's moderately priced and stands up well to weather, but it's often wet from the treatment process, which means it's more likely to shrink and twist, and less likely to glue up well. It's also difficult to apply a good-looking finish until the wood fully dries.

**DOUGLAS FIR.** This is the wood we used. It's more expensive than the more widely available "standard" dimensional lumber—often labeled H-F, S-P-F or "white wood"—but cheaper than the premium woods. It's about 20 percent harder, and stronger, heavier and more moisture resistant than standard lumber. Not all home centers and lumberyards stock Douglas fir; look for the "Doug Fir" or "DF" stamp. If in doubt, ask. In our area, Lowe's and contractor lumberyards carry Douglas fir.

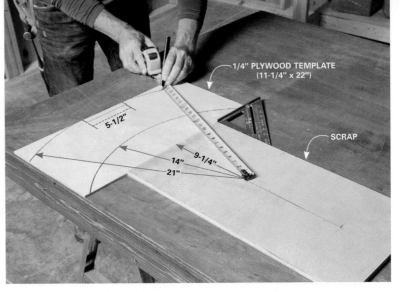

**1 Make the leg template.** Set a scrap of plywood against the template. Drive a screw 9-1/4 in. from the end of the scrap and use that screw as a pivot point for your tape measure. Then swing the two arcs to create the leg shape.

**2 Glue up the leg "sandwich."** Trace the leg shape onto two 22-in. 2x12s, lightly dampen the bottom piece, then apply polyurethane glue. Use a plastic putty knife to spread the glue slightly beyond the edges of the layout lines and across the main body of the leg.

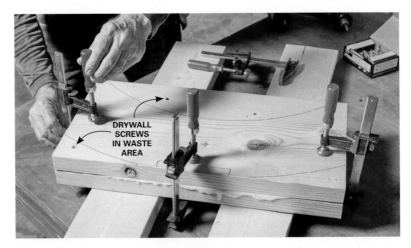

**3 Clamp the leg blanks together.** Line up the "mortise" edges of the boards, then drive a few drywall screws into the scrap wood to keep the boards aligned. Fasten clamps around the perimeter to force the boards tightly together.

# Figure A
## Viking Long Table
**Overall Dimensions: 110-1/2" Long x 40-3/4" Wide x 28-3/4" Tall**

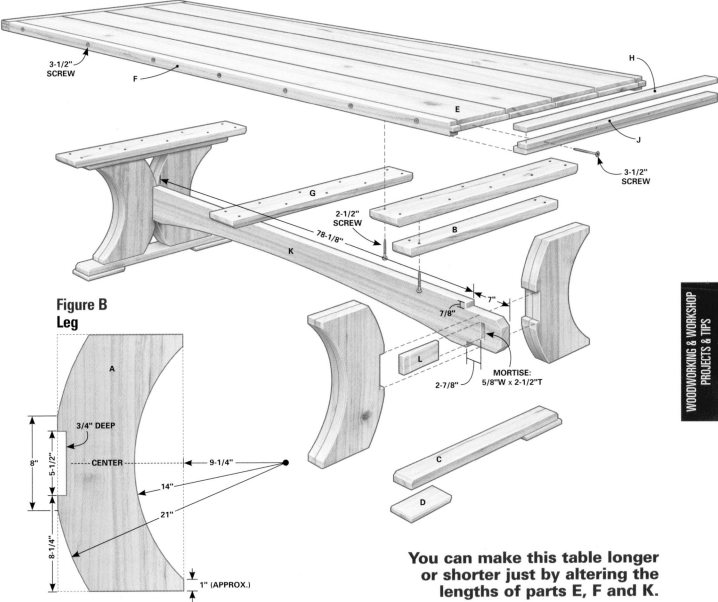

3-1/2" SCREW

F

H

E

J

3-1/2" SCREW

G

B

2-1/2" SCREW

78-1/8"

K

7"

7/8"

MORTISE: 5/8"W x 2-1/2"T

L

2-7/8"

## Figure B
## Leg

A

3/4" DEEP

CENTER

8"

5-1/2"

8-1/4"

9-1/4"

14"

21"

1" (APPROX.)

C

D

## You can make this table longer or shorter just by altering the lengths of parts E, F and K.

## CUTTING LIST

| ITEM | QTY. | SIZE | PART |
|------|------|------|------|
| A | 8 | 1-1/2" x 11-1/4" x 22" | Legs |
| B | 2 | 1-1/2" x 3-1/2" x 30" | Top leg plates |
| C | 2 | 1-1/2" x 3-1/2" x 30" | Bottom leg plates |
| D | 4 | 3/4" x 4" x 8" | Feet (white oak) |
| E | 4 | 1-1/2" x 9-1/4" x 108" | Top boards |
| F | 2 | 1-1/2" x 2-1/4" x 108" | Edge boards |
| G | 3 | 1-1/2" x 5-1/2" x 37" | Tabletop braces |
| H | 2 | 3/4" x 2" x 40-3/4" | Outside breadboard ends (white oak) |
| J | 1 | 3/4" x 1-1/4" x 40-3/4" | Middle breadboard end (white oak) |
| K | 1 | 1-1/2" x 7-1/2" x 92-1/8" | Stretcher |
| L | 2 | 3/4" x 2-1/2" x 7" | Wedges (white oak) |

## MATERIALS LIST

| ITEM | QTY. |
|------|------|
| 2x12 x 8' Douglas fir | 2 |
| 2x10 x 10' Douglas fir | 4 |
| 2x8 x 8' Douglas fir | 1 |
| 3/4" x 5-1/2" x 4' white oak | 3 |
| 2x6 x 10' Douglas fir | 2 |
| 2x4 x 10' Douglas fir | 1 |
| 2-1/2" exterior deck screws | 1 lb. |
| 2-1/2" exterior washer-head screws | 2 lbs. |
| 3-1/2" exterior washer-head screws | 2 lbs. |
| Construction adhesive | 1 tube |

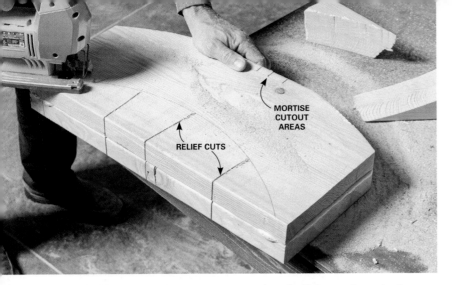

MORTISE CUTOUT AREAS

RELIEF CUTS

**4** **Cut the legs to shape.** Make a series of relief cuts along the "concave" side of the leg, then use a jigsaw with a coarse blade (or band saw) to cut the curves. Make a series of relief cuts for the stretcher mortise, then use a jigsaw and chisel to make the opening.

**5** **Sand the legs and rout the edges.** Clamp the legs to your work surface, then use a belt sander to smooth the curves and eliminate blade marks. Use a router with a 1/2-in. round-over bit to soften the curved edges, but leave the top, bottom and stretcher areas square.

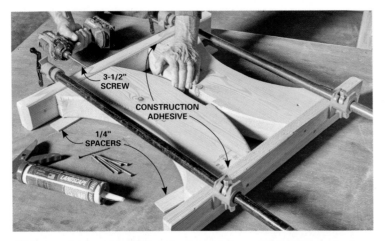

3-1/2" SCREW

CONSTRUCTION ADHESIVE

1/4" SPACERS

**6** **Create the leg assemblies.** Set the arches on 1/4-in. spacers, butt the arches together, then dry-fit the top and bottom plates. Check the stretcher opening with a 2x6 to make sure the tenon will fit. Finally, apply construction adhesive to the leg ends and clamp and screw the parts together.

We used white oak for the feet, the breadboard ends and the wedges. Other woods would work fine, but we liked the extra strength, hardness and contrast the white oak provided in these critical pieces. Red oak, the type you'll often find at home centers, isn't a good substitute, since it's much more prone to rot. You can find white oak at specialty woodworking stores and online.

How has the Douglas fir table I built four years ago stood up? We give it a quick sanding and a coat of Cabot Australian Timber Oil every spring and cover it with a tarp during the tough Minnesota winters. The table remains as beautiful as it was on the day it was made.

## Create the legs

Take your time at the lumberyard selecting flat, straight boards free of split ends, twists, cupping and loose knots—you'll spare yourself a lot of clamping and cussing down the road. If you have trouble finding perfect 2x12s, purchase an extra board—or longer boards and cut around the defects.

Cut your boards into eight 22-in.-long pieces; make sure the ends are square. Pair up your boards so when one is laid atop the other, there's little or no gap along the ends and edges. If you flip or rotate the boards, sometimes you'll find the perfect fit. Try to have any defects fall in the areas of the wood you'll be cutting away as you form the legs.

Mark out your leg template onto 1/4-in. plywood as shown in **Photo 1**. Cut just outside the line with a fine-tooth jigsaw blade, then use a belt sander to sand right up to the line. Use your template to trace the leg shape onto two leg sections (A). Lightly dampen the bottom piece—polyurethane glue needs moisture to work— then apply healthy squiggles of the glue across the main body of the leg (**Photo 2**). Use a plastic putty knife to spread the glue slightly past the edges of your template marks. Polyurethane glue is waterproof, and tightly glued seams mean less chance of moisture working its way between the boards.

Place the top board over your glued board, taking care to even up the edges. Install two or three screws in the waste area (**Photo 3**) to keep the pieces aligned and then use clamps—lots of them—along all the edges. Drive additional screws into the waste area to help draw the pieces tightly together. The glue will foam as it goes to work. Keep your boards clamped together at least two hours or overnight for good measure. Create three more leg blanks this way.

Cut out the legs. A jigsaw with a long, coarse blade (**Photo 4**) works fine, but a band saw works better, so use one if you have access to it. Whichever tool you use, make a series of "relief" cuts as shown. These allow you to remove waste material as you cut. They also allow your blade to get back on track if it wanders and begins making angled cuts, which jigsaws in particular are prone to do. If you have a jigsaw with reciprocating action, set it at zero; it will cut slower, but your blade will wander less.

Next use a belt sander to smooth and true up the curved sides (**Photo 5**). Begin with a coarse belt, then progress to finer grits. If you have access to a benchtop belt sander or spindle sander, use it; you'll get results faster.

Use a router with a 1/2-in. round-over bit to soften the edges of the curved parts. Don't rout the tops and bottoms of the legs or the flat area where the mortise cutout will be.

Position two leg sections next to each other (**Photo 6**) and check to make sure the mortise cutout (where the stretcher tenon will go) can accommodate a 2x6 test piece. It's easier to enlarge these areas now, before joining the legs. Set the legs on 1/4-in. spacers (so they'll be centered on the 2x4 top and bottom plates). Then apply construction adhesive to the ends to add a layer of moisture protection, and cinch the leg sections tightly together and to the 2x4 plates (B, C) with clamps. Secure the legs to the plates using 3-1/2-in. exterior screws. Repeat for the other leg assembly.

Cut the feet (D) to size and shape, then secure them with glue and screws to the bottom plates (**Photo 10**).

## Build the breadboard ends and tabletop

"Breadboard" ends have been used by woodworkers for centuries—and for good reason:

- They help keep the ends of the tabletop boards flat and aligned.
- They help protect the end grain of the boards from moisture and wear.
- They allow the top boards to shrink and expand more freely without cracking.
- They provide a smooth edge for your tummy to rest against.

The 2-1/4-in.-wide boards along the long edges give the tabletop more mass to match

**7** **Cut the tongues.** Position the top and edge boards "good side up," then, with your circular saw set 3/4 in. deep, make a series of cuts starting 3/4 in. from the end. Make one of these cuts across the very end to guide your chisel. Make these tongue cuts on both sides of the edge boards.

**8** **Build the breadboard ends.** Use waterproof glue and clamps to build the three-part breadboard ends. Make sure the center trough is 3/4 x 3/4 in. to accommodate the tongues of the top boards.

**9** **Assemble the top.** Position the top and edge boards "good side down," then screw the braces and breadboard ends to top boards.

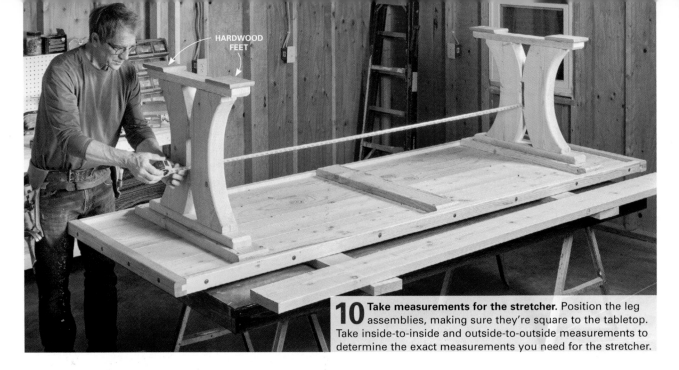

**10** **Take measurements for the stretcher.** Position the leg assemblies, making sure they're square to the tabletop. Take inside-to-inside and outside-to-outside measurements to determine the exact measurements you need for the stretcher.

HARDWOOD FEET

the heft of the legs. Rip your two 2-1/4-in.-wide edge boards (F) from a 2x6. Cut these and your four 2x10 top boards (E) to length. To create the "tongues" that slide into the breadboard ends, set your circular saw to cut 3/4 in. deep, then make one cut 3/4 in. from each end of each board (**Photo 7**), another cut right along the end, and then a couple more cuts in between. Place your chisel along the end cut and use it as a guide to remove the waste material. When you're done, each end will have a 3/4-in. x 3/4-in. tongue. Make the same cuts on the top and bottom of the edge boards (F) as shown.

Next, make your board ends (H, J) as shown in **Photo 8**; they're essentially three-board sandwiches with the middle board inset 3/4 in. to accommodate the tongues you've created. We made ours from white oak for strength, appearance and durability, but you can make yours from the same wood as your table. Be sure to use waterproof glue. Rout the outer edges and cut the breadboard ends to length; make them 1/2 in. longer than the width of the finished tabletop to accommodate board movement.

Place your two edge boards (F) and four tabletop boards (E) on your work surface upside down. Space your top boards 1/8 in. apart using

drywall nails or shims. Even up the ends of the six boards, then tap the breadboard ends into place. Position the braces (G) and make sure everything is tight and square (**Photo 9**). Then drill 3/8-in.-diameter holes through the support braces and secure the braces to the four tabletop boards using 1/4-in. x 2-1/2-in. washer-head screws. Note: The slightly oversize holes give the boards wiggle room to shrink and expand to help prevent cracking. Predrill holes in the breadboard ends—one centered on each of the four wide boards—and secure them with 3-1/2-in. washer-head screws. Finally, drill holes along the center of the edge boards (F); angle them slightly toward the top of the table so the screws will have plenty of meat to bite into, then drive home the 3-1/2-in. washer-head screws.

## Assemble the table

Position the two leg assemblies as shown in **Photo 10**. Make sure they're square to the tabletop, then measure the distance between them. This will give you the dimensions you need to create your stretcher. Note that we provide an exact stretcher length in the **Cutting List**, but your length will most likely differ.

There are a few key measurements you need to get right in

order for your stretcher and draw-bore wedges (**Photo 11**) to do their jobs.

- **THE SHOULDER MEASUREMENT.** This is the distance between leg assemblies. This distance is key because the shoulders hold the leg assemblies the right distance apart and "wiggle-proof" the table.
- **THE TENON LENGTH AND WIDTH.** The tenon extends 7 in. past the shoulder and should be 5-1/2 in. wide.
- **THE MORTISE CUTOUT.** The cutout is centered on the tenon and is 5/8 in. wide and 2-1/2 in. long. The edge of the mortise near the outside of the leg should be inset into the leg by about 1/8 in. so that when the wedge is installed, it will draw the shoulder tightly against the leg. When done properly, this joint is amazingly strong, so take your time to get it sized and positioned just right.

With all of this in mind, make the stretcher (**Photo 11**). Once you've marked the key stretcher length, tenon and mortise measurements, bend a thin piece of wood to create the arched bottom of the stretcher. Use a jigsaw to cut out the parts. Drill 5/8-in. starter holes in each end of the 2-1/2-in.-long mortises to give your jigsaw an entry point.

To make your wedges (L), first cut a 3/4-in. board 24 in. long, then rip it 2-1/4 in. wide. Use a belt sander to taper each end of the board, then cut them to their final 7-in. length and soften the edges.

Separate the legs and install the stretcher. Drive the wedges into place as shown in **Photo 12**. The screw driven through the end of the tenon helps reinforce it to prevent the wedge from blowing out the end of the tenon when driven in tightly.

Once the stretcher and legs are locked together, secure the leg assemblies to the tabletop crosspieces (**Photo 13**). Sand and smooth out any rough areas, then apply your exterior finish.

**11** **Lay out and cut the stretcher.** Use your measurements to lay out the overall length of the stretcher and establish the positions of the shoulders, tenons and mortises. Bend a flexible piece of wood and trace the edge to create the curved lower edge. Use a jigsaw to cut out all the parts, then rout the edges.

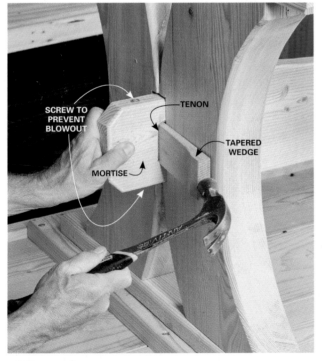

**12** **Install the stretcher and wedge it tight.** Slide the tenons through the leg openings, then tap wedges into the mortises to pull the shoulders tightly against the legs. The long screw at the end of the tenon helps prevent the wedge from splitting out the end of the stretcher.

**13** **Screw the leg assemblies to the braces.** Center the leg assemblies on the end braces. Drill oversize holes through the leg plates, then secure the legs to the top with washer-head screws.

# CEDAR **BATH MAT**

## It's just right for an entryway or a closet, too

By **Matt Boley**

**1 HOUR PROJECT**

**WHAT IT TAKES**
**TIME:** 1 hour
**COST:** $20
**SKILL:** Beginner
**TOOLS:** 1x2 or 1x6 lumber, 1-1/4-in. brads or nails, paint stir stick, sandpaper, antiskid pads, finishing supplies

**1** **Cut the slats.** If your local home center doesn't have good-quality 1x2 stock for the slats, buy a 1x6 and cut 1-1/2-in. strips. An 8-ft. 1x6 provided all the slats I needed.

**2** **Round the edges.** I rounded the slat edges with a 1/4-in. round-over bit. If you don't have a router, ease the edges with 100-grit sandpaper.

I saw a cedar mat like this online for $35 and thought, "Hey, I can make a better one for less." The project is super simple, practical and versatile: It can be a bath mat, an entry mat for a patio or a drip-dry platform for wet shoes. Here are some planning and building tips:

■ I chose cedar for its looks and rot-resistance. But any wood would be fine.

■ My mat is 14-1/2 x 30 in., but you can make yours any size. Just be sure the slats are supported by runners no more than 15 in. apart.

■ Large knots create weak spots, so you may need to buy extra lumber to get sections that are free of knots.

■ Although the nail holes won't show, I patched them with wood filler before sanding and finishing. Left exposed, the nail heads may rust and stain the floor.

■ I finished my mat with tung oil. Oil finishes aren't as durable as some others, but they're easy to renew when the finish starts to wear—just wipe on a fresh coat.

■ Be sure to apply antiskid pads on the bottom to keep the mat from sliding on hard floors.

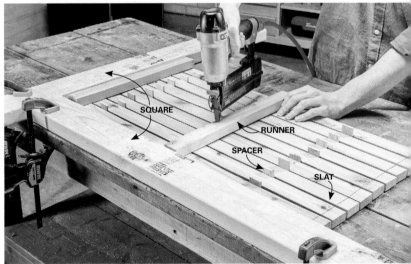

SQUARE

RUNNER

SPACER

SLAT

**3** **Assemble the mat.** Clamp wood scraps to your workbench to form a square. Lay out the slats against the guide using spacers cut from a paint stir stick. Then cut three runners 1 in. shorter than the width of the mat. Fasten the runners to the slats with 1-1/4-in. brads or nails.

# FRENCH CLEAT
# TOOL WALL

## Easy to build, easy to reconfigure as your tool collection grows

By **Travis Larson**

Just think of it—a tool storage system for your garage or shop that you can endlessly reconfigure to accommodate all your tools. They'll be right at your fingertips whenever you need them. And when it's time to straighten up at the end of the day, you'll know right where everything goes, making cleanup quick and easy.

How much you spend depends not only on the size of your storage wall but also on the level of finish you're after. We spent about $500 on the materials for our wall, but you could build it for about half the price by using 3/4-in. CDX construction plywood.

**WHAT IT TAKES**
TIME: 2 weekends as shown
COST: $500 as shown (about $10 per square foot)
SKILL: Intermediate
TOOLS: Miter saw, table saw, drill/driver

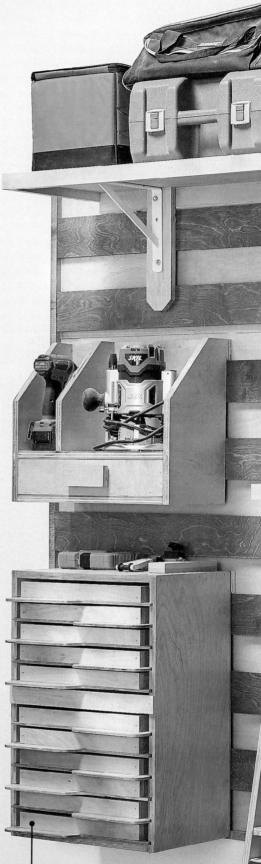

To learn how to build this, go to familyhandyman.com and search for "tray tower."

## MEET AN EXPERT

Travis Larson has been building homes, decks and additions and doing serious woodworking for well over 40 years. He's been an editor at *Family Handyman* for the last 20 of those years.

### What is a French cleat?

French cleats are an ingenious means of hanging just about anything. Mating 45-degree bevels—one on the wall, the other on the tool holder—interlock to form a rock-solid connection. You just drop the tool holder over the cleat and it's done—perfectly level, perfectly solid. No fasteners!

ACCESSORY CLEAT

45° BEVEL

WALL CLEAT

**1** **Mount a temporary ledger.** Cut one of the wall cleats to width (**Photo 4**) and then level it and screw it to the wall studs.

TEMPORARY LEDGER (CLEAT)

**2** **Hang the plywood.** Rest the first sheet on the temporary ledger and screw it to the studs with 2-in. screws spaced every 12 in. Rest the second sheet on top of the first and screw it to the studs as well. Remove the temporary ledger.

## BUILD THE WALL

### Size to fit your needs

Our wall is two horizontal sheets of 3/4-in. birch plywood (a 4 x 8-ft. sheet and a 2 x 8-ft. sheet; **Photo 2**), with 1x2 maple trim (**Photo 3**). The size of your wall depends on how much you want to store and how much space you have. The construction techniques are the same for any size wall.

### Apply the finish to full sheets before cutting

We prefinished the plywood and trim boards. You should too, because it saves lots of time and gives you a smoother finish. You'll still have to coat the cut edges, but that's a lot easier than finishing the entire wall after it's built.

We used Varathane Summer Oak and American Walnut stain to create the light and dark parts. We rolled on the stain with 4-in. foam rollers and then wiped it off with cotton rags. Topcoat with a water-based polyurethane.

### A table saw makes the project much easier

The best tool for ripping the parts and cleats is a table saw. However, if you don't have access to one, you can also make the cuts with a straight-edge and a circular saw. If you go that route, it's worth building a dedicated straightedge. To find out how, search for "create circular saw cutting guides" at familyhandyman.com.

A miter saw works well for cutting miters on edge banding and the 45-degree angles on many of the components. Flatten the point of each bevel (**Photo 4**) so they won't cut you or splinter off when you hang your tool holders. You can assemble your tool holders with either glue and 2-in. brads, or 2-in. and 1-1/4-in. trim-head screws.

**3** **Add the border.** Cut the 1x2 to fit around the perimeter and nail it into place with 2-in. 18-gauge brads.

1x2 TRIM

**4** **Cut the wall cleats.** Rip the French cleat strips for the wall to 4 in. wide. Then reset the saw to 45 degrees and adjust the fence to leave about a 1/8-in. flat area at the point of the bevels. Cut the 45-degree bevels on the strips. Repeat the process for the accessory cleats, but rip them to 2-1/2 in. wide.

1/8" FLAT SPOT

**5** **Mount the wall cleats.** Space the cleats with a 2x4 block and secure them with a pair of 1-1/4-in. trim-head screws spaced every 16 in. Keep the screws 1 in. from the top and bottom of the cleats.

2x4 SPACER

# BUILDING TIPS

Most of the tool holders take less than 20 minutes to build. Have fun and don't be afraid to toss your failures and try again. Here are tips to help you build your wall and make custom holders for your tools and gear.

1-1/4" SCREW

## Fasten with trim-head screws

Use 1-1/4-in. screws for 3/4-in. to 3/4-in. joinery. Use 2-in. screws for edge joints.

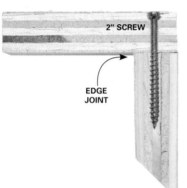

2" SCREW

EDGE JOINT

TEST WALL

## Build a test wall

Mount three cleats on a half sheet of plywood to mock up a test wall. Use it to test and assemble your shelves, bins, hangers and more.

## The plywood is optional

If your garage or shop wall has exposed studs, you'll find the plywood in our plan ideal for finishing the wall. But you could also screw the wall cleats right through existing plywood or drywall or even directly to the studs.

## Plan your tool holders

Lay out the tools or other items to help you decide what type and size holder will work the best.

TOP CLEAT

BOTTOM CLEAT

**Small shelves** can get by with minimal support. They'll only need vertical supports that cover one wall cleat.

**Medium-size shelves,** depending on their design and the weight of their contents, may need to span more than one cleat.

**Support large,** heavy units with double cleats. Screw the top cleat to the tool holder, then hang it on the wall with the bottom cleat already nested in the wall cleat. That way you can screw the tool holder to the bottom cleat from the front in exactly the right position.

### Plan for outlets

If you have existing outlets near the floor, you can tap into those outlets to feed new outlets in the slat wall itself. These new outlets can be at workbench level to feed battery chargers or up high to power lights.

You can cut holes in the drywall and feed cable up to those locations. You don't need to patch those holes because they will be covered by the slat wall. Leave the cables coiled behind the plywood and note their locations. Then you can cut outlet holes in the plywood and insert "remodeling" junction boxes.

## Take advantage of the hardware aisle

Stroll through the hardware section at your favorite home center. Choose hooks, racks and shelf brackets and build components to suit them.

# FLOATING SHELF
## (WITH A SECRET DRAWER)

**2 HOUR** PROJECT

**Floating shelves are fashionable and functional. But this one offers something more. It can act as a hiding place for valuables and any other items you want out of sight.**

By **Matt Boley**

**W**e'll show you how to build a 12 x 24-in. floating shelf, but you can easily size this design to suit your space. We built ours in several sizes. The shelf is wrapped with wood veneer— choose a color and species to match your trim or furniture.

## Tips & details

- Everything you need is available at home centers, including peel-and-stick wood veneer. Veneer is also available online in species and sizes you won't find at home centers. A 2 x 4-ft. sheet of wood veneer costs about $20.

- Don't be intimidated by the veneering process. Peel-and-stick veneer makes it easy, even for novices. Don't choose traditional glue-on veneer unless you have experience with it.

- We recommend that you limit the depth of this shelf to 12 in. A shelf that protrudes farther from the wall may tilt down a bit if it's filled with heavy items. And keep in mind that it's designed for lightweight items, not your rock collection or aquarium.

- Before finishing, lightly sand the veneer with fine sandpaper (180 or 220 grit). Veneer is paper-thin, so be careful not to sand through it. We gave our shelves a standard wood finish of stain followed by polyurethane.

- Your shelf will be strongest if the inner box can be screwed to two studs. If that doesn't suit your plans, fasten it to the drywall with heavy-duty fasteners. E-Z Ancor Toggle Lock anchors are one good choice.

### WHAT IT TAKES
**TIME:** 2 hours
**COST:** $40
**SKILL:** Beginner
**TOOLS:** Miter saw, table saw, brad nailer, drill, utility or knife

WOODWORKING & WORKSHOP
PROJECTS & TIPS

**1 Build the outer box.**
Cut parts E, F and G to length and width (see below) and assemble them with glue and brad nails. Where the parts meet, sand the joints flush to provide a flat, smooth surface for the veneer. But be careful not to round over the edges.

SAND JOINTS FLUSH

## Figure A
## Floating Shelf

**Overall Dimensions:**
**24" Long x 12" Wide x 3-3/8" Tall**

1/4" PLYWOOD

E

OUTER BOX

F

INNER BOX

B

G

E

C

A

D

2x4

3-1/2" SCREWS

F

B

1-3/4"
BRAD OR NAIL

1/8" GAP

2" SCREW

## MATERIALS LIST

**ITEM**
4' 1x3 board
4' 1x4 board
2' 2x4 board
2' x 4' of 1/4" plywood
Self-adhesive veneer
1-3/4" brads or nails
2" and 3-1/2" construction screws
Wood glue
180- or 220-grit sandpaper

## CUTTING LIST

| ITEM | QTY. | MATERIAL | DIMENSIONS | PART |
|------|------|----------|------------|------|
| A | 1 | 1/4" plywood | 1/4" x 11-1/8" x 22-3/8" | Inner box bottom |
| B | 2 | 1x3 board | 3/4" x 2-1/2" x 11-1/8" | Inner box sides |
| C | 1 | 1x3 board | 3/4" x 2-1/2" x 20-7/8" | Inner box front |
| D | 1 | 2x4 board | 1-1/2" x 2-1/2" x 20-7/8" | Cleat |
| E | 2 | 1/4" plywood | 1/4" x 12" x 24" | Outer box top/ bottom |
| F | 2 | 1x4 board | 3/4" x 2-7/8" x 12" | Outer box sides |
| G | 1 | 1x4 board | 3/4" x 2-7/8" x 22-1/2" | Outer box front |

**2** **Apply the veneer.** Set the outer box on the veneer and rough-cut it with a utility knife, making each section at least 1/2 in. larger than the surface it will cover. Don't forget to check the grain direction of the veneer before you cut. Begin to peel off the backing paper, set the veneer in place and then pull off the remaining backing as you press the veneer into place. Force the veneer firmly against the box with a roller or a smooth block of wood.

**3** **Trim the veneer.** After applying each section of veneer, place it face down on a flat surface. Slowly and carefully trim the veneer with a utility knife. A fresh, sharp blade will give you cleaner, more accurate cuts. After all the veneer is applied, gently sand the corners by hand with 180- or 220-grit paper to slightly round the sharp edges. We finished the box with stain and polyurethane.

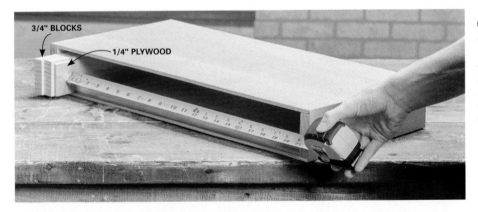

**4** **Measure for the inner box.** To size the inner box parts, you could do some math, but here's a goof-proof method: Set two 3/4-in.-thick blocks and a scrap of 1/4-in. plywood in the opening. Then measure to get the lengths of parts C and D. For the inner box sides (B), measure inside to the front of the box and subtract 1/8 in.

**5** **Build the inner box.** Join the front, cleat and sides of the inner box. Be sure to use screws for a strong connection at the cleat. Then measure and cut the plywood bottom and fasten it with glue and brads. Fasten the inner box to the wall by driving screws through the cleat. Then slip the outer box over the inner box and you're done!

# MAKE YOUR OWN
# BARN WOOD

## It's easy to do, looks authentic and saves you a fortune!

By **Jeff Gorton**

W hether you're creating a rustic interior or adding aged wood accents to a modern decorating scheme, barn wood is a popular choice. And the good news is you don't have to pick through piles of splintery old lumber or pay exorbitant prices for the look of barn wood. You can easily transform inexpensive pine boards into rustic boards that are almost indistinguishable from the real thing. In this story we'll give you a recipe for doing just that. The 8-ft. 1x6 boards we used for creating our authentic-looking "aged barn wood" cost about $4 each.

## A FOOLPROOF RECIPE:

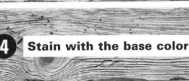

**1** Grind the edges

**2** Grind the surface

**3** Make wormholes

**4** Stain with the base color

**5** Add dark stain

**6** Top it off with gray

### MEET AN EXPERT

Jeff Gorton is a carpenter and editor, as well as our in-house forgery expert.

WOODWORKING & WORKSHOP
PROJECTS & TIPS

FINISH NAIL

**1** **Grind the edges and ends.** With the grinder spinning in the direction shown here, make random gouges on the edges of the board. While you're at it, round over the sharp factory edges. Then grind the ends of the boards to look weathered as shown here.

KNOT CUP BRUSH

CUP BRUSH

**2** **Erode the surface.** Remove some of the soft wood from between the growth rings (darker wood grain) by running the cup brush along the board. Follow the grain pattern. The growth rings are harder and will remain, while the brush will wear away the softer wood between them.

**3** **Make realistic wormholes.** Punch groups of "wormholes" in a random pattern with the awl. Elongate some of the holes by tipping the awl down after punching. Space groups of holes 6 to 12 in. apart.

AWL

## What you need

There are a few essential tools for this project. The first is an angle grinder. It doesn't have to be expensive. The one we're using is from Harbor Freight Tools and cost only $30. The second essential tool is a knot cup brush attachment for the grinder ($8 to $24). Make sure the arbor diameter of the cup brush matches the arbor on your grinder. In addition, you'll need an awl, a utility knife and a claw hammer for further distressing.

Grinding throws a lot of dust and even an occasional wood chip, so wear safety glasses and a dust mask.

You'll also need a roller to apply the first coat of stain, and cotton rags for the remaining two coats. We used Varathane Summer Oak for the first coat, Varathane Kona for the splotchy dark layer, and Varathane Weathered Gray for the final coat.

You don't have to be too picky about choosing knotty pine boards. As long as they're reasonably straight, they'll work fine.

## Getting started

Since clamps would get in the way of the grinding process, tack the board to sawhorses with 6d finish nails. Then follow **Photos 1 – 5** to distress the surface of the wood. **Photo 6** shows an additional technique, one for making curved wire brush lines that resemble sawmill marks. You can use this technique on a few of the boards for variety. If both sides of the boards will be visible, flip the board over and repeat the steps.

## Apply the finish

When you've completed the distressing steps for all of the boards, follow the staining process shown in **Photos 7 – 9**. Don't worry if the finish looks a little different from one board to the next. Variation will add to the authentic look. When you're done with the stain rags, hang them over the edge of a bucket or garbage can to dry before disposing of them. Wadded-up, stain-soaked rags can spontaneously combust. Your boards will look most authentic without a clear coating, but if you need a more durable finish, let the stained boards dry overnight before brushing on a coat or two of polyurethane. Choose a flat or matte sheen to retain the weathered look.

UTILITY KNIFE

**4** **Add dents.** You can make dents with almost any blunt tool, metal pipe, or even a chain. A hammer claw is handy and works well. Group dents in random patterns along the board.

**5** **Carve out splits.** Carve out the soft wood along the grain to simulate a crack. Make fake cracks on the ends of boards, or along the edges. You can also simply enlarge an existing crack.

**6** **Make saw blade marks.** Sweep the grinder across the board in a series of arcs to create the look of old, "rough-sawn" lumber. Add this pattern to a few of your boards for variety.

**7** **Start with a base coat.** Roll on the first coat of stain. Cover the board entirely. Then wipe off the excess with a cotton rag. Let this coat dry about five minutes before moving on to the next layer of stain.

**8** **Dab on dark stain.** Dip a wadded cotton rag into the dark stain and apply it to the board in random patches. Spread out the patches with the rag to create an uneven layer of dark stain.

**9** **Finish with gray stain.** With a separate cotton rag, wipe on a coat of gray stain. This coat can be more consistent than the dark coat. Wipe off excess stain with a dry cotton rag until you achieve the aged look you desire. If you want the additional protection of a clear finish over the stain, let the stain dry overnight before brushing on a coat or two of flat polyurethane.

# ONE-OF-A-KIND BIRD FEEDER
# BACKYARD CANTINA

**Invite birds to your place for countless happy hours!**

By Matt Boley

## WHAT IT TAKES
**TIME:** 2 hours
**COST:** $30
**SKILL:** Beginner
**TOOLS:** Jigsaw, drill/driver, clamps, Speed Square, hot glue gun, utility knife

**B**ird-watching lets you enjoy the best of wildlife, and getting started is easy. You can hang a bird feeder and delight in your new visitors as you sit and read a book on your porch or work in the yard. Feeders are available in a wide price range, and you can pay a lot for one that only looks handmade. So why not build your own? With a splash of creativity and a twist of effort, you can have a hangout that will please both you and your hungry guests.

**1** **Cut the sides.** Angle your jigsaw to 45 degrees and cut the sides (C) to the combined heights of your bottle and glass, minus 2 in. Ours ended up being about 15-1/2 in., but your measurement will almost certainly be different.

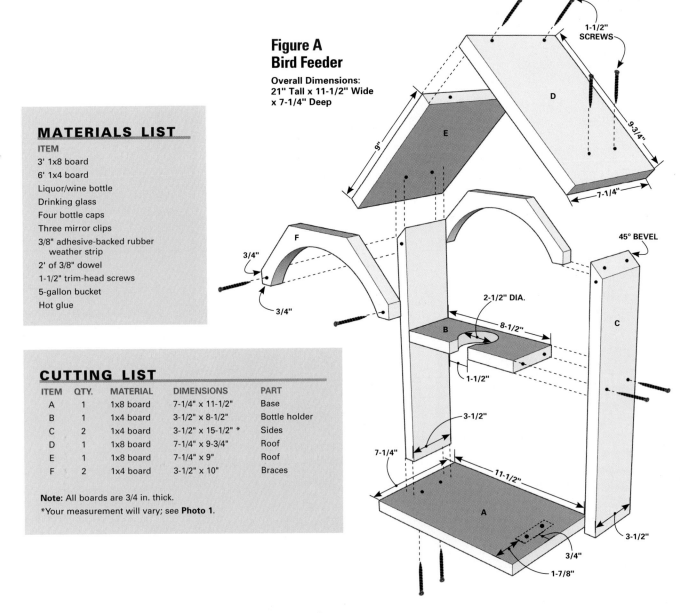

**Figure A**
**Bird Feeder**

**Overall Dimensions:**
21" Tall x 11-1/2" Wide
x 7-1/4" Deep

1-1/2" SCREWS

9-3/4"

7-1/4"

45° BEVEL

2-1/2" DIA.

8-1/2"

1-1/2"

3-1/2"

7-1/4"

11-1/2"

3-1/2"

3/4"

1-7/8"

3/4"

3/4"

## MATERIALS LIST

**ITEM**

3' 1x8 board
6' 1x4 board
Liquor/wine bottle
Drinking glass
Four bottle caps
Three mirror clips
3/8" adhesive-backed rubber
    weather strip
2' of 3/8" dowel
1-1/2" trim-head screws
5-gallon bucket
Hot glue

## CUTTING LIST

| ITEM | QTY. | MATERIAL | DIMENSIONS | PART |
|------|------|----------|------------|------|
| A | 1 | 1x8 board | 7-1/4" x 11-1/2" | Base |
| B | 1 | 1x4 board | 3-1/2" x 8-1/2" | Bottle holder |
| C | 2 | 1x4 board | 3-1/2" x 15-1/2" * | Sides |
| D | 1 | 1x8 board | 7-1/4" x 9-3/4" | Roof |
| E | 1 | 1x8 board | 7-1/4" x 9" | Roof |
| F | 2 | 1x4 board | 3-1/2" x 10" | Braces |

**Note:** All boards are 3/4 in. thick.
*Your measurement will vary; see **Photo 1**.

**2** **Make the keyhole for the bottle.** Cut a circle with a 2-1/2-in. hole saw in the center of the bottle holder board (B). Then use your jigsaw and square to create a channel for the bottle that will fit the neck of your bottle.

CUT FOR BOTTLE

3/4" SCRAP

**3** Fasten the sides to the base. Use a scrap piece of wood as a guide and screw the sides 3/4 in. in from the ends of the base.

## Materials

You can build this bird feeder from standard pine boards or pressure-treated lumber. Treated lumber will give you long-term rot resistance but also a dis-advantage: It contains a lot of moisture, so you'll have to let the wood dry for at least two weeks before painting it. Treated boards also tend to cup or bow as they dry. Both pine and treated lum-ber contain knots. If you don't like the knotty look, buy an extra board or two so you can use the knot-free sections.

You can use just about any wine or liquor bottle for this pro-ject. **Photos 1** and **4** show how to customize the parts to suit your bottle. Similarly, you can use any glass that has a flat base.

It's important to secure the bottle in the feeder. Wind and rain can knock the bottle out of its perch, breaking it or just spill-ing a lot of birdseed. We used 3/8-in. adhesive-backed rubber weather strip on the inside of both braces (F) to secure the bottle. You can find this product in the hardware section in most home centers and online.

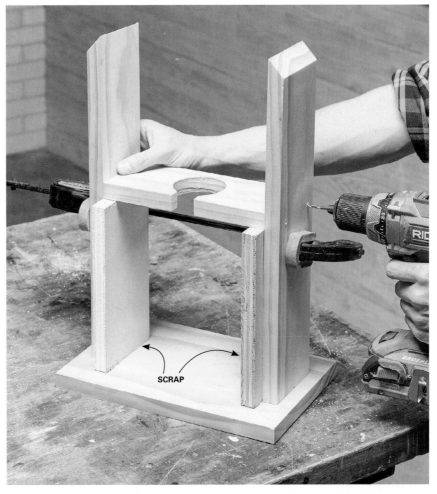

SCRAP

**4** **Attach the bottle holder to the sides.** Mock up the assembly to find the correct height of the bottle holder (B). Cut scrap wood to hold the bottle holder level and at the right height. Drill pilot holes and screw into the bottle holder from the outside of the feeder.

**5** **Mount the roof.** Screw the longer roof section (D) to one end of the shorter roof section (E) and attach the roof to the tops of the sides with screws.

3/4"

PLACE
WEATHER
STRIP HERE

**6** **Cut the braces.** Cut the 1x4 into 10-in. pieces. Mark the miters as shown in Figure A and trace a 5-gallon bucket to make an arc. Cut the arc with a jigsaw. Screw the braces to the sides. Cut adhesive-backed weather strip to 3 in. with a utility knife. Peel the backing and attach the strips to the inside of the braces.

**7** **Attach the glass.** Mark a centerline on the base. Set your glass in the center of the base and screw the mirror clips to the base, securing the glass to the assembly.

**8** **Install the bar stools.** Cut your dowel into 4-in. pieces. Plan where you want the bar stools and drill 1/4-in.-deep pilot holes with a 3/8-in. drill bit into the base. Use an "L" guide made from scrap 1x4 to ensure you drill plumb into the base. Finish the bar stools by hot-gluing bottle caps to the top of the dowels.

# BOTTLE CADDY

By **Des Sikowski-Nelson**

PHOTOS: DES SIKOWSKI-NELSON

WOODWORKING & WORKSHOP
PROJECTS & TIPS

OPEN HERE

**A handmade gift is better than store-bought. And building this caddy is a lot more fun than shopping at crowded malls. Here's how our family mass-produced 20 of them to share with friends.**

O ur whole family—father Val, son Aaron and daughter Des—got involved in the building of these caddies. We used reclaimed lumber from a 100-year-old barn in Wisconsin. But you can select any type of wood available at your local home center.

It took us three days in the shop to transform that gorgeous barn wood into 20 handsome caddies. Each one holds eight longneck bottles or six heritage bottles, which have fatter bottoms. Along with a plan for the caddy and a list of materials, we show a couple of jigs to help streamline the process so you can build a bunch of these at the same time.

### Get Dad's help
Here's 91-year-old Val stacking the parts after the angles were cut. Thanks, Dad!

### A family that builds together
Aaron, a pro woodworker for 41 years, and Val have been working together on special projects for more than 30 years.

### It all starts with an idea
Recently Des and Aaron designed and built several musical instruments, including cigar box and lap steel guitars.

PHOTO (1): TIM ABRAHAM

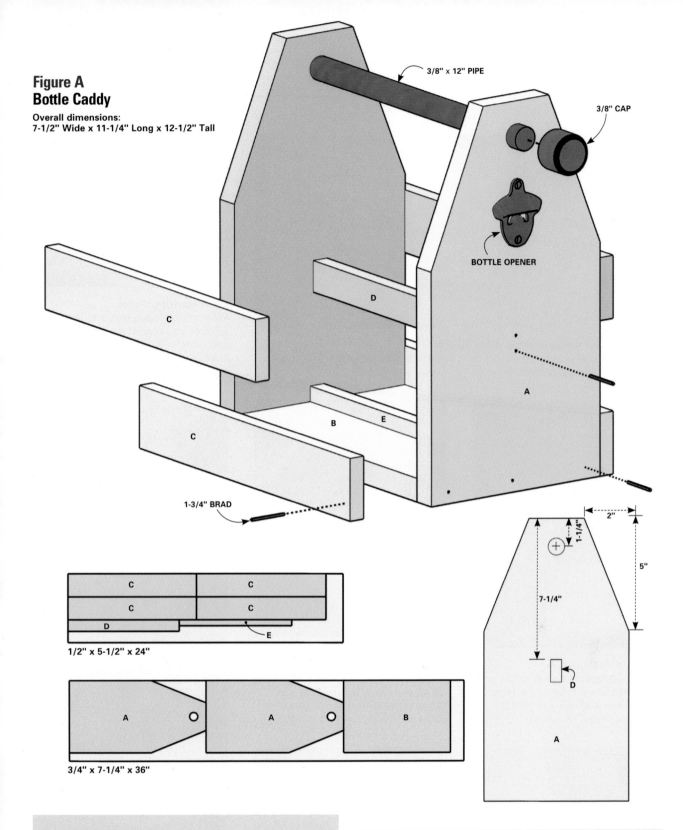

## Figure A
## Bottle Caddy

**Overall dimensions:**
7-1/2" Wide x 11-1/4" Long x 12-1/2" Tall

3/8" x 12" PIPE

3/8" CAP

BOTTLE OPENER

C

C

D

B

E

A

1-3/4" BRAD

C

C

C

C

D

E

1/2" x 5-1/2" x 24"

A

A

B

3/4" x 7-1/4" x 36"

2"

1-1/4"

5"

7-1/4"

D

A

## CUTTING LIST

| ITEM | QTY. | NAME | DIMENSIONS |
|------|------|------|------------|
| **FROM 1x8** | | | |
| A | 2 | Ends | 12-1/2" x 6-1/2" |
| B | 1 | Bottom | 9-3/4" x 6-1/2" |
| **FROM 1/2x6** | | | |
| C | 4 | Slats | 11-1/4" x 2" |
| D | 1 | Upper divider | 9-3/4" x 1" |
| E | 1 | Lower divider | 9-3/4" x 1/2" |

## MATERIALS LIST

| ITEM | QTY |
|------|-----|
| 1x8 x 3' | 1 |
| 1/2x6 x 3' | 1 |
| 3/8" x 12" black threaded pipe | 1 |
| 3/8" threaded end caps | 2 |

Wood glue, 1-3/4" brads, nails or screws. Search online for "wall mount bottle opener" to find endless options starting at $4 each.

## MASS PRODUCTION
If you want to build a bunch, here are some labor-saving tips.

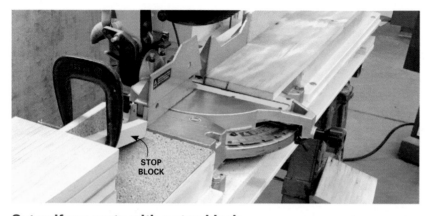

### Cut uniform parts with a stop block
Clamp a block to your fence so you can cut parts to precisely the same length without measuring and marking.

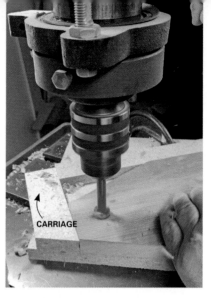

### Drill handle holes
Clamp the carriage to a drill press table so you can set each end in place and bore the handle hole. We used a 3/4-in. Forstner bit, which is about right for 3/8-in. black pipe.

### Make a carriage jig
Mark the angle cut on one of the end parts (A) and set it on a 10 x 14-in. scrap. Then add cleats to hold the end in position.

### Soak off labels
Labels on steel pipe are tough to remove. To make it easier, we picked up an aluminum foil roasting pan ($5 at home centers) and soaked the pipes in mineral spirits overnight.

### Line 'em up and spray 'em
We finished our bottle caddies with two coats of spray varnish. After the first coat, we lightly sanded with a fine sanding sponge. Then we added the handles and sprayed again. When the finish was completely dry, we attached an old-style metal bottle opener to one side of the caddy.

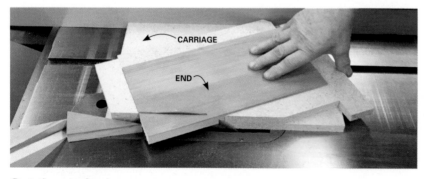

### Cut the angles
Set the table saw fence at 10 in. and slide the carriage against it to cut the angled ends. After the first angle is cut, flip the board and cut the other side.
**CAUTION:** Guard removed for photo. Use yours!

# WIPE-ON POLY

## The fast, easy, goof-proof finish

**T**he best choice for a clear coating is often a specialized finish like pre-catalyzed lacquer—but that assumes you have a spray booth outfitted with high-end equipment. For most of us, polyurethane provides a combination of cost and durability that's hard to beat. With wipe-on poly, you also get goof-proof simplicity, speed and convenience.

**MEET AN EXPERT**

Tom Caspar has been a professional woodworker and custom furniture builder for more than 40 years.

## Meet the team

We tried four versions of wipe-on poly. In terms of results, we found only small differences and were happy with each. Most home centers carry various sheens, but only one brand. All these options, and more, are available online. Prices start at about $15 per quart.

Minwax is the most common brand of oil-based wipe-on poly. Like other oil-based coatings, it adds a slight amber color to the finish. That can be good or bad, depending on the project.

Minwax water-based wipe-on poly dries faster than oil-based products, so you have to move fast. Unlike the others, it has no amber hue.

General Finishes Arm-R-Seal is formulated for brushing or wiping. It's slightly less amber than the other oil-based finishes.

Watco wipe-on poly is most like the Minwax oil-based product. Be careful when shopping; Watco's beloved Danish oil finishes comes in a similar container, and it's easy to grab the wrong product.

## THE PROS AND CONS OF WIPE-ON POLY

+ **FAST.** You can coat a project in less than half the time it takes to brush on a finish.
+ **EASY.** Unlike brushing, wiping on a flawless coat of poly doesn't require skill or an expensive brush.
+ **DUST TOLERANT.** Because the coating is thin and dries fast, "nubs" caused by airborne dust are much less likely. That makes it great for on-site finishing.
+ **NO CLEANUP.** Just dispose of the cloth, container and gloves. No brush to clean!
- **EXPENSIVE.** On average, wipe-on poly costs twice as much as brush-on poly.
- **SLOW BUILD.** As a rule, it takes three coats of wipe-on to match the buildup that you get from one coat of brush-on poly. That said, the speed of wipe-on application often makes up for those extra coats.

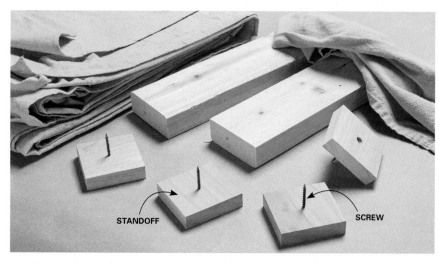

STANDOFF          SCREW

## Set the stage

Drips happen, so use resin paper, a drop cloth or newspaper to protect your worktable. If your project has legs, make standoffs for them to perch on. Standoffs allow you to wipe finish all the way down to the ends of the legs. They poke holes in the wood, so if you have parts that must be finished on both sides, such as a shelf, set them on blocks covered with cloth instead.

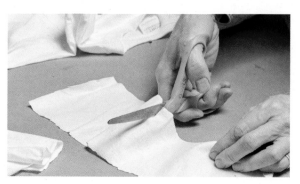

## Cut up an old T-shirt

Cut a T-shirt into 6-in. squares. Fold each square in half, twice, to make applicators. White fabric is best because any lint left in the finish is less likely to show.

MISSED A SPOT!

## Bright lighting is critical

Good light helps you avoid leaving drips, sags and "holidays" (spots that you accidentally skip). When you've just applied finish to an area, check to see that all of it looks shiny and wet. Use a portable light if you're working in a dim room.

## Wear gloves

Protect your hands with disposable vinyl or nitrile gloves. You can usually reuse them two or three times before they get too gummed up.

## Pour it into a plastic tub

A margarine or cottage cheese tub is just right for wipe-on. Dip your rag into the finish, squeeze out the excess and wipe on. With the lid in place, the poly will remain fresh for a couple days. After a few days, the solvent will begin to degrade the plastic, so don't use plastic for long-term storage.

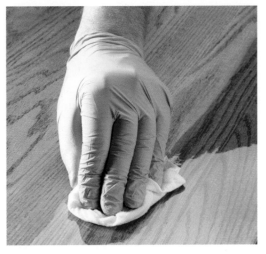

## Brush first, then wipe

When you need a thick, protective buildup of poly on a door or tabletop, you have three choices: Go with brush-on poly, apply several coats of wipe-on or do a combination of both. You can, for example, brush on two coats for a heavy build, then apply wipe-on for a flawless surface. Sand the brushed-on finish absolutely smooth and apply at least two wipe-on coats for a consistent sheen. To make sure the two finishes bond to each other, they should both be oil-based or water-based. Using products from the same company is a good idea too.

## Keep the coats light

Three thin coats of wipe-on finish will look smoother than one or two thicker coats. For the best results, don't sand after the first coat. (You might sand through it!) Apply a second thin coat, then lightly sand with 220-grit sandpaper. Then apply a final thin coat.

PAINT PAD

## Cover large areas fast

A paint pad holds more finish than a rag and wipes it on faster. You can reuse a paint pad, too. After each coat, just store it in a sealed plastic tub or plastic bag. Get a paint pad at any home center for about $5.

## Wipe off intricate projects

On most surfaces you wipe on the finish and just let it dry. If your project has lots of hard-to-access surfaces, try a different approach. Apply the finish to a limited area, then wipe it off after a few minutes using dry rags. This way, you don't have to worry about accidentally smearing finish on an area you've already covered. Just wipe it off.

### Perfect for tricky surfaces
Wipe-on is a slick solution for hard-to-brush items. Sometimes it even beats spraying. You can work the finish into tight spots where spray would "bounce" out.

## Freshen up an old finish

If your old furniture or wood-work looks dull and lifeless, try renewing it with a few coats of wipe-on finish. Wash it first with dish soap and water, then lightly sand the old finish with 220-grit sandpaper. Vacuum off the dust, then apply the finish as usual. Apply at least two coats to achieve an even sheen.

## Let stain dry overnight

Applying poly too soon after staining is always risky. And it's even riskier with wipe-on poly. If the stain isn't complete-ly dry, wiping it with a rag soaked with finish will cause it to smear. Ugly!

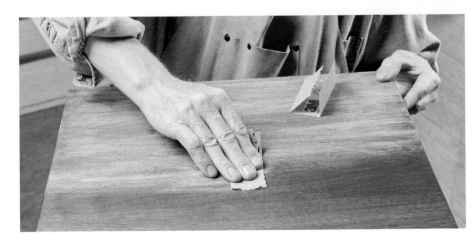

## Sand by hand

Don't use an electric sander between coats. It will remove too much finish. Sand by hand instead. Fold the paper in thirds so it doesn't wrinkle, then hold it flat with two or three fingers. Be careful near sharp or slightly rounded edges, though. Sanding too hard might cut through the finish and leave bare wood. It's best not to sand them at all.

## Want ultra smooth?
## Try steel wool

If you're using an oil-based finish and you want to make a surface smooth as glass, apply the last coat with "00" steel wool. Rub hard. The steel wool will cut through any nibs or dust on the surface. To capture the grit and to maintain an even sheen, use a bunch of dry rags to wipe off the finish before it dries. This will leave only an ultra-thin film of finish on the surface.

## Wet rags are a fire hazard

Take no chances. If rags wet with finish are wadded up, they can heat up, smolder and catch on fire as they dry. However, wet rags are safe if you dispose of them properly. Take them outside and separate them. Place them on concrete or asphalt or hang them with clothespins to dry overnight. Be sure to keep them away from kids and pets. Once the rags are stiff, they're no longer a fire hazard. You can put them in the trash.

## Check for drips

There isn't much that can go wrong with wipe-on. But you can end up with a few drips or sags. Immediately after you wipe on the finish, give the whole project a quick inspection and wipe away any mistakes.

## Correct bad brushwork

When brush-on poly goes wrong—dust nubs, sags, brush marks—you can correct it. After the finish has fully dried, wet-sand with soapy water or mineral spirits and 400-grit wet/dry paper. After you've sanded the finish flat and smooth, a couple light coats of wipe-on poly will give you a perfect surface.

WET/DRY SANDPAPER

# COMPRESSOR **CART**

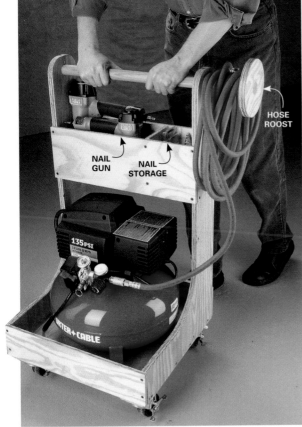

HOSE ROOST

NAIL GUN   NAIL STORAGE

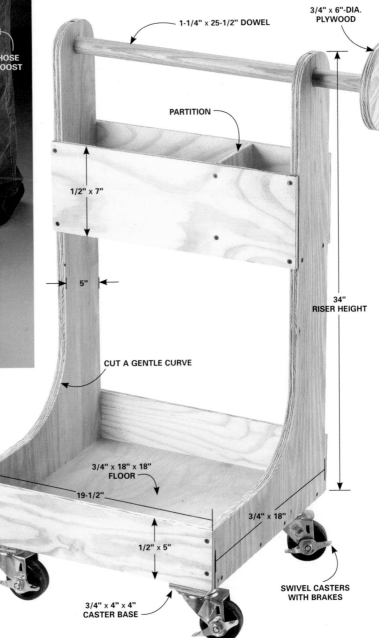

1-1/4" x 25-1/2" DOWEL

3/4" x 6"-DIA. PLYWOOD

PARTITION

1/2" x 7"

5"

34" RISER HEIGHT

CUT A GENTLE CURVE

3/4" x 18" x 18" FLOOR

19-1/2"

3/4" x 18"

1/2" x 5"

SWIVEL CASTERS WITH BRAKES

3/4" x 4" x 4" CASTER BASE

WOODWORKING & WORKSHOP PROJECTS & TIPS

Here's a smart way to mobilize your air compressor and neatly store air nailers, nails and air hoses on board. Our cart's dimensions fit a pancake-style compressor, but you can easily adapt the dimensions for another style.

To build one like ours, you'll need:

- Two 2 x 4-ft. sheets of 3/4-in. plywood
- Scraps of 1/2-in. plywood
- 1-1/4-in. x 3-ft. dowel
- Four 3-in. casters with brakes and miscellaneous hardware

Cut the floor from 3/4-in. plywood and screw four square pieces of 3/4-in. plywood under it to attach the casters to. Cut the side risers from 3/4-in. plywood and screw them to the floor. Then cut the front and back pieces of 1/2-in. plywood and screw them together to box in the compressor. Build the tool storage box on the risers with a 3/4-in. floor and 1/2-in. sides, adding a plywood partition to organize the storage space.

Drill 1-1/4-in. holes in the ends of the risers, then screw and glue in the dowel, leaving a protruding end for keeping the hose on board. Add a 3/4-in. plywood disc to the end of the handle for hose storage. Attach the casters with 1/4-in. x 1-in. screws, load up your cart and head for your next project!

# HandyHints®

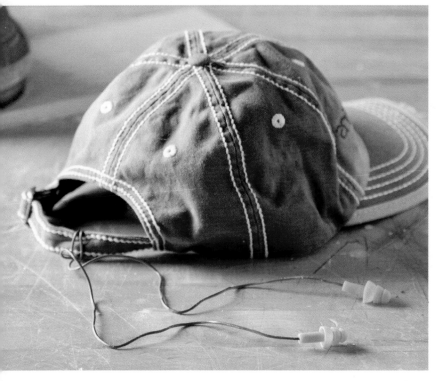

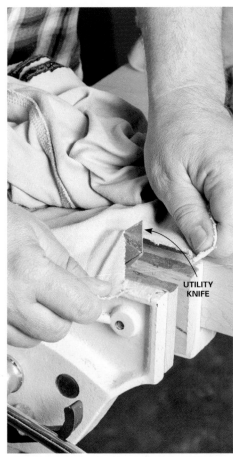

UTILITY
KNIFE

## EARPLUG TETHER

My earplugs were never around when I needed them, and too often I'd go without rather than search. I started tethering my earplugs to my cap, so there's no longer an excuse for skipping the hearing protection.

—Rick Wisz

## HANDY RAG CUTTER

I cut up old T-shirts and towels to use as rags in my shop. To speed up the process, I clamp a utility knife in my bench vise and make a cut to help me tear the scraps. If you're careful, you can make the entire cut with the knife.

—Isaac Richardson

## HANDY SANDING DISC CLEANER

Sandpaper loses its effectiveness when it's clogged with sawdust or pitch. Gum eraser–type sandpaper cleaners work really well, but if you don't have one, the sole of an old sneaker works too. Turn on your sander and slide the rubber sole along the disc or belt, using just enough pressure to remove the sanding debris.

—Lee Wright

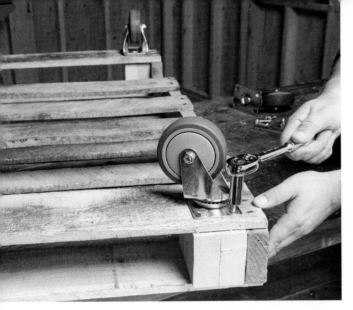

## PALLET DOLLY

I had a truckload of lumber to transport down a long hallway to my shop, and I wasn't looking forward to carrying it an armload at a time. Then I noticed the pallet it was on. I didn't have a pallet jack, but I did have a set of casters. After I installed some reinforcement blocking, it took just a few minutes to attach a 4-in. caster to each corner of the pallet. Now it's my all-around heavy-stuff mover.

—Keith Jones

## NO-WAIT GLUE

I don't like waiting for the glue to reach the bottle's tip when I'm in the middle of a big glue-up. To make sure the glue is ready to flow immediately when I pick up the bottle, I just turn the bottle upside down in a can that sits on my workbench.

—Brad Holden

## AROUND-THE-SHOP CURVE GUIDES

When I need to draw a curve on a project, instead of reaching for a ruler and a compass, I start looking around my shop. There are dozens of round objects available for tracing a perfect curve or radius—anything from a 5-gallon bucket to a roll of tape to the dime in my pocket.

—Bob Turner

# HandyHints®

## QUICK MIXING SURFACE

Instead of using a container to mix a little epoxy, make a mixing surface on your workbench using painter's tape. Lay down several strips, overlapping the edges so the epoxy doesn't get on your bench. When you're done, peel off the tape and throw it away.

—Chris Whiting

## NUT + NUT = BOLT HEAD

Hanger bolts are tricky to install. One end is threaded for wood, the other end has machine threads, and there's no head. So I thread two nuts on the end with machine threads and tighten them against each other. This allows me to use a wrench to install these otherwise tricky bolts.

—Jay Norman

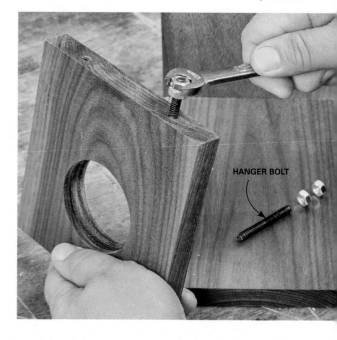

HANGER BOLT

## BLADE-HEIGHT GAUGE BLOCK

Here's a quick way to set the height of a table saw blade. I cut notches on the end of a 4x4 block at the blade heights I use most often: 1/4 in., 3/8 in., 1/2 in. and 3/4 in. To use the block, position the desired notch over the blade and raise the blade until its highest point just touches the block.

—Vern Hauser

## CONVENIENT BENCH CLAMPS

Trigger-style bar clamps make perfect workbench hold-down clamps. First, punch out the split-tube stop at the end of the clamp's bar and then slide the trigger head off. Slip the bar through a bench-dog hole and reinstall the trigger head. If your bench doesn't have dog holes, just drill a hole wherever you need it.

—Will Leighton

## SHORTENING FURNITURE LEGS

Got a bar stool that's too tall? Just cutting a little off the legs is easy, but if the legs are angled, how do you maintain the proper angle to the floor? It's pretty simple. Decide how much you want to cut off, and find a block of wood or any object of that height. Set the block on the floor and lay a pencil on it. Holding the pencil and the block, trace around the leg. Cut with a handsaw, and then round over the sharp edges with sandpaper. The same technique applies to metal legs, but you'll have to cut them with a hacksaw and round the sharp edges with a metal file.

WOOD BLOCK

## MAGNETIC TOOLBOX LABELS

Tired of trying to figure out which toolbox drawer had the tool I was looking for, I bought magnetic business cards at an office supply store ($25 for a pack of 100). I peeled the film off the front, stuck a piece of card stock on top of it (old business cards work great) and labeled each drawer.

—Laura Vogel

# Secret Hiding Places

## 12 clever ideas for keeping your valuables pilfer-proof

**W**hether it's jewelry, important papers or emergency cash, we all have stuff we want to keep safe. We'll show you 12 clever hiding places to safeguard your treasures. Be sure to catalog the location of everything you've hidden and share it with someone you trust, just in case.

**1 Key house**

An unoccupied birdhouse makes a handy spot for a spare key. Screen off the bird entrance to keep out tenants.

## 2 Not IN the drawer

Drawers don't go all the way to the back of a cabinet, and there's typically a little space on the underside too. Put cash or important papers in an envelope and tape them to the back or underside of a drawer.

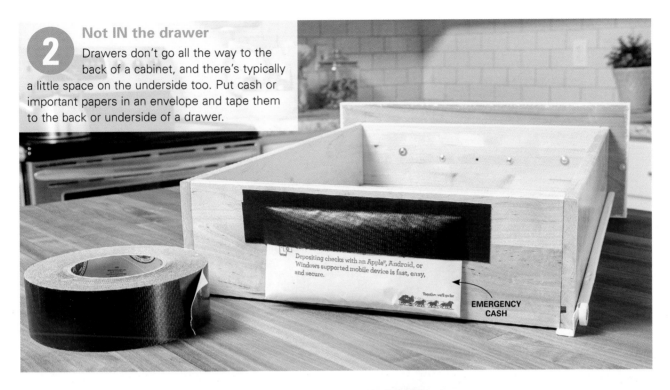

EMERGENCY CASH

## 3 Time well spent

Store a few small items in a wall or mantel clock, as long as the clock itself isn't worth stealing! Tape them to the back or put them in any open cavities.

HARD DRIVE

FAMILY JEWELS

WINTER CLOTHES

## 4 Slip a box inside a box

Store a container of valuables inside a larger bin full of unappealing stuff. Label it accordingly.

# Secret Hiding Places

**5** **Good venting is key**
Stick a magnet to a spare house key using hot glue, and tuck the key up out of sight inside the dryer vent hood. If your vent hood is aluminum or plastic, glue a magnet to the inside of the hood as well as the key.

**6** **It's magic, all right**
Pop the end cap off a marker and remove the ink cartridge. Just right for a spare roll of cash.

**7** **Spare tire**
Pick up a spare wheelbarrow wheel and tire (about $20 at a home center). Deflate the tire, tuck in your goods and reinflate it.

### 8 A roll in the roll

Take apart the spring bar that holds your toilet paper. Roll up a stack of bills, stash them inside and reassemble the bar.

### 9 Secret cash stash

Keep some emergency cash rolled up in a clean, empty sunblock tube. Tuck it in a drawer or medicine cabinet where you can easily grab it when you need it.

### 10 Don't kick this ball!

A soccer ball makes a perfect spot for little items. Let some air out of the ball and cut one of the seams using a utility knife. After inserting your items, tuck the seam back into place.

# Secret Hiding Places

**11** **Sitting pretty**
Dining chairs often have space under the seat for a drop-down hinged panel.

HINGED PANEL

**12** **"Litterally" buried**
Put small containers of valuables in a tub of cat litter (unused!) and then pour the cat litter back into the tub.

## CUTTING THE DECK

I was demolishing a 1950s built-in buffet in my basement as part of a remodel and decided to cut it into pieces for easy removal. I didn't have any extra cash to buy a reciprocating saw, but I felt my trusty chain saw would do the trick.

First I ripped off the plastic laminate top and took a quick look inside to avoid hitting any nails. With my next cut, I noticed paper flying out with the wood chips. I found that I had cut through five vintage baseball cards! They included 1954 editions of Willie Mays and Roy Campanella—valued at over $400!

That money could have bought a nice reciprocating saw or helped pay for the remodel...I guess I'm just really unlucky at cards.

—William F. Price IV

# 5 Exterior Repairs & Improvements

## IN THIS CHAPTER

Home Care & Repair .................................190
   *Emergency Roof Patch, Installing*
   *Gutters and more*

Easier Paver Patios..................................192

Finding & Fixing Roof Leaks ..................196

Handy Hints .............................................201
   *Easy Concrete Mixing and more*

# HomeCare&Repair

## TIPS, FIXES & GEAR FOR A TROUBLE-FREE HOME

FLASHING

## EMERGENCY ROOF PATCH

A section of flashing is the perfect patch for smaller holes, which are often caused by blown-down tree branches. Slide the flashing under the shingles above the hole and nail down the exposed corners of the flashing. Don't forget to caulk around the hole and the nail heads. Special roof sealant is best, but any type of caulk is better than nothing.

## INSTALLING GUTTERS

If you're installing your own gutters, check out an option called "chop & drop," which is offered by many pro installers. The installer drives a seamless-gutter truck to your house, churns out the gutter lengths you need and drives away. This is a much better option because you won't have seams in your gutters from joining the precut lengths available at home centers. If you choose a gutter color other than white, be sure you get all the end caps, downspouts and fasteners to match from the supplier. Home centers typically carry only white.

### MEET AN EXPERT

Before Mark Petersen joined our editorial team, he owned and ran a siding and gutter installation company for 18 years.

## EASY ICE SCRAPING

Sick of freezing your tail off while you're scraping the rock-hard ice off your windshield? Try this cool tip. Just mix two parts water with one part isopropyl (rubbing) alcohol in a spray bottle and spray it on your windshield. The ice will melt almost instantly. The alcohol won't harm your car's paint, but it will remove car wax, so try to keep it off waxed surfaces.

To prevent ice buildup, try Prestone Ice & Frost Shield ($5). "You spray it on before heading in for the night or when you arrive at work," says automotive expert Rick Muscoplat. "Any snow or freezing rain won't stick to your windshield. I gave it to my daughter and she uses it when she arrives at work. If it snows during the day, she just has to turn on the wipers and go."

## STOP MICE BEFORE THEY COME IN

At my rental properties, I control mice by exterminating them before they come inside. I place these bait stations outside near the foundation and load each of the vertical tubes with several poison bait blocks on a rod. A six-pack of JT Eaton 902 Top Loader Bait Stations costs about $70 online. You can also zip-tie them to a roof rafter or to the top of a fence to get mice that travel those routes. They've dramatically decreased my mouse issues.

—Tom Dvorak

**MEET AN EXPERT**

**Tom Dvorak is a remodeler and property manager who buys and renovates homes in the Twin Cities area.**

# EASIER PAVER PATIOS

### Plastic panels eliminate TONS of labor

By **Jeff Gorton**

**A** traditional base for a paver or stone patio is a 6-in.-deep layer of compacted gravel. For a typical 10 x 12-ft. patio, that means carting away about 2-1/2 tons of soil, and hauling in the same amount of gravel. But there's an easier way. Let plastic panels take the place of the gravel base. For that same patio, you would need only 24 paver base panels weighing a total of about 30 lbs. to replace the 2-1/2 tons of gravel.

**Lay panels on leveled sand**
After removing a few inches of soil and compacting the site, spread about 3/4 in. of sand over the soil and level it. Then place the paver base panels over the sand, staggering them to avoid continuous seams.

**Install the pavers**
Install the pavers as you would over a conventional gravel base. An advantage of this system is that the screeded sand is protected by the panels, so you're unlikely to mess it up as you work.

## What it is and how it works

Paver base panels are made from light-weight high-density polypropylene. The panels typically have tongue-and-groove or shiplap edges to keep the panel edges flush with one another.

You may wonder how a thin plastic mat can effectively replace a 6-in.-deep layer of compacted gravel. The answer is that the panels spread out the load, so the weight of a person walking on the patio is distributed more widely. Distributing the load puts less pressure on the soil and prevents the paver bricks from becoming uneven.

The panels have the added advantage of providing an insulating layer that reduces problems caused by soil that thaws and refreezes. And finally, paver base panels have built-in channels and holes to drain water to the sand layer below.

Paver base products have been around for only a few years, so it's uncertain how they'll perform long-term. But results are good so far. Studies from independent engineers have concluded that the panels are equivalent to a compacted gravel base for load distribution and superior for thermal resistance.

## BENEFITS OF A PANEL BASE

- Requires less digging.
- Eliminates heavy gravel fill.
- Saves time.
- Reduces the cost of digging and hauling.
- Prevents damage to the landscaping caused by excavating equipment.
- Allows patio installations in fenced areas or areas with limited access.
- Protects the screeded sand while you're installing pavers.

**Paver base panel**
Lightweight panels spread the load and eliminate the need for a thick gravel base.

**Sand**
A thin layer of screeded sand provides a level platform for the paver panels.

**Landscape fabric**
Nonwoven fabric allows drainage while preventing the sand from mixing with the soil.

## 5 THINGS YOU'LL NEED

As with any other outdoor paving project, the first steps are to plan the size and mark out the area with paint, a garden hose or string. Then measure the width and length and figure out how much material you'll need. Plan to build the patio base 1 ft. wider and longer than the size of the finished patio so that it will extend 6 in. beyond the paving on all sides.

**LANDSCAPE FABRIC:** The purpose of the landscape fabric is to prevent the sand from mixing in with the soil. But it's important to use a nonwoven fabric. Woven landscape fabric isn't very permeable and can act like a swimming pool liner, trapping water under your patio. Also look for fabric with at least a 20-year life span.

**SAND:** You'll need a layer of sand that's an average depth of 3/4 in. Buy all-purpose or fill sand, not sandbox sand. It's too fine. If you're buying bags of sand, figure about one 50-lb. bag for every 8 sq. ft. of patio.

**PAVER PANELS:** Divide the square footage of your patio by the square-foot coverage of each panel to determine the number of panels you'll need. Add about 20 percent if your patio is an irregular shape.

**PAVER EDGING:** You'll need a way to hold the paver bricks in place along the edges of the patio. The most common and convenient method is to stake down plastic paver edging. The Gator brand sells special screws that allow you to attach the edging directly to the paver mats. You'll find paver edging at home centers and landscape supply stores.

**PAVER BASE**
Step 1

Base Pard Pavment/Adouinee

Use to stabilize and fill hardscape project areas.

Materials specified by the Concrete Paver Institute.

Step 1

0.5 Cu. Ft. (14.1L)
Covers approx. 4 to 6 sq. ft. x 1"

**SAND OR POLYMERIC JOINT SAND:** Some manufacturers specify filling the joints between pavers with polymeric sand. This helps lock the pavers together and provides a maintenance-free joint that sheds water well. If you use polymeric sand in the joints, follow the installation instructions carefully to avoid discoloring the paver surface and to prevent problems.

In addition to these five materials, you'll need digging equipment like wheelbarrows and shovels, a place to put the excess sod and soil, a rented plate compactor, and in most cases, a rented brick saw. You can speed up sod removal by renting a sod cutter. And if you rent a trash bin, you can get rid of soil without making trips to the landfill.

## BUILDING WITH PAVER BASE PANELS

Paver base panels don't eliminate the need for careful site preparation. You'll have to remove grass or other vegetation and skim off 2 to 4 in. of soil. You also must remove soil evenly, leaving a flat surface because there's no thick layer of gravel to make up for uneven ground. After digging and grading, there shouldn't be more than about 1/2-in. variation in flatness over the area.

Since there is no gravel base, it's important to use a plate compactor to tamp down the soil before covering it with landscape fabric and a layer of sand. The sand layer must be screeded to provide a flat, properly sloped surface for the paver base panels.

Lay the paver base panels over the sand bed. The lightweight, easy-to-cut panels make this a quick task. Follow the manufacturer's instructions for offsetting the panels and for edge details. If you're planning to install stones that vary in thickness, you'll have to put a layer of sand over the panels to allow leveling of the stones.

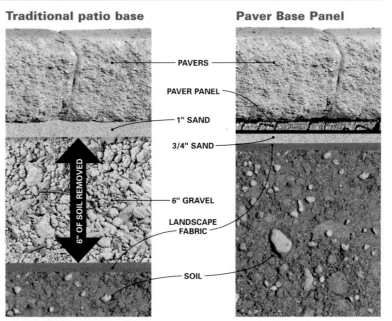

**Traditional patio base**

**Paver Base Panel**

PAVERS
PAVER PANEL
1" SAND
3/4" SAND
6" OF SOIL REMOVED
6" GRAVEL
LANDSCAPE FABRIC
SOIL

### Cost and availability

Some paver base panels are available at home centers; others are distributed through landscape supply stores. The cost of the panels ranges from $2 to $3 per square foot. There are several brands of paver base panels, including:
alliancegator.com/products/gator-base
brockpaverbase.com
ultrabasesystems.com

# FINDING & FIXING
# ROOF LEAKS

**FIX IT YOURSELF AND SAVE MONEY!**

ROOF VENTS

SMALL HOLES

CHIMNEY FLASHING

PLUMBING VENT BOOTS

WALLS AND DORMERS

STEP FLASHING

**If** you have water stains that extend across ceilings or run down walls, the cause is likely a roof leak. Tracking down the leak can be hard; the fixes are usually pretty easy. We'll show you simple tricks for finding and repairing the most common types of roof leaks.

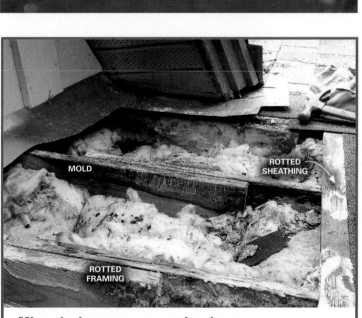

## Find the leaks

When you're trying to track down a leak, start by looking at the roof uphill from the stains. Roof penetrations are the first thing to look for. Items that penetrate the roof are by far the most common source of leaks. In fact, it's rare for leaks to develop in open areas of uninterrupted shingles, even on older roofs. Penetrations can include plumbing and roof vents, chimneys, dormers or anything else that projects through the roof. They can be several feet above the leak or to either side of it.

If you have attic access, the easiest way to track down a leak is to go up there with a flashlight and look for evidence. There will be water stains, black marks or mold. But if access is a problem or you have a vaulted ceiling, you'll have to go up onto the roof to examine the suspect(s). The photos on the following pages will show you what to look for.

If the problem still isn't obvious, enlist a helper and go up onto the roof with a garden hose. Start low, soaking the area just above where the leak appears in the house. Isolate areas when you run the hose. For example, soak the downhill side of a chimney first, then each side, then the top on both sides. Have your helper stay inside the house waiting for the drip to appear.

Let the hose run for several minutes in one area before moving it up the roof a little farther. Tell your helper to yell when a drip becomes visible. You'll be in the neighborhood of the leak. This process can take well over an hour, so be patient and don't move the hose too soon. Buy your helper dinner.

Water stains can also indicate condensation or ice dam issues. Condensation problems can often be caused from bath, cooking or even dryer vents exhausting into attics rather than through the roof.

Ice dams usually happen in cold climates in the spring or on mild winter days. Have a big chunk of ice along the eaves during winter? That's an ice dam.

### Minor leaks can cause major damage

Discover a roof leak? Well, you'd better fix it, even if it doesn't bother you much or you're getting a new roof next year. Over time, even small leaks can lead to big problems, such as mold, rotted framing and sheathing, destroyed insulation and damaged ceilings. The flashing leak that caused this $950 repair bill was obvious from the ceiling stains for over two years. If the homeowner had dealt with it right away, the damage and subsequent repairs would have been minimal.

## LEAKY WALLS & DORMERS

Water doesn't always come in at the shingled surface. Often, wind-driven rain comes in from above the roof, especially around windows, between corner boards and siding, and through cracks and knotholes in siding. Dormer walls provide lots of spots where water can dribble down and enter the roof. Caulk can be old, cracked or even missing between the corner boards and between window edges and siding. Water penetrates these cracks and works its way behind the flashing and into the house.

Even caulk that looks intact may not be sealing against the adjoining surfaces. Dig around with a putty knife to see if the area is sealed. Dig out any suspect caulk and replace it with a siliconized latex caulk. Also check the siding above the step flashing. Replace any cracked, rotted or missing siding, making sure the new piece overlaps the step flashing by at least 2 in. If you still have a leak, pull the corner boards free and check the overlapping flashing at the corner. Often, there's old, hardened caulk where the two pieces overlap at the inside corner.

**CRACKED CAULK**

**PROBLEM:** Water that sneaks behind walls and dormers dribbles down into your house just like a roof leak.

MISSING SIDING    FRESH CAULK

**SOLUTION:** Recaulk the corner flashing. Lift the overlapping section, clean it thoroughly and add a generous bead of fresh caulk underneath. Make sure the gap at the corner is filled with caulk.

## ROOF VENTS

Check for cracked housings on plastic roof vents and broken seams on metal ones. You might be tempted to throw caulk at the problem, but that solution won't last long. There's really no fix other than replacing the damaged vents. Also look for pulled or missing nails at the base's bottom edge. Replace them with rubber-washered screws.

In most cases, you can remove nails under the shingles on both sides of the vent to pull it free. There will be nails across the top of the vent too. Usually you can also work those loose without removing shingles. Screw the bottom into place with rubber-washered screws. Squeeze out a bead of caulk beneath the shingles on both sides of the vent to hold the shingles down and to add a water barrier. That's much easier than renailing the shingles.

**YEAH, RIGHT!**

**CRACK**

**PROBLEM:** Plastic roof vents can crack and leak. Duct tape is not the solution this time!

**SOLUTION:** Replace the old vent. If you're careful, you won't have to remove any shingles to slip out the old one and slide the new one into place.

## PLUMBING VENT BOOTS

Plumbing vent boots can be all plastic, plastic and metal, or even two-piece metal units. Check plastic bases for cracks and metal bases for broken seams. Then examine the rubber boot surrounding the pipe. That can be rotted away or torn, allowing water to work its way into the house along the pipe. With any of these problems, you should buy a new vent boot to replace the old one.

However, if the nails at the base are missing or pulled free and the boot is in good shape, replace them with the rubber-washered screws used for metal roofing systems. You'll find them at any home center with the rest of the screws. You'll have to work neighboring shingles free on both sides. If you don't have extra shingles, be careful when you remove shingles so they can be reused. Use a flat bar to separate the sealant between the layers. Then you'll be able to drive the flat bar under the nail heads to pop out the nails.

**PROBLEM:** When the source of a leak is gasket-type vent flashing, the culprit is usually a cracked gasket or missing or loose nails.

TORN RUBBER

LOOSE NAIL

MISSING NAIL

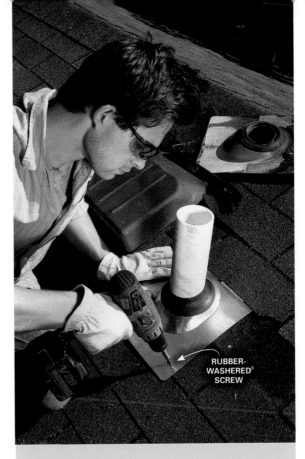

RUBBER-WASHERED SCREW

**SOLUTION:** Replace the old boot. Screw the base to the roof with rubber-washered screws. Don't use nails. They'll just work loose over time.

## ROOF VENTS

Tiny holes in shingles are sneaky because they can cause rot and other damage for years before you notice the obvious signs of a leak. You might find holes left over from satellite dish or antenna mounting brackets or just about anything. And exposed, misplaced roofing nails should be pulled and the holes patched. Small holes are simple to fix, but the fix isn't to inject caulk in the hole. You'll fix this one with flashing as shown here.

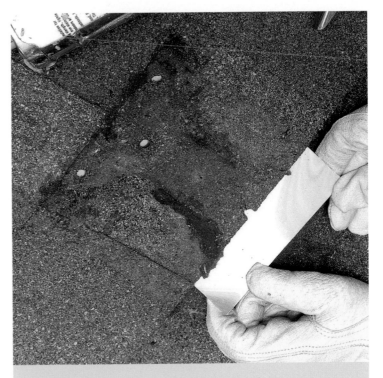

MOUNTING HOLES

**PROBLEM:** Leftover mounting holes can let in vast amounts of water.

**SOLUTION:** Seal nail holes forever. Slip flashing under the shingle and add a bead of caulk under and over the flashing to hold it in place.

## STEP FLASHING

Step flashing is used along walls that intersect the roof. Each short section of flashing channels water over the shingle downhill from it.

But if the flashing rusts through, or a piece comes loose, water will run right behind it, and into the house it goes. Rusted flashing needs to be replaced. That means removing shingles, prying siding loose, and then removing and replacing the step flashing. It's that simple. But occasionally a roofer forgets to nail one into place and it eventually slips down to expose the wall.

**PROBLEM:** Unnailed step flashing can slip down and channel water into the wall.

WATER INLET

SLIPPED FLASHING

**SOLUTION:** Push a loose piece of step flashing right back into place and then secure it with caulk above and below.

## BRICK CHIMNEYS

All kinds of bad things can happen around brick chimneys. In fact, there are far too many to cover in this story. Flashing around chimneys can rust through if it's galvanized steel, especially at the 90-degree bend at the bottom. A quick but fairly long-term fix is to simply slip new flashing under the old rusted stuff. That way any water that seeps through will be diverted.

The best fix, though, is to cut a saw kerf into the mortar and install new flashing. If you want to see what's involved, search for "chimney flashing" at familyhandyman.com.

## WET CEILINGS AREN'T ALWAYS FROM ROOF LEAKS!

Water stains on the ceiling don't always indicate a leak up on the roof. Many times the stains come from, or are caused by, problems up in the attic. Here are three of the main culprits:

**ATTIC-MOUNTED A/C COMPRESSORS.** Clogged condensate tubes will cause collection trays to overflow. And improperly sealed or insulated ducts can cause condensation to form and drip into the house. A quick look around the attic will help you track down this problem.

**BATH AND KITCHEN VENTS.** These vents are often vented directly into the attic (or become detached from roof vents). They can pour gallons of water vapor into the attic, where it'll freeze or condense and drip back into the house. Again, a visit to the attic will locate it. Even an uninsulated exhaust vent that is vented through the roof can create condensation on the duct. That moisture then leaks back into the house, usually around vent grilles. Those ducts should be replaced with insulated ones.

**ICE DAMS.** Ice buildup on eaves, coupled with water coming in along outside walls, is a sure sign of ice dams. They're usually caused by some combination of improper attic venting, attic bypasses and inadequate attic insulation. To learn more, search for "attic bypasses" and "ice dams" at familyhandyman.com.

# HandyHints®

**FROM OUR READERS**

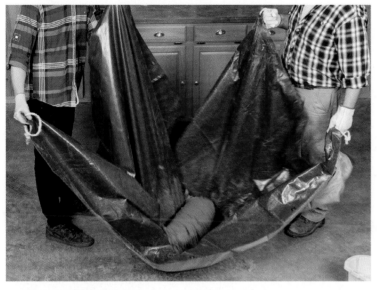

## EASY CONCRETE MIXING

I needed to pour a concrete pad for a brick mailbox I was building. My neighbor, a retired mason, offered to help, and his first instruction was to skip the concrete mixer rental. He had an easier way, using two people, a 6 x 6-ft. heavy-duty tarp with rope handles at each corner, and a water bucket.

Here's how it works. Pour a bag of concrete mix in the center of the tarp, make a crater in the center and then add the recommended amount of water. Each person grabs two tarp corners like they're going to fold the tarp. Lift one corner at a time going in one direction, like you're doing "the wave" at a football game, and continue for a minute or two until the bag is mixed. Pour the concrete right from the tarp into the form and start a new bag. My project, requiring eight bags of concrete mix, was mixed and poured in less than an hour, including washing the tools and tarp.

—Travis Dunford

## PREPAINTING NAIL HEADS

When you're installing prepainted wood or engineered-wood siding, paint the tops of galvanized nail coils the color of the house before loading them into the gun. It's much faster than going back and painting them one at a time later. Use a foam brush and apply the paint sparingly so it doesn't drip over the edges of the nail heads. Let the paint dry completely before loading the coils into the nail gun.

—Nate Schluter

MAGNETIC TOOL BAR

## MAGNET DRAGNET

After you've had remodeling or roofing work done on your home, it's not unusual to get a flat tire from old nails or other hardware left behind. As soon as the roofing contractors' taillights were out of my driveway, I rigged up this drag using rope and a 24-in. magnetic bar tool holder (No. YA161; $40 at store. snap-on.com). I drag it everywhere I'll be driving. It picks up much more metal debris than the wheeled type, which doesn't actually touch the ground. It sure beats the cost and hassle of a flat tire.

—Steve Rodgers

# Hole Saw
## Smarts

**W**hen you need to drill a large hole, bigger than 1-1/2 in. in diameter or so, a hole saw is simply the right tool for the job. However, hole saws have a well-deserved reputation for being no fun to use. If the prospect of using one conjures memories of an ice pack on your wrist and the smell of burning wood, relax and read on. Here are 14 tips to help ensure safe, successful cutting.

## 1 A bit is better for some holes

For holes 1-1/2 in. in diameter or less, a spade, auger or Forstner bit is a better choice than a hole saw. These bits are far less likely to catch and twist your arm, and there's no plug to pry out, just wood shavings. So start building your hole saw kit with sizes that are larger than 1-1/2 in.

## 2 Keep it clean

Hole saws are often tasked with cutting through studs and joists, which are typically pine, spruce or Douglas fir. All of these species contain lots of pitch and resin, which build up on the saw's teeth. This buildup adds friction, slows cutting and increases heat. This excess heat causes the teeth to dull very quickly.

Clean off the pitch after use to greatly extend the life of your hole saws. You can buy specially formulated cleaners, such as CMT Formula 2050 Blade & Bit Cleaner ($13 for an 18-oz. bottle) at home centers. Or, do a quick search online to find plenty of homemade solutions.

WORN TEETH

ARBOR

## 3 Don't struggle with worn-out saws

Like any other cutting tool, a hole saw will get dull with use. If your hole saw cuts slowly or starts to smoke, it's likely dull and needs replacing. If you're adept at sharpening, you can give it a shot, but a new saw makes life much easier.

## 4 Build your own kit

A quality hole saw kit costs $50 to $200, depending on the number of saw sizes and the type of teeth (bimetal, carbide or diamond; bimetal teeth are sufficient for most work). If you can't afford to buy the whole kit at once, don't worry. Most manufacturers sell individual hole saws and arbors. Build your kit one saw at a time as needed, sticking with one brand so you can use the dedicated arbor for new hole saws. That way, you won't end up with odd-sized hole saws that you'll never use.

# Hole Saw Smarts

**BACKER BOARD**

**8** **Back up your workpiece**
When you're cutting holes that need to look tidy on both sides, clamp a sacrificial backer board under the workpiece to prevent blowout (splintering on the exit side). If you're at the drill press, a backer board also serves to protect your drill press table.

**5** **Use a drill press**
Whenever it's an option, use a hole saw in a drill press. A drill press ensures that the hole is straight and enables you to clamp the workpiece down securely. The drill press's handle gives you total control over the pressure you're applying, and you can easily adjust the drill press to run at the proper speed.

**6** **Avoid cheap hole saw kits**
These cheap kits seem like a great deal, but you get what you pay for. The teeth dull very quickly and the saws are often shallow, limiting the thickness of the material you can drill through.

**PILOT BIT**

**PILOT HOLE**

**7** **Don't burn out your drill**
Cutting holes with a hole saw is hard work for a drill, and if you're not careful, you can burn out the motor. If you feel your drill's motor housing getting hot, stop and let it cool off.

**9** **Cut from both sides**
When possible, drill from both sides. This does two things. First, it helps prevent blowout. Second, you don't end up with the cutout plug stuck in the hole cylinder. Start cutting from one side, stopping as soon as the pilot bit comes out the other side. Next, insert the pilot bit in the hole on the other side of the workpiece and finish the cut.

**10** **Watch your speed**
Whatever the material, slow is the way to go with hole saws. The larger the diameter of the hole, the slower you'll need to go. For wood, aluminum, brass and mild steel, 500 rpm is about right for a 3/4-in. hole, all the way down to 75 rpm for a 5-in. hole.

**11** **Rock the drill**
Cutting holes goes much faster if you slightly rock the drill in a circular motion so not all the teeth are cutting at once. You're also less likely to burn the wood than with constant, even pressure.

**12** **Don't use the trigger lock**
Using your drill's trigger lock might seem like a good idea, but it's quite dangerous. If the hole saw catches and jerks the drill out of your hands, you'll have a spinning airborne cutting tool.

AUXILIARY HANDLE

**13** **Use an auxiliary handle**
Although you'll often use a hole saw in a handheld drill, sawing large holes is a tough job, so use your most powerful drill. Besides power, the drill should have an auxiliary handle, as hole saws don't act like drill bits. They have a tendency to "catch," giving your wrist a nasty twist. It can even yank the drill right out of your hand while the spinning drill handle crashes into anything in its path. An auxiliary handle lessens the chance of losing your grip.

CLEARANCE HOLE

**14** **Drill clearance holes**
As a hole saw is cutting, there's nowhere for the sawdust to effectively exit the kerf. So it gets packed into the teeth, causing slow cutting, heat, burning and premature dulling. Drill a couple of 1/2-in. clearance holes to give the sawdust a way out. To get the clearance holes in the right place, start the pilot bit and let the teeth cut in about 1/16 in. Drill clearance holes through the workpiece, just inside the kerf.

# HOLE SAW JACK-O'-LANTERN

## Frightening, fast & fun

### By Gary Wentz

**A** few years ago, I promised to provide 20 jack-o'-lanterns for a Halloween party. I stared at my truckload of pumpkins, regretted my promise and wondered how to produce good-looking jack-o'-lanterns fast. The answer: hole saws! Here are the gory details:

ARBOR

I used 1-1/4-in. and 2-1/4-in. hole saws, but it's best to have several sizes to choose from. I removed the drill bits from my hole saws so there wouldn't be holes in the center of the eyeballs.

Instead of using a drill, I cut holes by hand. Here's why: First, starting a hole without the center drill bit is more difficult with a drill. Second, I was able to feel when the hole saw was starting to break through to the inside of the pumpkin. At that point, I would stop and push the cutout plug into the pumpkin with my fingers. If you drill completely through, the plug will be stuck in your hole saw and you'll have to pry it out with a screwdriver.

DRILL BIT

PLUG

You can cut holes faster with a drill, but you're more likely to end up with a plug stuck in your hole saw.

**1** **Cut out the lid.** A jigsaw works slick for cutting the lid. Just plunge the blade into the pumpkin, start up your saw and cut. Don't forget to clean off your tools. Pumpkin goop is surprisingly tough to remove after it dries.

**2** **Start the hole.** A hole saw tends to wander as you start the cut. To avoid that, push hard so all the teeth sink into the pumpkin. Then twist. Cut slowly enough to stay focused on keeping the hole saw centered.

**3** **Drill without a drill.** When your cut is about 1/4 in. deep, grab the arbor with locking pliers (such as Vise-Grip pliers) to make cutting easier. As the hole saw begins to break through the pumpkin, stop. Then push out the plug by hand. Cut an "eyeball" out of the plug using a smaller hole saw. Or you can cut the eyeballs first, then cut out the larger eye opening. I used the leftover rings as ears and fastened them with screws.

**4** **Screw in the eyeballs.** Slippery pumpkin parts are hard to hold steady, so it's best to hold each eyeball on your benchtop while you start the screw. Then drive it into the pumpkin. Fasten the ears with shorter screws. Form the mouth by making overlapping cuts with a hole saw.

LOCKING PLIERS

SCREW

# 6 Outdoor Structures, Landscaping & Gardening

## IN THIS CHAPTER

Home Care & Repair .....................208
  *Multipurpose Garden Tools, Planning a
  Retaining Wall and more*

Restore a Weedy & Patchy Lawn ..........213

Sprinkler System Fixes............................218

Living Wall................................................224

Digging Holes .........................................230

Concrete Basics .......................................234

Choose a Lawn Tractor.............................237

Install an Irrigation System.....................242

Handy Hints .............................................247
  *Chimney Flue Planters, Measuring
  Stick for Firewood, Easy Apple
  Cleanup and more*

**ASHLAR BLOCKS:** Ashlar walls contain blocks of different sizes, shapes and sometimes, colors. These blocks were tumbled, which breaks off the sharp edges.

## PLANNING A RETAINING WALL

When you're choosing concrete block for a retaining wall, keep in mind that some types of block allow more design options than others. There are two key differences:

- Some block systems allow graceful curves, even tight curves. Others allow only large-radius curves—or no curves at all.
- Some systems include a variety of options such as capstones to top off the walls, blocks for above-ground "seating" walls, matching stair blocks or patio pavers. Others primarily offer plain blocks.

Designing a wall and selecting block can get complicated. To start, snap a few photos of the wall site and sketch a rough plan. Then visit a garden center that specializes in hardscaping. That's where you'll get the best advice and widest selection. Most stores have several types of block on display. Be prepared for huge cost differences. Some block systems cost as little as $4 per sq. ft. of wall surface. Others, depending on the features you choose, can cost $20 or more.

**STANDARD BLOCKS:** Blocks of a single size and shape are easier to work with than ashlar blocks. This is "straight face" block, but tumbled is available too.

**THREE-WAY SPLIT BLOCKS:** Because the corners are split off, these blocks are best for tight curves. They're easy to stack and usually less expensive.

CHAIN-SAW
ATTACHMENT

POWER
HEAD

## MULTIPURPOSE GARDEN TOOLS

If you're in the market for a string trimmer, consider this new trend in lawn and garden gear—multipurposing. You buy one power head, which usually comes with a straight-shaft string trimmer. But then you can buy other attachments, like the pole chain saw shown, a cultivator, a leaf blower, a grass edger or even a hedge trimmer.

Some manufacturers offer battery-powered models with interchangeable attachments, but if you want the power and run-time of a gas engine, check out this two-stroke gas-powered Troy-Bilt base model. It comes in at about $129, with additional accessories costing $60 to $100 each. You can switch from one attachment to another in less than 30 seconds. You save money by not having to buy a dedicated machine for each task, and you have only one engine to maintain for all these different tools. To learn more, visit lawncare.familyhandyman.com.

## SMALL IS BEAUTIFUL

If you live in suburbia and you're thinking of buying a riding lawn mower, here's something to consider. A lawn tractor may be your first instinct, but a wiser choice might be a much smaller riding mower, like this Troy-Bilt TB30R Hydro Neighborhood Rider.

Here's why. With this riding mower, the engine is under the seat, not in front of you, so its wheel base is much shorter than a lawn tractor's. That gives you a tight, 18-in. turning radius—better for maneuvering around trees and gardens. It also has a much narrower mowing deck, 30 in., so you can easily drive through 3-ft.-wide gates. And consider the space you'll save in your garage or shed.

The TB30R (about $1,400) also features a hydrostatic transmission with smooth speed control and adjustments. To learn more, visit lawncare.familyhandyman.com.

# Home Care & Repair

## MATE HOSE ENDS FOR STORAGE

Apparently, an empty garden hose makes a cozy home for various critters. Mine has housed a snake and a frog, but most frequently it has hosted ants. Too many times I've hooked up my oscillating sprinkler, only to have it immediately plugged with ants. I finally learned my lesson. In the fall, I drain the hoses and mate the ends before storing them for the winter. If I forget to mate the ends, or if I haven't used the hose for a while in the summer, I make sure to run water through the hose before connecting it to the sprinkler.

—Travis Larson

## KEEP FEEDERS CLOSE TO WINDOWS

At a conservative estimate of at least 1 billion deaths per year in the United States alone, window strikes are the main killers of wild birds. Here's a way to prevent some of these collisions at your home. Whenever you're placing feeders near the house, keep them no more than 3 ft. away from windows. That way a bird can't build up enough speed to sustain a fatal injury after feeding. This also brings the birds closer for better viewing.

### MEET AN EXPERT

**Daniel Klem is a professor of ornithology at Muhlenberg College in Pennsylvania.**

## DON'T PUT OFF PRUNING

With every year of delay, trees and shrubs become harder to prune. As branches get bigger, so does the task of trimming them. A job that would take 20 minutes now might consume an hour next year. You may also need bigger tools. Worse, neglected trees or bushes can become so hopeless that you'll have to cut them down and start over.

## CHOOSING A DECK FINISH

A wooden deck that's coated with a finish will likely need to be refinished every three to five years. With an entire aisle devoted to finishing products at the home center, how do you decide what's best?

The steps involved with using oil-based vs. water-based finishes, and the maintenance required, will help drive your decision. Manufacturers' claims about how long a finish lasts should be taken with a grain of salt; the life span of any finish on wood that's exposed to the elements is unpredictable.

As you choose a deck finish, keep these facts in mind:

### Oil-based

- Easy to apply because of the slower drying time.
- Penetrates the wood and doesn't form a film.
- Takes longer to dry.
- The wide temperature parameters for application let you apply it earlier or later in the season than water-based finishes.
- Doesn't crack or peel.
- You can refinish just a small area.
- Regular cleaning is recommended.

### Water-based

- Dries fast, making application more difficult than oil because it's harder to keep a wet edge.
- Forms a protective film.
- Will likely crack and peel.
- Must be completely removed before refinishing.

### No finish

- Use pressure-treated lumber or a rot-resistant species such as cedar or redwood.
- No refinishing or the accompanying prep work required.
- Requires periodic cleaning as needed.
- Boards will weather to a silver/gray patina.
- With good airflow, the deck will last for decades.

### Prep work is everything

When it's time to refinish, the first step is cleaning. Pressure washing can loosen the wood fibers and hasten the breakdown of the wood, so don't do it unless you're experienced with the proper pressure and angles for cleaning wood. Deck cleaners and scrub brushes are a much safer option.

The remaining prep work depends on the type of finish that's currently on the deck. You can apply an oil finish over an old oil finish with minimal prep and expect good results. But if the old finish is water-based and you haven't thoroughly removed it before applying an oil-based finish, the penetration of the oil-based finish will be blotchy. If you don't know whether the old finish is water- or oil-based, here's how to tell:

- If the old finish absorbs water and isn't peeling or cracking, it's most likely oil-based. In this case, use a deck cleaner with a scrub brush to clean the surface. Apply

your new finish according to the directions on the can.

- If the old finish is cracking or peeling and/or doesn't absorb water, it's likely water-based. To remove water-based finishes, you'll need to use paint stripper as well as a fair degree of sanding before applying your new finish.
- For a new deck that's never been finished, wait a year before applying any finish. During the waiting period, clean with a deck cleaner and a scrub brush at three to six months, and then again right before finishing.

# HomeCare&Repair

## DID THE WEEDS WIN IN YOUR YARD?

If weeds have taken over your lawn, spot treatment just isn't practical. Use a dial sprayer attached to your garden hose and add concentrated broadleaf killer to the pot. Set the dial at the top to the ratio called for on the herbicide container.

Hook up the garden hose and apply an even treatment to the weedy areas. Be sure to clear the yard of anything that can get contaminated by overspray. And protect your flowers and bushes with plastic sheeting or cardboard. Broadleaf killers will kill or harm anything with leaves—including your flower bed.

ADJUSTABLE DIAL

DIAL SPRAYER

ORTHO DIAL N SPRAY

## KEEP COOL WITH SHADE

Shade from trees, trellises and vines blocks direct sunlight through windows, which is responsible for about half the heat gain in your home. Carefully positioned trees and horizontal trellises on the east and west sides can save up to 30 percent of a household's energy consumption for heating and cooling.

# RESTORE A **WEEDY & PATCHY LAWN**

## Work a little, water a lot—and then enjoy!

By Joe Churchill

## RESEEDING SAVED MY PATHETIC LAWN

One of the best things about working at *Family Handyman* is having lots of pros at my fingertips. This time it was Joe Churchill, our lawn expert. Last summer we met in my backyard, and he told me exactly how to restore my ugly lawn. And by fall, I had the best-looking lawn in the neighborhood. Aside from the weed killing and watering, the restoration took just one weekend, and the results speak for themselves!

Vern Johnson,
Art Director

Reseeding is a job you can do in a weekend if you have an average-size lawn. You'll have to wrestle home a couple of engine-powered rental machines. And once your work is done, be prepared to keep the soil damp with daily watering for the first month or so. It's the key to a successful reseeding job.

Before you establish this beautiful new lawn, be sure to do any hardscaping or landscaping—such as retaining walls, patios or tree planting—that might tear up your new lawn with heavy equipment or excavating. If an inground irrigation system is in your future, install that beforehand as well. You'll avoid damaging your new lawn by trenching in irrigation lines and sprinkler heads, and you'll have the benefit of using the system to water the new grass. Flag the sprinkler heads to avoid hitting them with the aerator or power rake.

**1** **Kill the weeds.** Use a hose-end sprayer to spray the lawn with a broadleaf weed killer at least three weeks before you plant the new grass seed. Wear eye protection, gloves, a long-sleeve shirt and pants, and waterproof shoes.

## Get better grass

Grass has improved dramatically in recent years, with varieties bred for better color, thicker turf or shade and drought tolerance. So reseeding doesn't just fill in the bare spots; it also improves the mix of grass varieties in your lawn.

## Save the existing grass?

The steps we show here are for a lawn that's at least 50 percent grass. Take a close look at the lawn. If you see plenty of healthy grass among the weeds or large areas of good grass throughout the lawn, you can save the existing grass and fill in the rest of the lawn by planting new seed. That

**2** **Aerate the soil.** Make at least three passes from three different directions with an aerator to loosen the soil.

**WHAT IT TAKES**
TIME: One weekend for an average-size lawn
COST: About $10 per 100 sq. ft., including rental costs.
SKILL: Beginner
TOOLS: Two rental power tools, plus a rake and a broadcast spreader

calls for applying a broadleaf herbicide, which kills the weeds but doesn't harm the grass. It should be applied three to four weeks before starting the project. A hose-end sprayer with concentrated weed killer is the fastest, easiest application method (**Photo 1**). But if your lawn is hopelessly bare or completely covered with weeds, it's best to go "scorched earth" and kill all the vegetation with a nonselective herbicide like Roundup and start over. If after two weeks, some weeds reappear, apply another treatment to the survivors.

## Late summer or early fall is best

Timing is important when it comes to lawn reseeding. When summer heat begins to wane, it's much easier to stay on track with watering newly sprouted grass shoots because they won't be stressed by high heat and humidity. Plus, there will be plenty of time for the grass to get established before winter.

You'll be far less successful planting and growing grass from seed during spring and summer. If you must seed in the spring, wait for soil temperatures to reach a consistent 55 degrees F. Also watch for weeds! They can outcompete new grass seedlings as they both vie for space, sunlight and water. Using a seed-friendly herbicide is recommended in the spring or early summer if you have to treat emerging weeds after reseeding. And when choosing the starter fertilizer, look for one containing siduron or mesotrione pre-emergent herbicide, or be prepared for disappointing results.

Reseeding can be a crapshoot. A big thunderstorm could wash your seed away. So pay attention to long-range forecasts and plan accordingly. That's especially true if your yard is sloped enough that it doesn't take much water to wash away seed. Before you start the soil prep, set your mower to its lowest setting and give your yard a buzz cut.

## Rent an aerator and power rake

There's no reasonable way to prep the soil by hand, so you should plan to rent an aerator (**Photo 2**) and power rake (also called a dethatcher; **Photo 3**) for about $100 each per day. Lifting them into and

**3** **Prepare the surface.** Pulverize the aerating plugs and loosen dead foliage with a power rake. Rake up and remove any vegetation that completely covers the soil.

**4** **Outline garden beds.** Sow seed with a drop spreader near or around gardens or other areas where you want to avoid sowing grass seed.

**5** **Seed the large areas.** Spread seed with a broadcast spreader in large areas away from gardens. Use half the recommended drop rate to spread the seed in one direction. Spread the remaining seed in the opposite direction to ensure even distribution.

**6** **Rake in the seed.** Lightly rake the seed to establish good seed-to-soil contact.

out of the pickup will require a helper, but operating them doesn't require an athlete's physique. The worst part is that you'll be marching around the yard following the self-propelled machines for many, many passes. Unless you have a small yard, plan to aerate it in one day, then return the aerator the following day and rent the power rake to finish the heavy work. Day two would also include planting, raking and fertilizing.

### Aerate like crazy

Aerators pull small plugs from the soil and deposit them on the surface (**Photo 2**). That loosens the soil, making it easier for roots to grow deep into the soil. The plugs will be pulverized in the next step, power raking (**Photo 3**), to form loose soil for the seeds to germinate in. The holes you create will allow fertilizer and water to penetrate deep into the soil for better retention. When you're using a core aerator to prepare soil for reseeding, the key is to make at least three passes—more if you have the stamina—each from a different direction.

### Next step: power raking

Power rakes spin metal tines at high speed to scarify and loosen the soil as well as break up the aerator plugs. They also lift thatch from your lawn. Go over the whole lawn from two directions, then rake up and remove dead debris if it completely covers the ground and would prevent seed from contacting the soil.

### Choose the right spreader

In most cases, a broadcast spreader (**Photo 5**) is the best choice because it evenly distributes seed or fertilizer for thorough coverage. If you have a large yard bordered by flower beds or vegetable gardens, use a drop spreader (**Photo 4**) to spread the seed near them before doing the majority of

the yard with a broadcast spreader. Since the seed drops straight down, you won't be casting grass seed in your gardens by mistake.

Whichever spreader you use, set the feed rate at half (or less) of the recommended rate. When using the drop spreader around border gardens, overlap subsequent passes slightly for more even seed distribution. But when using the broadcast or drop spreader for the open areas, make two or more passes from

different directions for even distribution. This is especially true when you're using a drop spreader so you don't wind up with a striped lawn. If you don't own a broadcast spreader, buy one—don't rent it. You'll need it to keep your new lawn in tip-top shape after it's established.

### Sow the seed

Applying too much or too little seed is a mistake. Here is a little hands-

## HOW TO BUY QUALITY SEED

Quality seed mixtures contain different species and varieties of lawn grasses that will better adapt to your lawn's conditions. Don't try to save money when you shop for grass seed. Look for the highest-priced seed on the shelf and follow these tips:

- Pay attention to the label. The lower the amount of weed seed, crop seed and inert matter, the better.
- Consult your local county or university extension service for a list of recommended lawn seed varieties for your area. You can also check university websites for tips on how to purchase quality grass seed.
- For quality lawns in full sun, look for a high percentage of Kentucky bluegrass in the mix.
- Lawns containing heavy shade should be seeded with a mix containing 70 percent or more fine fescue.
- Fine fescues (creeping red, sheep's, hard, chewings) use less water and need less fertilizer and fewer mowings.
- Avoid mixtures containing annual ryegrass because it lasts for only one year!
- Stay away from unnamed varieties or "Variety Not Stated" (VNS) ingredients.

and-knees observation to let you know if you're applying the right amount. Picture a square inch of area on a freshly seeded area and count the seeds. Strive to get about 15 or so seeds per square inch. After spreading, lightly rake the seed into the soil for good contact. It doesn't have to be completely buried. Some of the seed can still be showing.

## Fertilize with a starter

Fertilizers used to contain nitrogen, phosphorus and potassium. But due to water pollution concerns, many states no longer allow phosphorus in ordinary lawn fertilizers. However, phosphorus is very helpful for root development, so it's important for starting new seed. At the garden center, look for fertilizer labeled "Starter" or "New Lawns." Your state may allow its sale for establishing new lawns or in gardens.

## Water, water, water

An oscillating sprinkler works best for getting your lawn started. It covers a large area with even, light streams of water to prevent washing away seed. You'll only need to water for about 20 minutes at a time depending on your soil type. Unless it rains, you'll likely need to water at least twice daily. On hot or windy days, you may need to water even more frequently.

Closely monitor the soil to keep it damp, not saturated. Strive to maintain soil dampness to a depth of about 1/2 in. You'll need to do this for at least three weeks. If you're not diligent, you may throw away all your hard work and money. One dry, hot sunny day is all it takes to wipe out a new lawn. A $25 timer for your hose, available at any garden or home center, might be helpful if you can't be home to water as needed. After the grass is 3 in. high, you can start mowing and begin a normal watering regime.

**MEET AN EXPERT**

**Joe Churchill is a senior turf specialist for Reinders Inc. For over 30 years, he has helped lawn care companies, golf course superintendents and sports turf managers grow healthy, high-performing turf.**

**7** **Distribute the fertilizer.** Spread starter fertilizer over the yard. Follow the directions on the bag to determine how many pounds per 1,000 sq. ft.

**8** **Water daily.** Water lightly daily or twice daily in hot, dry or windy conditions to keep the soil damp, not wet.

### Soil watering gauge
Your goal is to water to a depth of 1/2 in. As a test, water for about 20 minutes, then drive a spade into the ground and look for the dark line near the surface indicating water penetration. That'll tell you if you should water for longer or shorter periods.

**DIY**
SOLUTIONS
TO IRRITATING
IRRIGATION
PROBLEMS

# SPRINKLER SYSTEM FIXES

**Y**our irrigation system may seem complex, but it's made up of simple components you can repair or replace yourself in just an hour or two. Don't be intimidated: The pipes are plastic and much easier to repair than the plumbing in your house. The electrical lines are low voltage, so they're not hazardous. You may need a multimeter ($30) to diagnose electrical problems, but you can master that step in just a few minutes.

### Solution 1: Replace a broken sprinkler head

Broken sprinkler heads are easy to identify. Just look for cracked or broken plastic casing on the heads, heads that don't pop up, or heads that spray water wildly or not at all. It's common to find the top of the head completely broken off. This typically happens to heads that are set too high and get run over by vehicles or hit by lawn mowers.

Replacing the head is one of the simplest fixes. Replacement heads are available at home centers and online, starting at $5. Be sure to buy the same type of head that you're replacing.

To remove a broken head, turn off the system and dig a 2-ft.-diameter hole around the head. Using a square shovel, slice the sod into easy-to-remove pieces. Set the sod on a tarp so you can put it back in place at the end of the job.

Dig down to the "riser" (the vertical pipe that branches off the main line), which is connected to the sprinkler head. Dig gently to avoid damaging the plastic water line, which is 8 to 12 in. underground.

Turn the head counterclockwise to remove it from the riser. While the head is off, take care not to spill dirt into the riser. Sprinkler heads are installed only hand-tight, but after they've been in the ground for several years, you may need a wrench to unscrew them. If the head doesn't turn easily, hold the riser with a slip joint pliers to keep it from twisting loose from the fittings below.

Attach the new sprinkler head by placing it on the riser and turning it hand-tight (**photo right**). Don't use Teflon tape or joint compound on the riser threads.

Sprinkler heads are tested at the factory to make sure they work. As a result, they're often packaged still wet, so don't be surprised to see water in a new head.

Before filling in the hole and replacing the sod, set the desired sprinkler pattern (see "Reset the Spray Pattern," p. 220).

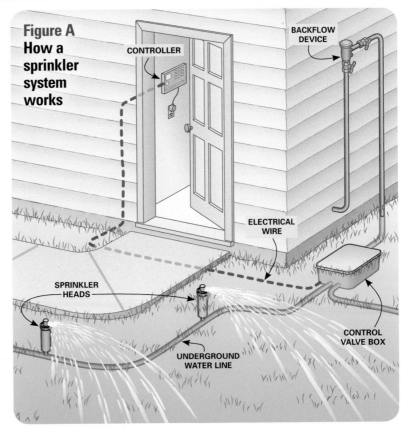

**Figure A
How a sprinkler system works**

CONTROLLER
BACKFLOW DEVICE
ELECTRICAL WIRE
SPRINKLER HEADS
CONTROL VALVE BOX
UNDERGROUND WATER LINE

**How a sprinkler system works**
The controller sends a signal to the control valves in the control valve box. The valves open, sending water through the underground water line, which causes the sprinkler heads to pop up and spray.

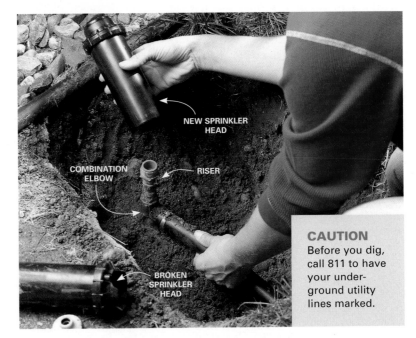

NEW SPRINKLER HEAD
COMBINATION ELBOW
RISER
BROKEN SPRINKLER HEAD

**CAUTION**
Before you dig, call 811 to have your underground utility lines marked.

**Screw on a new head**
Dig around the sprinkler head to expose the riser. Unscrew the broken sprinkler head from the riser and screw on the new one.

## Solution 2: Clean a clogged head

A head that's clogged with dirt may rise but not spray, stay up after watering, or produce an erratic spray pattern.

To clean the head, dig it out and remove it from the riser (see p. 219). Take the head apart by holding the bottom of the canister and turning the top of the head counterclockwise. Once it's unscrewed, lift it out of the canister (**Photo 1**).

Remove the screen basket, which serves as a filter, at the base of the head. If you can't pop the screen out with your fingers, pry it out with a screwdriver or pull it free with a pliers. After rinsing the screen (**Photo 2**), clean the rest of the sprinkler head. Reinstall the head. If it still doesn't work, replace it with a new head.

## Reset the spray pattern

When you install a new head or reinstall an old one, you may need to adjust it to water a specific area. Adjustment methods vary. You can adjust some head types by turning a slot at the top with a screwdriver. Others require a special key that you insert into the head and turn (**Photo 3**). Some heads also allow you to adjust the spray pattern by turning a tiny screw located next to the nozzle.

Adjust the heads before installing them, then fine-tune them once they're in place, with the sprinkler running.

First, turn the top clockwise until it stops. That nozzle location is the starting point (the head will turn counterclockwise from there). Adjust the head to set the watering rotation anywhere from 40 to 360 degrees counterclockwise from the starting point.

Set the head in the canister. Standing behind the head, align the nozzle with the right edge of the area you want to water, such as along a driveway. Tighten the head in the canister. Carefully backfill the hole and replace the sod.

Turn on the sprinklers and allow the head to rotate a few times, then make additional adjustments while the system is running.

**1 Take the head apart.** Unscrew the top from the canister. Rinse away soil and debris in a bucket of water.

**2 Clean the screen.** Remove the screen basket from the bottom of the head, then rinse it clean.

**3 Adjust the pattern.** Set the watering range of the sprinkler head before installing it. Place the head in the canister so the nozzle is at the edge of the area to be watered. Make final adjustments with the water running.

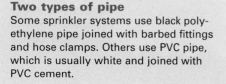

**Two types of pipe**
Some sprinkler systems use black polyethylene pipe joined with barbed fittings and hose clamps. Others use PVC pipe, which is usually white and joined with PVC cement.

## LOW WATER PRESSURE

### Solution 1: Turn on valves at backflow device

Low water pressure will result in the sprinkler heads barely shooting water. In extreme cases, many of the heads won't even pop up. Start with the easiest solution. Make sure the valves at the backflow device are fully open. The backflow device is located above ground, with the valve at least 12 in. above the highest sprinkler head in the yard. Most backflow devices have two valves, one on the horizontal pipe and one on the vertical. Turn the valves to their open positions as shown. The valve is open when the handle is parallel with the pipe.

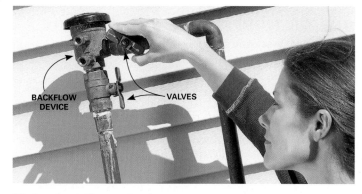

**Make sure the water is on**
Check the valves on the backflow device to make sure they're open. Turn the valve on the horizontal pipe first, then the vertical pipe valve.

### Solution 2: Find and repair leaks

Check for leaks in the water line. Look for a series of sprinkler heads that aren't watering properly. A water line problem is always located between the last working head and the first nonworking head.

Look for signs of leaking water, such as water bubbling up from the soil when the sprinklers are running, a depression in the ground, or a very wet area. If you find running water, follow the water to the highest point to locate the source.

Once you locate the approximate leak site, dig straight down to the water line. Then enlarge the hole along the line, following the flow of the leaking water until you find the break or crack. Before making the repair, be sure the system is turned off at the controller.

To fix the leak, cut out the damaged section of pipe. A hacksaw cuts plastic pipe easily. Replace the damaged section with a repair coupling ($5 at irrigation supply stores). Turn on the system to check for leaks, then backfill the hole with dirt and replace the sod.

**Replace damaged pipe**
Cut out the damaged section of line and replace it with a repair coupling. Repair couplings come in several styles. This one expands and contracts like a telescope.

REPAIR COUPLING

### Solution 3: Check for crushed pipes

If you can't locate a leak, the water line may be crushed or obstructed. Sometimes roots wrap around the line and squeeze it closed over the course of several years (**photo below**). Or vehicles can compress the soil, causing the line to collapse.

These problems are harder to find and often require a lot of digging.

Again, look for the problem after the last working head. Dig along the water line until you find the damaged section. If the line runs near a tree, start your digging there.

Once you locate the damaged section, cut it out with a hacksaw. If the line was damaged by tree roots, reroute the line by digging a new trench away from the tree.

Cut a new section of pipe to replace the damaged one. Then install the new section of pipe, connecting it at each end with regular couplings and hose clamps (**photo right**).

**Replace crushed pipe**
Cut out the damaged section. Replace it with a new pipe, making connections with couplings and hose clamps.

TREE ROOT

CRUSHED LINE

### Solution 1: Check for voltage to the bad zones

Your watering system is divided into a series of zones. Each zone has an electrically activated valve that controls the heads for a designated area.

Generally, if you have a zone that's not turning on, you have an electrical problem. To solve the problem, make sure the zone wires are firmly attached to the terminals in the controller, the transformer is plugged in and the circuit breaker at the main panel is on.

Next, test for voltage to the nonworking zone, using a multimeter ($30 at home centers and hardware stores). Turn on the nonworking zone at the controller. Turn the multimeter dial to voltage and place one lead on the common terminal (marked "c" or "com"). Place the other lead on the terminal of the zone that's not working (**photo below**). It doesn't matter which lead goes to which terminal.

Refer to your owner's manual to see whether the voltage reading falls within the required range (usually 24 to 28 volts). If it doesn't, the controller needs to be replaced. (If you don't get any voltage reading, see "Check Fuse and Transformer.")

Fortunately, controllers rarely go bad unless they're struck by lightning. New ones start at $175 and can cost upward of $400. Replace a damaged controller with the same brand and model as you currently have. To replace it, label each wire that's connected to the controller with a piece of tape. Unhook the wires, then attach them to the new controller in the same sequence.

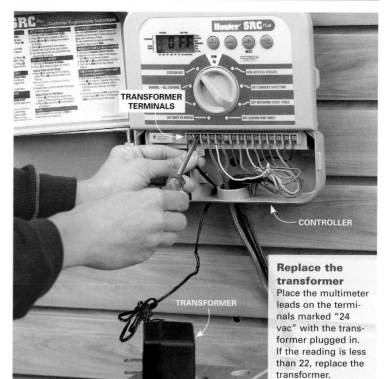

**Replace the transformer**
Place the multimeter leads on the terminals marked "24 vac" with the transformer plugged in. If the reading is less than 22, replace the transformer.

### Solution 2: Check fuse and transformer

If no zones will turn on, first turn the controller to the manual setting to see if the system will run. If it turns on manually, the controller is good, but the rain sensor may be stopping the automatic programmed watering, which is what it's designed to do.

Rain sensors conserve water by preventing the system from running when the ground is already saturated. Some states require rain sensors on all new systems. (Your rain sensor is bad if the system runs when the ground is already wet.)

If the system doesn't run in the manual position, check the controller for power. If it has a fuse, make sure it's not blown. Or, if it has a circuit breaker reset button, press the button, then try the system again. If the system is plugged into a GFCI receptacle, press the GFCI reset button.

If it still doesn't turn on, make sure the outlet that the power transformer is plugged into is working by plugging in a power tool. If it's working, plug the transformer back in, turn the system off and test the transformer for voltage. Using a multitester, place a lead on each of the two transformer terminals. It doesn't matter which lead goes to which terminal.

The transformer terminals are marked "24 vac." A 24-voltage transformer should normally test between 24 and 28 volts. If the voltage falls below the manufacturer's range, replace the transformer ($25). Simply unscrew the terminals that hold the two transformer wires in the controller and remove the transformer (**photo above**). Insert the wires on the new transformer through the designated opening in the controller. Attach the wires to the controller terminals marked "24 vac" by placing the wire ends under the screws, then tightening them.

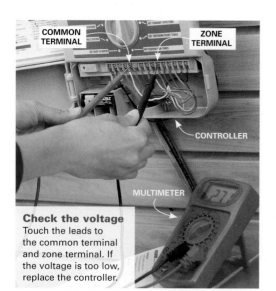

**Check the voltage**
Touch the leads to the common terminal and zone terminal. If the voltage is too low, replace the controller.

CONTROL VALVE

SOLENOID

### Solution 3: Repair a bad valve

If the controller, fuse and transformer check out OK, test the resistance "ohms" between the common terminal and the nonworking zone. Turn off the system, turn the multimeter to test for ohms (the omega symbol), and place the leads on the common terminal and zone terminal, just as you did to test for voltage.

Compare the ohms reading with the range listed in your owner's manual (usually 20 to 60 ohms). If the ohms fall below the required amount, the switch (solenoid) that operates the control valve for that zone is defective and needs to be replaced. The defective solenoid will be connected to the same color wire as the zone wire at the controller. (If the reading is too high, see "Repair Damaged Wires.")

Control valves are typically grouped with three to six valves in one box (**Photo 1**). The boxes are located in the ground with a cover that simply lifts off. They can be located anywhere in the yard but are usually close to the main water supply.

Although valves themselves rarely need to be replaced, solenoids do occasionally fail. Replacing them is quick and easy.

Be sure the controller is in the off position (you don't need to shut off the power) and the water valves on the backflow device are turned off (see top photo, p. 221). Inside the control valve box, remove the wire connectors and disconnect the two wires on the defective solenoid. Turn the solenoid counterclockwise to unscrew it from the valve (**Photo 1**). Water will slowly seep out of the valve opening, even with the water turned off. Place a new solenoid in the valve.

Twist the ends of the new solenoid wires onto the same common and field wires that the old solenoid was attached to (**Photo 2**). It doesn't matter which solenoid wire goes to the common and which one goes to the field wire. Twist a new waterproof wire connector over

**1** Replace a solenoid. Disconnect the wires and unscrew the defective solenoid from the control valve. Insert a new one and turn it until it's finger-tight.

**2** Reconnect the wires. Connect the two wires on the new solenoid to the common wire and a field wire, using waterproof connectors.

each connection (**Photo 2**). To make waterproof connections, use a silicone-filled "direct bury" connector, available at home centers for $15 for a package of 10.

### Repair damaged wires

If the ohms reading between the common terminal and the nonworking zone terminal is too high (it's sometimes an infinity reading), the problem is a severed or bad wire to the control valve. If only one zone isn't working, the field wire is damaged. If none of the zones in a control valve box are working, the common wire is damaged, although the field wires could also be bad.

To find a bad wire, bypass each in turn by temporarily substituting a 14-gauge wire for the original that you run above ground. Make the wire connections with the controller turned off. Then turn the controller back on. Test the field wire first. If the zone turns on, the old field wire is bad. Replace it with an 18-gauge wire rated for underground burial. Bury the wire at least 8 in. underground. Follow the same procedure to test the common wire.

WATERPROOF CONNECTOR

OUTDOOR STRUCTURES, LANDSCAPING & GARDENING

# LIVING WALL

## Plant a vertical garden, and let the automatic watering system keep it thriving.

By Travis Larson

## WHAT IT TAKES

**TIME:** One weekend with a helper
**COST:** $100 per lin. ft. for cedar, $40 for treated lumber
**SKILL:** Intermediate (same skills as for building a fence)
**TOOLS:** Posthole digger, 4-ft. level, drill/driver, circular saw, miter saw (optional)

**If** you have a ground-level deck or patio and would like a bit of privacy, consider building a living wall. It can shield you from the neighbors, surround you with flowers and provide fresh herbs just steps away from your kitchen or grill. The planter boxes are easy to build, and a drip irrigation system provides automatic watering all summer long—no worries about missing a day of watering or losing all your plants when you go on vacation.

**EXTRA!**
THE PLANTER BOXES ARE EASY TO MOVE AROUND. YOU COULD EVEN TAKE YOUR PLANTS INSIDE FOR THE WINTER.

## The perfect patio project

Every project has its benefits, but few projects bring as many bonuses as this one. Just consider all the features this wall can add to your deck or patio:

- **PRIVACY.** This wall blocks the view and—covered with plants—even muffles noise a little.
- **SHADE.** At 7 ft. tall, the wall blocks late afternoon sun and screens the wind.
- **ECONOMICAL.** We used cedar lumber and spent $1,800 for everything but the plants. Built with treated lumber, this wall will cost about $800. Whatever lumber you choose, the wall will cost about 40 percent less if you clad only one side. Even with the most expensive option, it's a relatively low cost for a project that transforms a deck or patio.
- **COLOR.** Flowers and greenery enliven a bland deck or patio.
- **FRESH HERBS.** A steady supply, just steps from your kitchen.
- **EASY TO BUILD.** Setting posts straight and plumb is the hard part of a project like this one. But with our process, positioning posts is goof-proof. The rest is a simple matter of screwing boards to the posts.

## Planning your wall

Our wall is about 16 ft. long including the small corner at the end. You can make your wall any length you want, but go with our height—about 7 ft. tall—or shorter. A 7-ft. wall will give you plenty of privacy but won't be so tall that it gets wobbly, and 10-ft. 4x4s work well for the posts. Whatever the length of your wall, space your 4x4s no more than 4 ft. apart so they're strong enough to support the planters, which weigh 20 lbs. or more.

We clad both sides of our wall with cedar 1x4s spaced 3/4 in. apart. If your wall runs along the wall of your house or garage, you can skip cladding the side that won't be seen.

## Buying the materials

With the overall length in mind, do some math to figure out how many 4x4s you'll need. Again, try to plan for a 4x4 every 4 ft. or less, adding one more for one end. You'll need 21 1x4s for each side you clad. If you're building a shorter wall, figure on three boards per foot of height. Your wall will look best if you buy lengths that will cover the entire wall without seams. We liked the look of rough-sawn cedar with an oil-based stain. But you could save a fair amount of money by using treated 1x4s instead of cedar. See the **Materials List** for more shopping information.

## Planter boxes

Go to the garden center and look at planter box liners. These thin-walled shallow plastic boxes hold the soil to protect wooden boxes from rotting. They come in a few different lengths. Pick narrow ones (6 in. or less). When filled with soil, wider ones may be too heavy for our system to support. Choose liners that are 5-1/2 in. deep or less so they won't show below the wood boxes. The lip will rest on the top of the boxes and support the liner, soil and plants (**Photo 15**).

## Building the wall

For dead-straight and foolproof post-setting, lay out, set and align your 4x4 posts using our 2x4 ribbon system (**Photos 1 – 5**). Once they're all placed, pour two bags of concrete mix around each post, leaving a few inches at the top for adding a couple of gallons of water.

## Figure A
## Living Wall

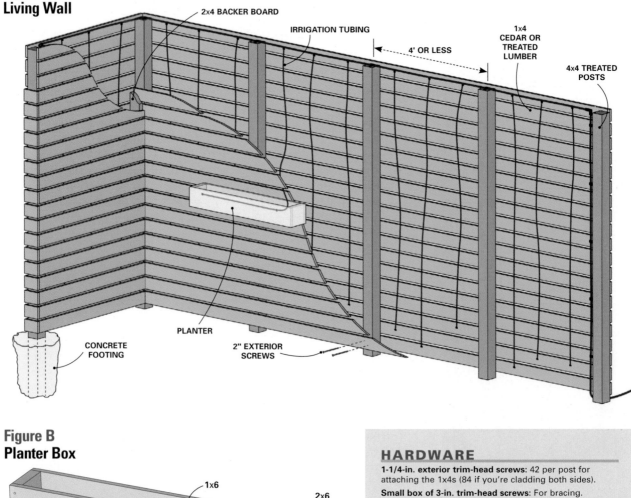

2x4 BACKER BOARD

IRRIGATION TUBING

4' OR LESS

1x4 CEDAR OR TREATED LUMBER

4x4 TREATED POSTS

CONCRETE FOOTING

PLANTER

2" EXTERIOR SCREWS

## Figure B
## Planter Box

1x6

2x6

2" SCREWS

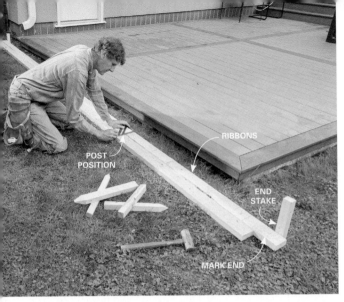

**1** Lay out the post locations. Drive stakes a foot or more beyond the end post locations. Push both 2x4 ribbons against the stakes and mark the ends so you'll know where to reset them later. Lay out the post positions on both ribbons.

**2** Mark the postholes. Drive stakes in the center of each post position, 2 in. away from the ribbon.

**3** Dig the holes. Set the ribbon aside and dig 8-in.-diameter, 30-in.-deep holes at each stake.

**4** Set the end posts. Reposition the ribbons using the marks you made earlier (see Photo 1). Screw one of the ribbons to the end stakes. Then screw each end post to the ribbon while a helper holds the post plumb both ways.

**5** Set the middle posts. Screw the top ribbon to the end posts, then set the middle posts, fastening each to the ribbons. Pour dry concrete mix into each hole, leaving the top 3 to 4 in. unfilled.

**6** Brace the end posts. Replumb the end posts in both directions and brace them in place. Eyeball the middle posts to determine if they need to be plumbed and braced. The dry concrete will absorb soil moisture and slowly harden, so don't leave this step for tomorrow!

**7 Add water.** Fill each posthole with a couple of gallons of water. If you used fast-setting concrete mix, you can resume the project after a couple hours. Otherwise, wait overnight.

**8 Clad the first side.** Level the first 1x4 and fasten it to each post with two screws. Space each row above that with 3/4-in. blocks. A 2x4 stop board aligns the 1x4s at the corner. At the other end, let the 1x4s overhang and cut them off later.

CORNER POST
3/4" SPACER BLOCK
STOP BOARD

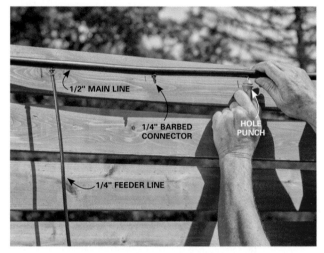

**9 Trim the posts.** When you have just two rows of 1x4s left to install, measure up 8 in. from the top of the one you just attached. Cut off the posts and then install the final two rows.

8"

**10 Install the irrigation system.** Pierce the main line with a special hole punch and use a 1/4-in. barbed connector to attach the 6-ft. feeder lines. Don't forget to plug the ends of the feeder lines.

1/2" MAIN LINE
1/4" BARBED CONNECTOR
HOLE PUNCH
1/4" FEEDER LINE

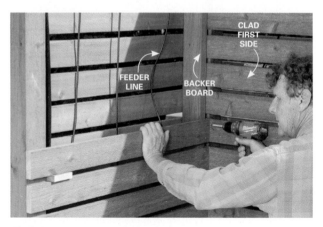

**11 Clad the inside corner.** Clad one side, overlapping the inside corner post(s). Then screw a 2x4 over the 1x4s to act as a backer for the remaining 1x4s.

FEEDER LINE
BACKER BOARD
CLAD FIRST SIDE

**12 Cap the ends.** Cut short lengths of 1x4s to finish off exposed post ends. Butt joints are best for these. Miters are tricky to cut and will open into ugly gaps later. Keep screws near the center to avoid splitting.

There's no need to hassle with pre-mixing the concrete. By the next morning, the posts will be firm enough for you to start adding the 1x4 cladding.

Begin cladding one side, making sure the bottom 1x4 is level. That 1x4 should be perfectly straight because if it's wavy, the ones above it will be too. Don't use the slab or patio as a reference; it's likely sloped. Then add each row of 1x4s using a 3/4-in.-thick spacing block, fastening it with two 1-1/4-in. exterior trim-head screws into each post. Screw a temporary 2x4 stop board to the post at one end to keep the ends perfectly aligned (**Photo 8**).

Leave off the last two rows of 1x4s so you can mark and cut off the 4x4s 8 in. above the last row you fastened (**Photo 9**). That'll keep the 4x4s 1/2 in. below the top row to help hide the irrigation tubing that will run across the top of the 4x4s. Leave off the 1x4s on the other side of the wall for now to give you easy access for installing the irrigation system.

## The irrigation system

We won't go into detail about how to install the drip irrigation system. Search for "drip irrigation" at familyhandyman.com for all the information you need. But here are

a few details on how it works for this project.

A timer valve at the hose bib meters the water going to the planters via a 1/2-in. vinyl line that runs up and across the tops of the 4x4s. We pierced that line (**Photo 10**) and plumbed in 6-ft.-long 1/4-in. feeder lines—three in each 4-ft. bay. Plug the ends of those lines for now. Once the planters are hung, you simply fish out a line just above each planter. Cut off the plug and replace it with an elbow. Slip a 1/4-in. weep line the same length as the planter over the elbow and plug the weep line. Any extra feeder lines can be used for more planter boxes. You'll find everything you need for the irrigation system at any home center or nursery. The components will cost about $100.

## Prefinish the wood

If you want to use a finish on your wall, apply it before you start building. The posts and the back side of the 1x4s will show through all those cracks, so it's important to finish all four sides of everything. We applied an oil-based stain with a 1/2-in. roller. The truth is that you'll likely spend as much time staining as building the wall. (Three of us built this entire wall in one day.)

**13** **Build the planter boxes.** Cut the 2x6 ends and 1x6 boards so that the completed planter frame will be about 1/4 in. wider and longer than the body of the plastic box liners. (The liner lips rest on top of the boxes.) Join the parts with 2-in. screws.

**14** **Add the hooks.** At both ends of each planter box, drill a 1/4-in. pilot hole 1-1/2 in. from the top. Turn hooks with a box wrench. Cut away any vinyl coating with a utility knife.

## Figure C
## Drip Watering Detail

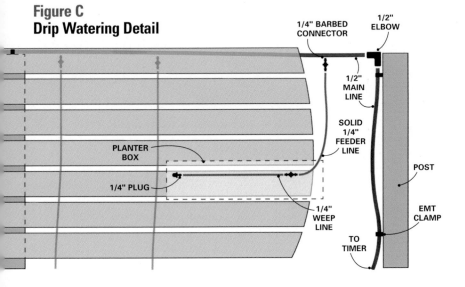

1/4" BARBED CONNECTOR

1/2" ELBOW

1/2" MAIN LINE

SOLID 1/4" FEEDER LINE

POST

EMT CLAMP

PLANTER BOX

1/4" PLUG

1/4" WEEP LINE

TO TIMER

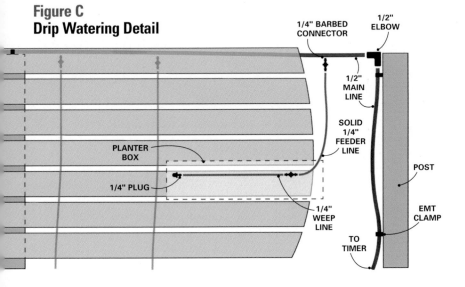

**15** **Test and adjust the hooks.** Fine-tune the depth of the hooks by hanging the boxes on the wall. Turn them in as far as they'll go while still hooking onto the 1x4. You'll have to twist the hooks slightly sideways to fit them through the 3/4-in. slots.

# DIGGING **HOLES**

## Smart tips for a dumb job

By **Gary Wentz**

**D**igging is bonehead simple. But as with any other job, a little know-how lets you do it smarter and faster and with less strain.

ELECTRICAL LINE

MARK EXCAVATION SITE WITH WHITE PAINT

### Color Code for Buried Utilities

| | |
|---|---|
| | Proposed excavation |
| | Electric power lines, cables, conduit, lighting cables |
| | Gas, oil, steam, petroleum or gaseous materials |
| | Telecom, alarm or signal lines, cables or conduit |
| | Drinking water |
| | Sewers and drain lines |

**1 Call before you dig.** Cutting into a buried utility line can kill or cost you—yes, you're responsible for damage to underground lines on your property. To avoid that risk, call 811 three or four days before you dig. It's a good idea, though usually not mandatory, to mark the area you plan to excavate with white spray paint before utility lines get marked.

**3** **Trench with a mattock.** A mattock is designed for digging narrow trenches—just right for running cable or pipe. Swing it like an ax to cut into hard soil, and then lift out the dirt with the wide blade. The chopping blade slices through roots. Wrap tape around the shaft to gauge the depth of your trench.

CHOPPING BLADE

TAPE

**2** **Sharpen your shovel.** A sharp edge makes all the difference when you're slicing through hard soil or roots. A file will do the job, but a grinder equipped with a metal-grinding disc is the fastest way to sharpen. A knife-sharp angle will dull instantly, so grind a blunter edge, about 45 degrees or so.

SOD FOLDED BACK

KNOCK BLOCK

**5** **Knock off sticky soil.** Soil clinging to your posthole digger makes progress almost impossible. To knock off the sticky stuff, keep a "knock block" within reach and slam your digger against it. It can be a stone, a brick or a face-down shovel.

**4** **Fold back the sod.** When you're digging a trench, slice the sod along one side of the trench's path and fold it over. Then, after refilling the trench, you can just flip it back into place.

POWER
SOD CUTTER

**7** **Rent a posthole auger—or not.** Gas-powered augers can make deck footings or fence-post holes fast and easy, but only in some types of soil. In hard clay, an auger is slower than a spade. In rocky soil, you'll have to stop occasionally to pull out rocks with a clamshell digger. Because of these frustrations, some deck and fence contractors don't bother with power augers and simply hand-dig every hole.

**6** **Save the sod.** Digging a hole is an opportunity to harvest some sod and patch bad areas of your lawn. With a square spade, you can neatly slice small pieces of sod, but it's slow going. For larger areas, rent a manual kick-type sod cutter. For major sod harvesting, rent a power sod cutter (about $80 for a half day).

**8** **Get a tile shovel.** The long, narrow blade is great for trenching. It also works well for breaking up tough soil and enlarging postholes. Prices start at about $20 at home centers.

**9** **Get tough on tough soil.** A long, heavy digging bar is the ultimate tool for loosening rock-hard soil and dislodging rocks. A 5-ft. version costs about $50 at home centers. That may seem like a crazy cost for a simple steel bar, but you won't regret it when you're in tough digging conditions.

**10** **Cover your grass.** To avoid raking soil out of the grass later, pile soil on cardboard or plywood. They work well because you can scoop dirt off them when refilling the hole. Tarps are fine too, but they're easily punctured by a shovel.

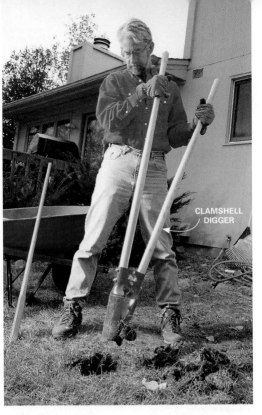

CLAMSHELL DIGGER

**13** **Mark the depth.** A tape measure isn't the tool for checking depth—it will get filled with dirt and wrecked. Instead, mark depths on your shovel or posthole digger. That way, you can measure as you dig.

**11** **Beware of auger-type diggers.** Just twist the handle and an auger-style digger drills a perfect posthole. Unlike a clamshell digger, it doesn't require you to enlarge the hole. But there's a catch: Augers work well only in soil that's soft, rock-free and not too sticky. In most soils, a clamshell digger is a better choice. Augers cost $50 or more.

**12** **Dig postholes with a clamshell digger.** A clamshell digger ($20 and up) is best for most jobs. Just plunge it into the ground, spread the handles and pull out the dirt. As your hole gets deeper, you have to enlarge the top of the hole so you can spread the handles.

HALF OF CLAMSHELL DIGGER

**14** **Improvised shovel.** A tile shovel is the best tool for flaring out the base of footing holes. But if you don't have one handy, remove the bolt from your clamshell-style posthole digger and use half of the digger as a tile shovel.

**15** **Mark with a hose and paint.** Lay out the footprint of your hole or trench with a garden hose. When you've got the layout right, mark it with spray paint.

# CONCRETE BASICS

## What every DIYer needs to know

By **Gary Wentz**

### Concrete recipe

Aside from cement, concrete contains sand and stones. Those stones, or "aggregate," are a carefully measured mix of various sizes. Small stones fill in the gaps between larger ones, and sand fills in between them. Cement is the glue that holds it all together.

CEMENT

FINE AND
COARSE SAND

INTERLOCKING
CRYSTALS

CRYSTALS TOO
FAR APART

**Trivia:**
Cement is often called "Portland cement." That's because it looks like stone found around Portland, England, where the cement was developed in the 1800s.

### It's not "cement"

Most people say "cement" and "concrete" interchangeably. But they're not the same thing. Cement is just one of the ingredients in concrete, and if you ask for cement at the lumberyard, you might get a bag of Portland cement.

**Vocab:**
The hardening process of concrete is called "curing."

### Water makes concrete "work"

Cement is mostly limestone that's been ground up and superheated. Adding water causes a chemical reaction; microscopic crystals develop, grow and interlock, binding the aggregate together and forming a rock-hard mass.

### Too much water makes it weak

It's tempting to add extra water to make concrete easier to work with or to soften concrete that has begun to harden. But don't do it. With too much water, cement crystals develop too far apart, leaving concrete weak and porous.

## Concrete doesn't "dry"

Concrete hardens while it's wet—not as it dries. If, for example, you throw a bag of concrete mix into a bathtub full of water, it will harden underwater (but we really don't recommend you do that).

**PLASTIC SHEET**

**Trivia:**
If kept constantly moist, concrete will continue to grow stronger for years. But those gains in strength are small after the first few weeks.

**AGGREGATE**

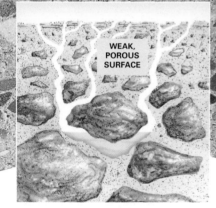

**WEAK, POROUS SURFACE**

## Keep it wet longer to make it stronger

Concrete will continue to harden until it dries out completely. That's why pros often use blankets, plastic sheets or spray-on coatings to retain moisture. Since most of the strength gain takes place in the first few days, experts often recommend a "wet cure" of three to seven days. Typically, concrete is considered fully cured after 28 days.

## Don't overwork it

To finish the surface, concrete is first "floated" with a float or a darby. This pushes the aggregate down and pulls fine sand and cement to the surface—just what you need to form a smooth, troweled finish or a rough-broomed finish later. But limit float work to two or three passes. Too much floating leaves a topping of watery cement. And that means a weak, porous surface. Too much troweling causes the same trouble.

## Simple safety

Cement is caustic. So it can cause anything from dry skin to nasty burns that require medical attention. Wear gloves and protect your eyes. Concrete dust is bad for your lungs. So strap on a respirator while mixing or cutting it.

## A little thicker is a lot stronger

A 4-in.-thick sidewalk is fine. But for driveways or slabs that will bear heavy loads, go for at least 5 in. That extra inch provides about 50 percent more strength but adds only a few hundred bucks to the cost.

CONTROL JOINT

GROOVER

**Beyond concrete:** Portland cement is also the key ingredient in other building materials such as mortar, stucco and tile grout.

## Does deicing salt damage concrete?

Some deicing chemicals, at very high concentrations, can damage concrete. But most often, damage occurs this way: Deicers turn the ice to water, which seeps into concrete pores. Later, the water freezes and expands, causing tiny craters in the surface. With each cycle, the damage grows worse. One way to reduce this damage is to sweep or shovel meltwater and slush off the concrete. Masonry sealers also help by plugging the pores in concrete.

## Allow for cracks

Concrete shrinks as it cures, which causes shrinkage cracks. Settling and frost heaves also lead to cracks. Instead of risking random, meandering cracks, provide "control joints" for straight, invisible cracks to occur. You can plow control joints into fresh concrete with a groover (as shown here) or use a saw when the concrete is partially cured. On sidewalks, control joints are needed every 4 to 5 ft. On wide slabs like driveways, place them 10 to 12 ft. apart.

## Speedy concrete

By adding an "accelerator" to the mix, manufacturers produce bagged concrete that hardens in an hour or less. That's great for small jobs but risky for big jobs that require ample finishing time.

**Convenient concrete:** In the 1930s, bagged concrete mix hit the market. Before that, folks had to mix up cement, sand and aggregate themselves.

# CHOOSING A LAWN TRACTOR

**Here's the info you need to choose the best model for your yard and budget.**

By **Rick Muscoplat**

WHOOPS! BAD DRIVING!

L awn tractors come in a wide price range: $1,200 to $2,200. Even the lowest-priced models can cut your mowing time in half compared with a walk-behind mower. So how do you choose the best machine for your yard? We talked to experts at the four largest manufacturers to get their take on which features are most important. Then we borrowed and tested four machines that span the price range. Here's what we learned.

# BEFORE YOU BUY: 6 QUESTIONS TO ANSWER

**1 Is a lawn tractor right for you?**

You're a perfect candidate for a lawn tractor if your yard is larger than a half acre and you spend an hour or more cutting grass with a walk-behind mower. If your yard is slightly smaller but you want to reduce mowing time, a riding mower might be a better choice.

**2 What size mower deck?**

Obviously, the larger the mower deck, the faster you'll finish. But keep in mind that a large mowing deck may not fit through your fence gate or between trees. Measure before you buy. As a general rule, choose a 42-in. deck for 1-acre lots, a 42-in. to 46-in. deck for 1- to 2-acre lots, and a 48-in. deck for larger yards.

**3 Where will you park it?**

Lawn tractors have a big footprint. You'll need a large storage space—at least 70 in. long by 50 in. wide, with about 48 in. of free space above the unit (for a machine with a 42-in. deck).

BUYING A MOWING DECK THAT'S TOO SMALL IS A MISTAKE TRACTOR OWNERS ONLY MAKE ONCE.

**4 Can you haul it?**

When your tractor needs routine service or repairs, you can pay a pick-up and delivery fee or haul it yourself—if you have a trailer or a truck and ramps. Lawn tractors weigh about 400 lbs.

**5 Will it climb your hills?**

Lawn tractor engines are sized to climb the grade listed in the specs. If you have a hilly yard, check those specs.

**6 Does the seat fit your seat?**

You'll be spending a lot of time on the machine and the ride can be rough, so you'll want a comfortable seat. Manufacturers equip their machines with mid-back or high-back seats that vary in width and comfort. Conduct a butt test before you buy.

If you'll be the only driver, you don't need an adjustable seat. However, if you're splitting mowing duties with others, choose a seat with a lever release to adjust the depth and height.

## RIDER, LAWN TRACTOR, GARDEN TRACTOR: WHAT'S THE DIFFERENCE?

**Some retailers use the terms "lawn tractor," "riding mower" and "garden tractor" interchangeably. But they're not the same.**

**Rear-engine riding mowers** do one thing: cut grass. Compared with lawn tractors, they're less powerful, slower and cut a smaller swath (maximum width: 30 in.). At $800 to $1,400, they're not always cheaper than a lawn tractor. The least expensive models are a good choice for smaller yards and limited storage space.

**Lawn tractors,** the focus of this article, have more power, cutting widths of up to 48 in., comfort features, faster cutting speed and a higher price tag ($1,200 to $2,200). They can tow a cart or vacuum attachment, and most models have a detachable mower deck, allowing you to add winter accessories like a snow thrower.

**Garden tractors** are the heavy-duty models. They start at about $2,200 and top out at about $8,000. They accept larger mowing decks (up to 72 in.!) and a wide range of implements such as tillers, seeders, snow throwers, front loaders and backhoes.

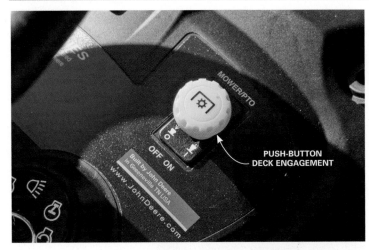

## Easy deck engagement

For safety reasons, the cutting blades don't automatically spin at start-up; you have to engage them with a mechanical lever or an easy electric push-button. Some of the lever mechanisms are awkward or stubborn, so try before you buy.

## Hour meter

All lawn tractors require maintenance based on hourly usage. A built-in hour meter takes all the guesswork out of maintaining your tractor. You can always add an hour meter later ($50), but the built-in models eliminate that hassle.

## Convenient gas gauge

Some models have a gas gauge you can check while driving, while others offer a see-through tank. The less expensive models require you to stop and lift the hood to check the fuel level.

## Bumper

Trust us on this: You're going to smack a tree someday, and that impact can destroy the hood. So buy a machine with a bumper or set aside some dough to buy an add-on bumper from the manufacturer.

OUTDOOR STRUCTURES, LANDSCAPING & GARDENING

GEAR-STYLE
TRANSMISSION

### 3 Transmission Types

**Gear-style transmissions** are common on the least expensive lawn tractors. They require you to manually move a lever to change speeds and to switch from forward to reverse.

**Continuously variable transmissions** (CVTs) are a step up from geared transmissions and are available in two styles. The less expensive designs have a foot pedal to vary speed and a manual shift lever to change from forward to reverse. The higher-priced CVT models don't use a shifter. Instead they have forward and reverse pedals. CVT transmissions provide great value and the same top-end speed as a hydrostatic transmission, but they can jerk a bit when you're starting out or maneuvering at slow speeds.

A **hydrostatic transmission** is the best choice but also the costliest. It works like an automatic transmission in a car and provides the smoothest operation, especially when you're maneuvering around gardens and trees at slow speeds.

CVT PEDALS

## Engine size and features

Lawn tractor engines are sized to match the mower deck and climb the grade listed in the manufacturer's specs. Buying a machine with a larger engine won't get you a higher top-end speed, but the larger engine is important if you plan to haul a cart or add a snow blade or a snow thrower accessory.

Most tractor engines have traditional carburetors. However, the Cub Cadet model XT1-LT42 has electronic fuel injection (EFI), which dramatically reduces the starting problems associated with carbureted engines and ethanol fuel. Plus, Cub Cadet claims its EFI system boosts fuel efficiency by 25 percent.

## Mow-in-reverse mechanisms

Lawn tractors automatically stop blade movement the instant you shift into reverse. To mow in reverse, you have to hold in a button the entire time you're mowing in reverse or turn the key to the reverse position and then reposition the key when you want to move forward. We slightly prefer the button system, but both are inconvenient.

## ZERO TURN RADIUS MOWERS:

### Are they right for you?

Zero turn radius (ZTR) mowers cut grass 40 percent faster than even the fastest lawn or garden tractor. They move faster, and the zero turn radius feature allows them to do a 180-degree turn at the end of the cutting path, totally eliminating the "loop around" needed by rear engine riders and tractors.

A ZTR mower is far more maneuverable than a rear engine rider or tractor, allowing you to closely follow a winding garden edge and cut around trees in a single loop. That eliminates the need to go back and clean up with a string trimmer.

Higher-end ZTR models include a seat suspension system that isolates you from the mower so you don't feel bumps and vibration—an especially important feature if you have bumpy terrain. ZTR mowers with a 42-in. cutting width start at about $2,300 and top out at about $5,000 for a 60-in. model.

TORO

# INSTALL AN
# IRRIGATION SYSTEM

Installing an irrigation system is a great way to keep a lawn green through even the doggiest days of summer. We spent a day with pro installers, who taught us how to pull pipe, make solid connections faster and get it done safely. The result: a well designed irrigation system that sips water instead of guzzling it.

We don't show how to connect an irrigation system to a home's water supply or install a vacuum breaker/backflow preventer in this story. This crew hires a licensed plumber for those steps.

## MEET AN EXPERT

**Brian Larson is the owner of Northway Irrigation in Ham Lake, MN. Northway has been installing residential and commercial irrigation systems for more than 30 years.**

## A good plan saves water

It takes a lot of know-how to figure out how many zones to install and which sprinkler head goes where. A poorly designed system will waste water—a lot of it! Luckily, irrigation product manufacturers such as Hunter, Toro and Rain Bird have extensive literature online to help. Rain Bird will even design your layout for you if you send in the measurements of the property.

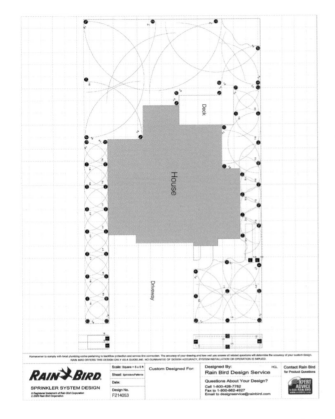

## Pull the pipes with a vibratory plow

Pulling polyethylene pipe through the ground is faster and easier than digging trenches and doesn't create a huge mess. Here are some things to consider when pulling pipes:

- Avoid tree roots. (To get an idea of how far they extend from the trunk, consider that the root structure is often the same size as the canopy.)
- Shoot for a depth of about 10 in.
- Feed the pipe into the hole as you pull.
- Avoid pulling pipes that are spliced (they could come apart underground).
- If you're renting a plow, pull all the pipes right away and return the machine. This may allow you to rent for only a half day and save money.
- A vibratory plow may not work in super-compacted soil. You may need a trencher instead. A local rental center should know what types of soil you are likely to encounter.
- **Caution:** Always call 811 to have the utilities located before you dig!

## Remove sod first

Slice off the sod before you dig a hole so it can be put back into place. If you do it right, the yard should show very few signs of your labor—besides the greener grass, of course.

## Hand-dig around utilities

No matter how deep you think a utility pipe or wire is buried, always hand-dig over and around those areas.

## Keep pipes clean

Dirt and other debris that get into the pipes will plug the heads. Keep all that out by covering the ends with duct tape. Besides dirt and rocks, these pros have found the occasional snake and frog clogging up the works...surprise! If you know you've kicked dirt down in the pipe, flush the line before installing that head.

Bore under obstructions

## Bore under obstructions

Some vibratory plows/trenchers are capable of horizontal boring as well. If you plan to rent a plow and have to dig under a sidewalk or driveway, you might as well rent the boring rods and the drill head at the same time.

## Don't cut pipes with a saw

Cutting pipes with a saw can leave behind plastic shavings that could clog the sprinkler heads. An inexpensive poly pipe cutter works great. If you have the option, pick a bright-colored one that will be easier to spot in the grass. A pipe cutter like this one costs less than $10 at home centers.

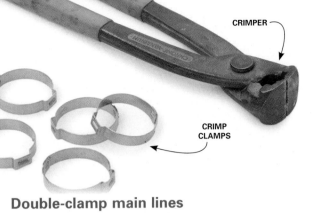

CRIMPER

CRIMP CLAMPS

STAGGERED EARS

## Double-clamp main lines

You can secure pipes to fittings quickly and easily with crimp clamps, but sometimes they can ever so slightly squish the pipe into an oval shape, creating a less-than-perfect connection. Main lines (the lines leading to the zone valves) are always pressurized, so install two crimp rings on each side of each fitting connection for extra protection against leaks. Stagger the ears on the two clamps to offset any pipe distortions.

SWING PIPE

## Install heads with swing pipe

Install a section of "swing pipe," often called "funny pipe," between the end of the poly pipe and the sprinkler head. Because funny pipe is flexible, you can much more easily position the head exactly where it needs to be. Funny pipe also allows the head to move a bit in case it's run over by a vehicle or pushed around by the frozen ground. When a head is connected directly to the rigid poly pipe, any movement could crack the fitting that connects them.

## Cut out kinks

A kink in poly pipe creates a weak spot. Don't try to straighten the pipe. Instead, cut out the kink and splice two pipes together with a coupler. If you must pull a pipe that has been spliced, add a couple extra clamps to the fitting and hook up the longest of the spliced sections to the plow.

COUPLER

## Smart controllers save water

According to the EPA, residential outdoor water use in the United States accounts for nearly 9 billion gallons of water each day, mostly for landscape irrigation. Experts estimate that as much as 50 percent of this water is wasted through overwatering caused by inefficiencies in irrigation methods and systems.

Traditional controllers turn each zone on and off for a predetermined amount of time. A rain gauge connected to a controller will monitor recent rainfall and shut down the system in the middle of or shortly after a rain event. That's helpful, but there are controllers and sensors available now that can track temperatures, sunlight and other seasonal conditions, and will adjust the watering schedule accordingly. A well-planned design along with a properly functioning smart controller can save a couple hundred gallons of water per day!

The one shown here, made by Rain Bird, connects to a home Wi-Fi, allowing the homeowner to control it or get updated on a smartphone.

## Protect wires from the elements

The wire connections in the valve box require connectors approved for direct burial. Basically tubes filled with dielectric grease, the ones shown are made by NorthStar Industries.

**GREASE-FILLED CONNECTORS**

OVERCUT ACCESS HOLES

## Leave room for the pipe

Overcut the access holes in the valve box to provide extra room for the pipes. If the pipes fit snugly, they could be crushed if the box is run over by a lawn tractor or other vehicle when the ground is soft or saturated.

### What do pros charge?
At Northway Irrigation, the total cost of installing an irrigation system in an average suburban yard is $3,000 to $4,000.

## Self-tapping fittings are fast and easy

**SELF-TAPPING FITTING**

When you pull pipes underground instead of trenching, traditional tee fittings can be difficult to install. The best way to tap heads directly into a continuous run of pipe is to install self-tapping fittings (saddles). Just snap the saddle onto the pipe and screw in the spike, which taps into the pipe. Hook up your funny pipe to the saddle and you're good to go.

## CHIMNEY FLUE PLANTERS

To make these terra-cotta planters, go to a
brick supplier and buy 3-ft. lengths of clay
chimney flue liner ($15 each). Cut them to
different heights using a circular saw fitted
with an abrasive cutting wheel. You can put
them on a deck or patio, or accent your yard
wherever you like—just pick your spots and
bury the ends in the soil a little.

Fill the liners with gravel for drainage,
leaving 8 in. at the top for potting soil. Since
the water can drain, the liners won't crack
if they freeze. Or just set pots on top of the
gravel and bring in the plants for the winter.

—Nancy Belmont

OUTDOOR STRUCTURES,
LANDSCAPING & GARDENING

# HandyHints®

## BERRY-BOX SEED SPREADER
If you have just a few small bare spots in the lawn, use a berry container to spread the seed. They have small holes just right for shaking out grass seed. Just clean and dry the container, fill it with grass seed and you're ready to go.

—Brad Holden

PUNCH HOLES
IN LID

## SALAD BAR GREENHOUSE

The next time you hit the salad bar for lunch, save the plastic container to make a mini greenhouse for starting seeds. Wash the container and then punch some air holes in the top. Fill the bottom with potting soil, plant your seeds, add a little water and close the lid. Set the container in a sunny spot and watch your seeds sprout! Once the seeds sprout, take off the lid.

—Diane Plowe

FIREWOOD LENGTH

CUT HERE

## MEASURING STICK FOR FIREWOOD

For a tidy stack, I like my firewood to be all the same length. The simplest measuring device I've found is my chain saw's bar.

—Travis Larson

# Car & Garage

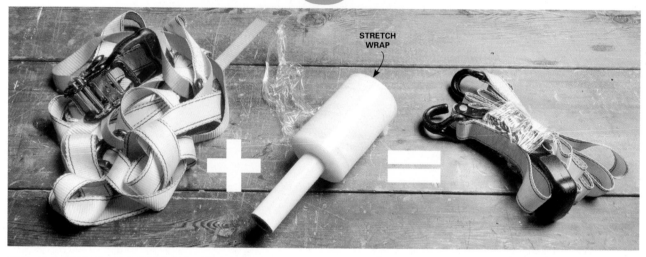

STRETCH WRAP

## NO-TANGLE RATCHET STRAPS

Ratchet straps must have a self-tangling feature—they're always twisted up when I want to use them. I've tried bundling them with rubber bands, but the bands break as they get old. So I bought a roll of stretch wrap and put it in a canvas bag with my ratchet straps. When I'm done using a strap, I bundle it up and wrap it tight with a few rounds of stretch wrap. I fold back the end portion so it's easy to unwrap the next time. Now my straps are always ready to use.

—Mike Coleman

## BLOW OUT THE GARAGE

Forget the broom—just open the door and blast out the dust and debris with an electric leaf blower. Works great on porches, too. Be sure to wear a dust mask as well as eye and ear protection.

## UNDER-THE-HOOD MAINTENANCE RECORD

My truck's air filter cover makes a perfect blackboard for my maintenance schedule. I use a chalk marker to write down the dates I last changed the oil, air filter, spark plugs, etc. The chalk marker isn't affected by water but is easily cleaned off with an ammonia-based cleaner (such as Windex). For me, this is much simpler than recording everything in the owner's manual. It's right where I need it!

—Hank Huff

## SAWDUST FOR OIL SPILLS

Sawdust won't remove the stain from an oil spill, but it can quickly get rid of the puddle. And if you have power tools, you've got a ready supply. Sprinkle a generous amount of sawdust over the oil and let the pile sit for about 20 minutes.

Using a stiff broom, sweep the sawdust over the spill a few times to soak up as much oil as possible. Scoop the oily sawdust into a plastic bag, tie it shut and toss it in the trash. You may need to use a degreaser to remove any oily residue.

**Note:** In most states, it's acceptable to throw oil-soaked sawdust in the trash (as long as the oil is no longer in liquid form). However, you should check your local regulations before doing so.

—Travis Larson

## FLY YOUR OWN FLAG

Home centers and lumberyards typically have red plastic flags and twine or staples to fasten the flags to your extra-long load. But it seems like they're almost always out of one of the above. Also, staples and twine usually come undone, liberating the flag before I've reached my destination. So I keep my own flag in my truck. It's a red shop rag with a bungee cord run through a hole in one corner of the rag. I've never had this fly off, and it's always there when I need it.

—Saul Carvajal

## MOTOR OIL SMART SPOUT

I had a hard time pouring motor oil into my snow blower engine without spilling, so I raided the kitchen for a solution. I found that the spout for olive oil and vinegar bottles screws right onto motor oil bottles. Now I can pour without a mess, but I need to buy a replacement before my wife finds out.

—Rich Gonzalez

ENTERTAINMENT CENTER!

# GARAGE
## MAKEOVER

**Get the garage of your dreams one step at a time. The high-capacity cabinets shown above are one upgrade, and here are the others:**

By **Jeff Gorton**

**A new garage door**
Add curb appeal, comfort and quiet. See p. 257 for details.

**SLIDING
DOORS!**

**STORAGE
GALORE!**

## A floor coating
The high-gloss surface looks beautiful and protects against stains and spalling. See pp. 258-259.

## A built-in entertainment center
If your garage serves as a gathering spot, consider including a bar and TV like we did. To do it, you just add inexpensive stock cabinets, put a bar inside one of the cabinet openings (see **Figure A**), then hang a TV above. Our stock cabinets cost about $300 for the pair.

# Car & Garage

**If** your garage looks like a junk shop, this storage project can solve the problem. With this simple system, you can build full walls of storage that are easily accessible behind the attractive sliding doors. We'll show you how to build the exact version shown on p. 252. To customize the cabinets for your garage, see the tips below.

**4' LEVEL**

**PLASTIC SHIM**

**2x4 FRAME**

**1 Level the base.** Rest the 2x4 frame in position and level it with shims. Attach the leveled 2x4 frame to the wall with screws.

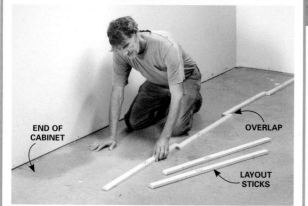

**END OF CABINET**

**OVERLAP**

**LAYOUT STICKS**

## CUSTOMIZE THE PLAN FOR YOUR GARAGE

Your cabinet can be any length you want. Using scrap lumber, cut layout sticks to represent the common door widths (24, 30, 32 and 36 in.). Mark the desired end of your cabinet with tape and lay out different combinations of sticks. The sticks should overlap by about 1-1/2 in., but you can adjust the overlap to get the exact cabinet length you want. Mark the overlap locations on the floor to later position the partition panels (F).

To customize the depth of your cabinet, start with the desired shelf depth. Add 4-5/8 in. to get the depth of the end, top and floor panels (C, D, E).

## CUTTING LIST

| KEY | QTY. | SIZE & DESCRIPTION |
|-----|------|--------------------|
| A | 2 | 2x4 x 122-3/4" bottom frame |
| B | 7 | 2x4 x 9-7/8" crosspieces |
| C | 2 | 3/4" x 15-7/8" x 92-7/8" top and floor panels |
| D | 2 | 3/4" x 15-7/8" x 32-7/8" top and floor panels |
| E | 1 | 3/4" x 15-7/8" x 84" finished end panel |
| F | 2 | 3/4" x 11-1/4" x 81-3/4" partition panels |
| G | 1 | 3/4" x 15-7/8" x 81-3/4" end panel |
| H | 2 | 3/4" x 11-1/4" x 31-3/4" shelf panels |
| J | 1 | 3/4" x 11-1/4" x 60" counter panel |
| K | 2 | 3/4" x 2-1/2" x 31-3/4" top ledgers |
| L | 1 | 3/4" x 2-1/2" x 60" top ledger |
| M | 2 | 3/4" x 1-1/2" x 31-3/4" shelf ledgers |
| N | 4 | 3/4" x 1-1/2" x 10-1/2" shelf cleats |
| P | 2 | 3/4" x 3/4" x 11-1/4" partition cleats |
| Q | 1 | 3/4" x 3/4" x 15-7/8" end cleat |
| R | 1 | 3/4" x 3/4" x 60" counter spacer |
| S | 3 | 3/4" x 3/4" x 10-1/2" counter spacers |
| T | 1 | 3/4" x 3-1/2" x 12-7/8" toekick |
| U | 1 | 3/4" x 3-1/2" x 123-1/2" toekick |
| V | 2 | 3/4" x 1-1/2" x 84" end trim |
| W | 1 | 3/4" x 2-1/2" x 123-1/2" top trim |
| X | 1 | 3/4" x 1-1/2" x 123-1/2" bottom trim |
| Y | 2 | 3/4" x 1-1/2" x 81-3/4" partition trim |
| Z | 2 | 3/4" x 2-1/2" x 31" shelf nosing |
| A1 | 1 | 3/4" x 1-1/2" x 60" counter nosing |

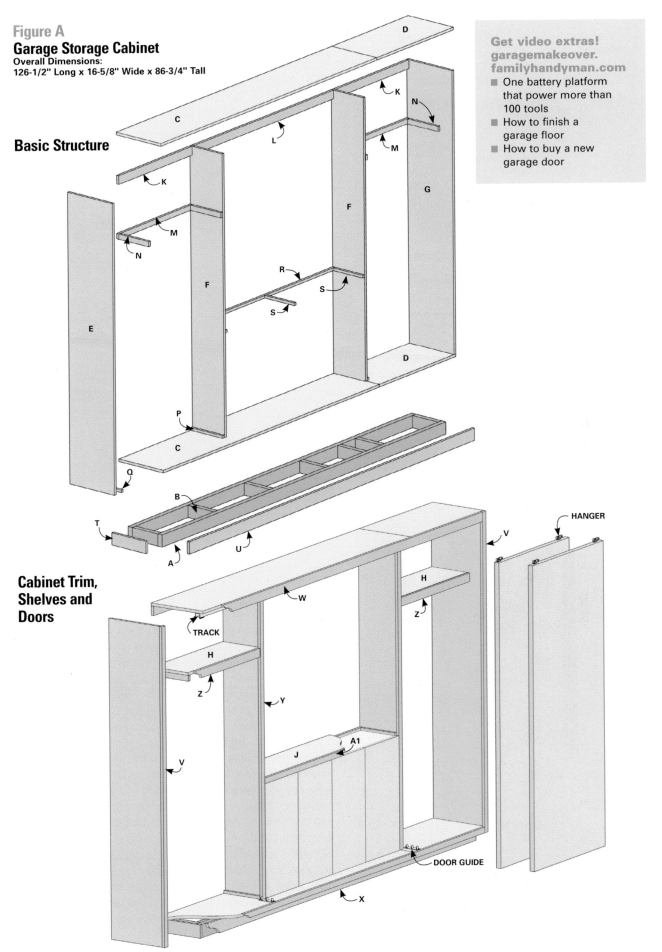

## Figure A
### Garage Storage Cabinet
Overall Dimensions:
126-1/2" Long x 16-5/8" Wide x 86-3/4" Tall

**Basic Structure**

D

C

K

L

K

N

M

F

G

E

F

N

R

S

S

M

P

C

D

Q

B

T

A

U

**Get video extras!**
garagemakeover.
familyhandyman.com
- One battery platform
  that power more than
  100 tools
- How to finish a
  garage floor
- How to buy a new
  garage door

**Cabinet Trim,
Shelves and
Doors**

V

HANGER

W

H

Z

TRACK

H

Z

Y

V

J

A1

DOOR GUIDE

X

# Car & Garage

Attach the floor. Screw the plywood floor to the 2x4 frame. Trim-head screws hold well and are less conspicuous.

Mark for the ledger. Align the edge of a partition panel with the end of the bottom plywood. Plumb it with a level and mark along the edge and along the top with a pencil.

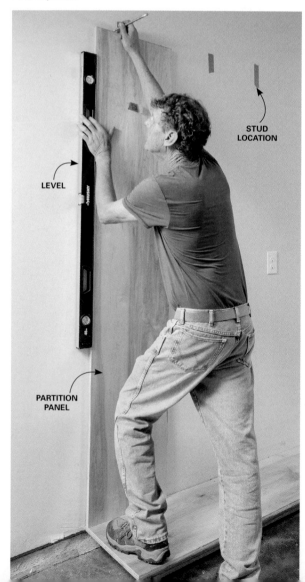

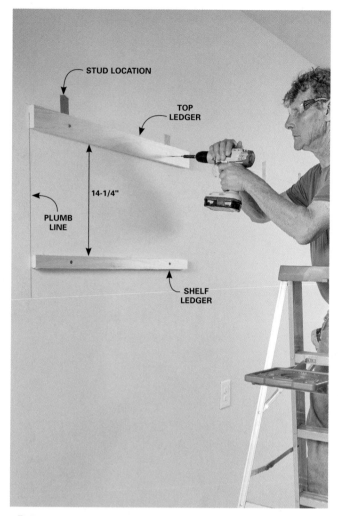

Attach the ledgers for the top and shelf. Align the end of the ledger with the plumb line and the top with the level line. Drive 2-in. screws through the ledger into the studs. Position the shelf ledger 14-1/4 in. below the top ledger.

We ordered hollow-core birch veneer doors for our cabinets, but you can use any 1-3/8-in.-thick doors. For a more traditional look, inexpensive six-panel composite doors would work well. To complement the birch doors, we found 3/4-in. maple plywood at a local home center to use for the cabinet construction. The four-door cabinet shown on p. 252 cost us about $600, or about $60 per linear foot. But you could reduce the cost by choosing less expensive doors and paint-grade plywood.

With help from a friend or two, you should be able to finish constructing one six-door section of cabinets in a weekend, not including the painting and varnishing. The most time-consuming and difficult part of the project is cutting the plywood parts. For this, a good-quality table saw is helpful. But if you don't have access to a table saw, you can use a straightedge guide and a circular saw to make accurate cuts. In addition to a table or circular saw, you'll need a drill, a level and standard carpentry tools like a tape measure and square. We used a miter saw to cut the trim and brad nailer to attach it, but these aren't required.

## ADD STYLE AND FUNCTION WITH A NEW GARAGE DOOR

A new garage door dramatically boosts the curb appeal of your home, but the benefits don't stop there. This Clopay door features top-of-the line polyurethane insulation for maximum insulation value and sound deadening. That, combined with the quiet nylon rollers, gets you one step closer to converting your garage to the perfect man-cave hangout. The door we chose cost about $3,000 including professional installation and removal and disposal of the old door. See more at garagemakeover.familyhandyman.com.

Before

END PANEL

END CLEAT

**5 Install the end panel.** Position the end panel by snugging the end cleat against the bottom of the floor plywood. Then drive screws through the end panel into the ledgers to hold it in place.

### MATERIALS LIST

| ITEM | QTY. |
|---|---|
| 2x4 x 12' treated lumber | 2 |
| 2x4 x 8' treated lumber | 1 |
| 4' x 8' x 3/4" plywood | 3 |
| 3/4" x 3/4" x 6' trim boards | 3 |
| 1x2 x 6' trim boards | 2 |
| 1x2 x 8' trim boards | 4 |
| 1x2 x 12' trim board | 1 |
| 1x3 x 6' trim board | 3 |
| 1x3 x 12' trim board | 1 |
| 1x4 x 12' trim board | 1 |
| 32" x 80" hollow-core doors | 4 |
| Composite or treated shims | 2 pkgs. |
| 3" wood screws | 1 lb. |
| 2" trim-head screws | 1 lb. |
| Trim nails | 1 lb. |
| 1-1/4" brads or finish nails | 1 lb. |
| 2" brads or finish nails | 1 lb. |
| 2200 36" 2-door hardware sets | 2 |
| (Johnson Hardware No. 2200722H) | |
| Wood glue | |

**6** **Add the partitions.** Screw a 3/4-in. cleat to the floor plywood. Press the partition panel against the cleat and ledgers and attach it with screws. Add the ledger and cleat for the second partition and attach it with screws.

**7** **Install the top.** Rest the top plywood on the ledgers and partitions. Drive screws through the plywood top into the ledger and partitions.

## DURABLE, BEAUTIFUL DIY FLOOR

If your garage floor looks a little shabby next to your beautiful new storage cabinets, Rust-Oleum's RockSolid Metallic Floor Coating Kit could be the answer. The two-part polycuramine coating creates a stunning high-gloss finish that's tougher than epoxy and impervious to oil and gasoline. Rust-Oleum RockSolid is available in kits (about $120 each) that cover 75 to 100 sq. ft. It comes in eight colors, including Brilliant Blue and Cherry Bomb. Careful prep work is critical. After that, applying the coating is an easy DIY project that you and a helper can finish in an afternoon. See more at garagemakeover.familyhandyman.com.

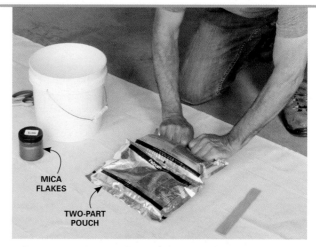

### After prepping, mix the floor coating

Prep the floors by first removing any oil or grease deposits with a heavy-duty degreaser. Then etch the surface with the citric acid supplied with each kit and thoroughly rinse the floor. After the concrete has completely dried, you can apply the polycuramine floor coating. Roll the pouch until the seal breaks and then mix the two parts together for two to three minutes. Pour it into a clean pail, add the mica flakes and stir for another couple of minutes.

## Getting started

Every garage is a little different. Before you order materials, take a close look at your garage walls to find the ideal location for your storage cabinet and to identify possible obstructions like pipes, outlets, windows or doors. Use a level to see if the floor is sloping, and note any protruding brick or concrete at the bottom of the wall. We had to modify our plan to avoid an outlet, and we shimmed the base to compensate for the sloping floor.

If you've found a suitable location to build the six-door version shown here, you can use the Materials List on p. 257 to order materials and the Cutting List for reference to cut the parts. To build a custom version, see the sidebar on p. 254 for helpful tips.

## Build the base

Begin construction by building the ladder-type 2x4 frame and set it in place against the wall. Then use a level and shims to level the frame from end to end and front to back (**Photo 1**). Screw the frame to the wall. We used masonry screws to attach the frame to the concrete curb.

## Cut the parts

Rip the plywood for the bottom, top, ends and partitions with a table saw or circular saw. For the best results, fit your saw with a blade that's labeled for crosscutting plywood. Cut the parts to length. We used a crosscutting guide for quick, accurate crosscuts. For instructions, search for "crosscutting guide" at familyhandyman.com. To save finishing time, we applied satin polyurethane to all of the plywood before cutting the parts. Label the parts with masking tape to simplify assembly.

**8** **Nail on the trim.** Cut the trim pieces to fit. Apply a bead of wood glue to the plywood before placing the trim and attaching it with brads or finish nails.

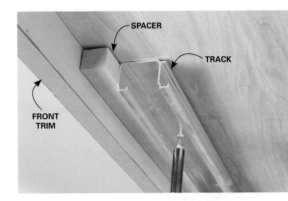

**9** **Mount the track.** Cut the tracks to length so they meet in the middle. Space the tracks from the front trim with a temporary 7/8-in. wood block and attach them with 3/4-in. screws.

### Mask, cut in, then pour a ribbon
Protect the walls with masking tape before mixing any of the coating. After a bucket is mixed, cut in along the walls with a synthetic paintbrush about 5 ft. in both directions from the corner. Pour a ribbon of coating onto the floor about 5 in. wide, 1 ft. away from the wall and 5 ft. long.

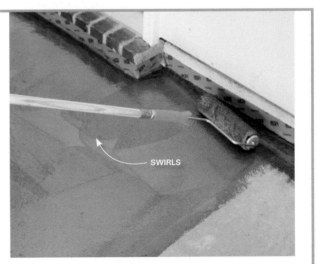

### Roll it out, then swirl
Roll out the coating into a 5 x 5-ft. square until it's evenly distributed. Then create circular patterns by swirling the roller throughout the patch of coating. After that section is complete, move immediately to pour another 5-in. strip and begin rolling and creating the same swirling look. Keep mixing, pouring and rolling until the entire garage floor is complete.

# Car & Garage

## Build the cabinet box

With the parts cut, building the box goes quickly. Start by attaching the floor (**Photo 2**). Next, locate the studs with a stud finder and mark them with masking tape. Then use one of the interior partitions and a level to mark the location of the top ledger board (**Photo 3**). **Photo 4** shows how to attach the ledger boards for the top and the shelf. With these in place, it's easy to attach

**10** **Hang the doors.** Starting with the inside doors, hook the hangers on the track and tilt the doors into place.

the end panel (**Photo 5**). The 3/4-in. cleat attached to the bottom of the end panel helps position the panel accurately. The top of the end panel should be exactly 3/4 in. above the ledger. After attaching the end panel, repeat this process for each of the partitions (**Photo 6**). Attach the partitions to the cabinet bottom with 3/4-in. cleats. Finally, nail or screw the opposite end panel to the wall and install the final two ledgers. Complete the cabinet box by adding the top (**Photo 7**).

We purchased two wall cabinets that were 30 in. x 30 in. x 12 in. deep to fit between the center partitions. If you decide to do the same, mount the cabinets and add 3/4-in. spacers to the tops to support the countertop that fits over the cabinets. This allows you to add a 1-1/2-in.-wide piece of trim to the front of the counter.

## Add the trim and door track

Using **Figure A** as a guide, cut the wood trim pieces to fit and use wood glue and finish nails or brads to attach the trim (**Photo 8**). Painting or finishing the trim before you install it will save you time. Later, you'll only need to fill the nail holes and touch up the paint or finish.

We used two 6-ft. door tracks and cut them with a hacksaw to meet in the middle of the cabinet. For best results, butt the uncut ends together when you install the tracks, being careful to keep them accurately aligned. **Photo 9** shows how to use a 7/8-in.-wide spacer to position the tracks before attaching them with 3/4-in. screws.

## Install the door hardware and hang the doors

Mark the less attractive side of each door with masking tape and mount the hangers to this side. Mount hangers 1 in. from the edge of the door. You'll notice that the hangers have different offsets. Doors with the wide offset hangers hang on the back of the track. The ones with the narrow offsets go on the front. After mounting the hangers, hang the doors to test how they fit (**Photo 10**). If the doors don't meet properly or appear crooked, loosen the two adjusting screws on the back of one hanger and move that door until it's aligned with the other. Then retighten the screws. When you're happy with the fit of the doors, mount the door guides to hold the bottom of the doors in alignment.

With the doors mounted, you're ready to add a storage system to the cabinet interiors. We mounted Rubbermaid FastTrack rails and slat wall panels to the walls in some of the bays. If you want more shelving, add cleats to the sides and back to support additional plywood shelves, or mount shelf standards to the walls and use shelf brackets to support the shelves. The result will be an attractive storage space in your garage neatly concealed by the convenient bypass doors.

# 7 Using DIY Tools & Materials

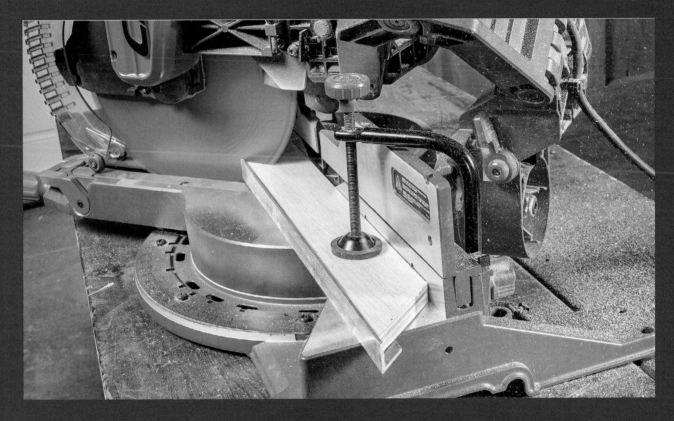

## IN THIS CHAPTER

Home Care & Repair ...............................262
   *Is Your Square Square?*

Cordless Brad Nailers.............................263

8 Easy Ways to Cut Metal Fast ..............269

Choosing Caulk.........................................273

Handy Hints ..............................................277
   *The Money Wrench Trick, Compressor
   Creeper, Pocket Magnet and more*

# HomeCare&Repair

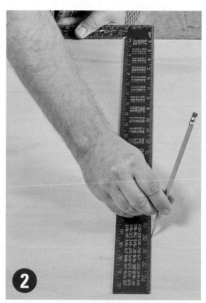

## IS YOUR SQUARE SQUARE?

Framing squares—even brand-new ones—aren't reliably square.

**1.** To test your square, place the tongue (the short part) against the factory edge of a sheet of plywood and make a line along the body (the long part) using a sharp pencil.

**2.** Flip the square and line up the body with the line you just made. If it lines up perfectly, you have a square square.

**3.** If it doesn't line up perfectly, you can try to fix it (next step). You'll need a center punch, a hammer and something to use as an anvil, such as your vise (a wood surface doesn't work).

**4.** If your square is less than 90 degrees, set it on your "anvil" and punch the inside corner hard enough to make a dimple. Squeezed between the punch and the anvil, the metal moves outward. Recheck the square, starting with a new line. Increase the dimple as needed, rechecking each time you strike the square.

**5.** If your square is more than 90 degrees, dimple the outside corner.

If you're shopping for a new square, grab a handful of them, take them to the plywood aisle, sharp pencil in hand, and test them first.

CENTER PUNCH

# CORDLESS
# BRAD NAILERS

## Speed and convenience—
## without the compressor and hose

By **Jeff Gorton**

USING DIY
TOOLS & MATERIALS

**O**ur shop is full of compressor-powered nail guns. But with all the advances in battery and motor technology, we wondered if cordless nailers had finally improved enough to replace our trusty pneumatic tools. To find out, we rounded up ten 18-gauge brad nailers and put them to the test. Here's what we discovered.

## THE BASICS

### Bare tool or kit?

Most of these nailers are available as kits containing a battery and charger. Six of them are also available as bare tools. If you own other battery-powered tools, you'll save money if you can find a brad nailer that uses the same battery. Otherwise, the kits are usually a better deal.

**BARE TOOL**

**CHARGER**

**BATTERY**

### HOW DO THEY WORK?

Paslode pioneered cordless nail guns with its fuel-powered nailers. Paslode nailers contain a canister of fuel that provides the driving force when a small amount of fuel is ignited in a cylinder. The advantage of this design is that the battery can be small and light since its main function is to provide ignition for the fuel. These nailers are also very powerful. But they do have some drawbacks: The exhaust fumes smell bad and you have to buy replacement fuel canisters.

Most of the nailers we tested use the motor to compress air in a cylinder. The compressed air pushes a piston that drives the brads.

DeWalt, Bostitch and Porter-Cable have taken a different approach from the two above. In their nailers, a spinning flywheel provides the driving force. To ensure rapid firing, a few of these nailers rev up as soon as you press the nose to the workpiece.

Other than the significantly lighter weight of the Paslode, we didn't find any advantage of one technology over the other. There's a split-second delay with the flywheel models, but it's not bothersome. They all drove brads well enough to install standard trim.

4.7 LBS.

### Tool weight matters

If you're installing crown molding overhead, a few pounds could make the difference between aching shoulders and a pain-free job. The Paslode nailer weighs a measly 4.7 lbs. At the other end of the spectrum is the 7.65-lb. Hitachi. The weights shown in the chart on p. 268 include batteries with ratings of about 2 amp-hours.

7.65 LBS.

## Look at the tip

When you're installing trim, it's important to place nails accurately. And to do this with a brad nailer, it helps to have a clear view of the gun tip. The Porter-Cable and Bostitch nailers are examples of guns with a clear view of the tip. The tip on the Milwaukee tool is harder to see.

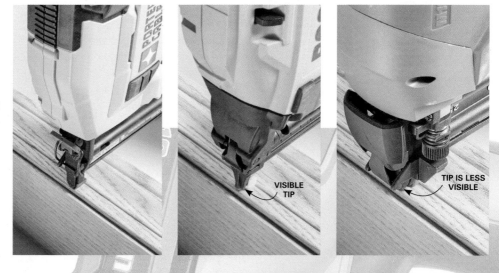

VISIBLE TIP

TIP IS LESS VISIBLE

SEQUENTIAL-FIRE MODE

SINGLE-FIRE MODE

## Do you need sequential firing?

All but two of these brad nailers include the option to switch from single-fire to sequential firing. In single-fire mode, you must release the trigger between shots. Switching to sequential firing allows you to hold the trigger down and "bump-fire" brads by simply pressing the nose against the workpiece. You should be aware of this feature, but don't let it drive your buying decision. Bump firing isn't critical to most trim carpentry or woodworking.

## Dry-fire lockout is a nice feature

Many of these nailers have a dry-fire lockout feature that prevents the gun from firing when there are no brads. Without this feature, you could keep on nailing without realizing that the gun had run out of fasteners. Also, most of the guns have a small window in the nail cover with some means of signaling that the brads are running low. We like Ridgid's transparent cover that allows you to see at a glance how many brads are left and what length they are.

## Do you need maximum power?

You'll probably never have to drive a 2-in. brad into solid oak. (Even some conventional nailers can't do that.) But we thought it would be an interesting test. The Makita and Ryobi nailers were the only ones that struggled in this test. But every model we tried is capable of driving 1-1/2-in. brads through 3/4-in. oak into a pine jamb. And this is probably the most difficult nailing job you'll encounter in normal circumstances.

## The brad depth is adjustable

Overdriving a brad can cause it to go completely through thin material so it won't hold. It can also leave unsightly driver marks in the trim. And underdriving a brad will leave it protruding. To avoid these problems, all of these brad nailers have adjustable tips that help regulate the fastener depth. Some of the adjusters operate more smoothly than others, but they all accomplish the task. The Ryobi tool also has an air-pressure adjustment for even more control of the fastener depth.

## MODELS WE TESTED

To see how the 18-gauge battery-powered brad nailers performed under adverse conditions, we drove hundreds of 2-in. brads into 2-1/4-in. solid oak. Then we tested in real-world conditions by nailing oak casing to an oak jamb. Here's what we discovered:

### Ridgid
**R09890K**
**$298**

This is a ruggedly built tool with the advantage of Ridgid's lifetime warranty. We like the transparent magazine cover and the two styles of no-mar tips that Ridgid supplies so you can choose your favorite.

### DeWalt
**DCN680D1**
**$299**

This nailer appears to be nearly identical to the Bostitch. Both nailers drove 2-in. brads consistently into solid oak and worked perfectly in our testing.

**EDITORS' CHOICE 2018** *BEST OVERALL*

### Milwaukee
**2741-21CT**
**$399**

From the sleek, compact body to the precision brad-depth adjuster, this tool has a high-quality feel. Our only gripe is that the view of the tip is obscured by the jam-release lever. The nailer responds instantly and performed well in our testing.

### Bostitch
**BCN680D1**
**$299**

This nailer has a flywheel-type drive system that revs up as soon as you press down on the tip, ensuring a quick response when you pull the trigger to drive the brad. The nailer has every feature you could want and performed flawlessly in our shop.

DEPTH ADJUSTER

18 GA BRAD NAIL

18 GA BRAD NAILER

BRUSHLESS

XR

DEPTH ADJUSTER

## Hitachi
**NT1850DE**
**$299**
Weighing 7.65 lbs., this is the heaviest tool of the lot. The nailer performed well in our testing and would be a good choice if you have other Hitachi tools to share batteries with. Our only complaint is the depth adjustment, which is hard to turn and disconnects from the safety tip if you turn the adjuster too far.

## Senco
**Fusion F-18**
**6E0001N**
**$309**

**EDITORS' CHOICE 2018**
*BEST OVERALL*

Senco uses a sealed cylinder in conjunction with a motor to drive the brads. This results in good power and almost instantaneous response. We like the balance and feel of this tool.

## Paslode
**IM200Li**
**$329**

**IN A CLASS BY ITSELF**

This brad nailer is in a class of its own. The gas-fuel technology is sort of old-school, but it's tried and true. In our test, this tool was the lightest (4.7 lbs.) and felt the most comfortable. If you're willing to shoulder the additional cost of fuel canisters and put up with the faint smell of exhaust, put this gun at the top of your list.

## Porter-Cable
**PCC790LA**
**$190**

**EDITORS' CHOICE 2018**
*BEST VALUE*

We like the weight and balance of this nailer. And it drives brads consistently without problems. The only downside is the lack of a dry-fire lockout to prevent firing when there are no nails in the magazine.

## Makita
**XNB01Z**
**$378**
We like how easy it is to see the tip, aiding in accurate brad placement. But the shape of this nailer gives it a back-heavy feel that we found uncomfortable. This is the only gun that requires a tool to take apart the nose to clear jams.

## Ryobi
**P320-P128**
**$188**

**EDITORS' CHOICE 2018**
*BEST VALUE*

This model performed well and has all the features of more expensive nailers. The unique adjustable air pressure could be handy for fine-tuning brad depth. It uses Ryobi's One+ battery—great if you own other tools using the same battery platform.

## How long will the battery last?

Manufacturer claims run from about 700 to 2,000 brads fired on one battery charge. But since there are no testing standards, it's hard to say what this really means.

Considering that it takes about 600 brads to nail on the baseboard, casing and crown moldings in an average-size room, we would expect all of these nail guns to complete the task on a single charge. And most would have power left to finish another room or two. So unless you're trimming out an entire house and have only one battery, we don't think the number of brads you can fire on a single charge is a key consideration.

TOOL-FREE
JAM CLEARING

## Clear jams easily

In our testing, we had very few brads get jammed in the tip of the tool. But when this does happen, it's nice to be able to clear the tip without tools. All but one of the brad nailers have tool-free jam clearing. On most tools, you release a latch on the front to access the jammed brad. To access a jam on the Milwaukee tool, you just release the nail clip cover.

Occasionally the driver in these brad nailers will get stuck. A few tools have a "stall release" lever to reset the driver. Other tools instruct you to remove and then replace the battery. Then you press the nose against a scrap of wood and pull the trigger to reset the driver. Be sure to read this section of your instruction manual to see how your tool works.

PNEUMATIC
BRAD NAILER

BATTERY-POWERED
BRAD NAILER

## Is a battery-powered brad nailer right for you?

If you're a pro, the answer is probably yes. For the small odd job, or to take care of punch-list items, it's hard to beat the convenience of a battery-powered brad nailer. But for DIYers, the choice is a little more difficult. Compressor-powered brad nailers have the advantage of being smaller and lighter, and you don't have to worry about keeping a battery charged. And you can buy a kit containing a brad nailer, small compressor and hose for about the same price as one of these battery-powered nailers. On the other hand, it's convenient to be able to grab a battery-powered brad nailer and start working without setting up the compressor and having to drag a hose around behind you.

## 18-GAUGE BRAD NAILER SPECIFICATIONS

|  | MODEL # | BARE TOOL | WEIGHT WITH BATTERY (LBS.) | DRY-FIRE LOCKOUT | BUMP AND SEQUENTIAL FIRING | TOOL-FREE JAM CLEARING |
|---|---|---|---|---|---|---|
| Bostitch | BCN680D1 | Not available | 6.4 | ✔ | ✔ | ✔ |
| DeWalt | DCN680D1 | $250 | 6.2 | ✔ | ✔ | ✔ |
| Hitachi | NT1850DE | Not available | 7.65 |  | ✔ | ✔ |
| Makita | XNB01Z | $249 | 7.4 | ✔ | ✔ |  |
| Milwaukee | 2741-21CT | $249 | 6.8 | ✔ | ✔ | ✔ |
| Paslode | IM200LI | Not available | 4.7 |  |  | ✔ |
| Porter-Cable | PCC790LA | $149 | 6.2 |  |  | ✔ |
| Ridgid | R09890K | $159 | 7.2 | ✔ | ✔ | ✔ |
| Ryobi | P320 | $129 | 6.3 | ✔ | ✔ | ✔ |
| Senco | 6E0001N | Not available | 6.4 | ✔ | ✔ | ✔ |

# 8 EASY WAYS TO **CUT METAL FAST**

**T**here's nothing wrong with using a good, old-fashioned hacksaw, but there are faster, easier ways to cut metal. In this article, we'll show you power tool tips and techniques for cutting the types and thicknesses of metal that DIYers handle the most.

### ① Ditch the abrasive grinder discs

An angle grinder fitted with an abrasive metal-cutting disc works well to cut all kinds of metal, including bolts, angle iron, rebar and even sheet metal. But the discs wear down quickly, cut slowly and shrink in diameter as you use them. Instead, we recommend using a diamond blade that's rated to cut ferrous metal. These will last much longer, cut faster and cleaner, and wear down much slower than abrasive discs. You'll find ferrous-metal-cutting diamond blades for $13 to $40 at home centers, hardware stores and online.

## ② Cut metal with your circular saw

It may not be an obvious choice, but fitted with the right blade, a circular saw is a great metal-cutting tool. In our test, it cut through rebar like a hot knife through butter. You can cut mild steel up to about 3/8 in. thick using a ferrous-metal-cutting blade. Be careful, though! Hot metal chips will fly everywhere. Put on your safety gear, keep bystanders away, and cover anything you don't want coated with metal chips. You'll find ferrous-metal-cutting blades at home centers, hardware stores and online. There are two types: inexpensive steel-tooth blades and carbide-tooth blades ($8 to $40). Carbide-tooth blades are more expensive but will last longer.

FERROUS-METAL BLADE

METAL ROOFING

NONFERROUS BLADE

WOOD BACKER

ALUMINUM ANGLE

## TIPS FOR CUTTING METAL SAFELY

Cutting or grinding metal sends tiny chips or shards of metal everywhere. And they can be hot and sharp. To avoid eye injuries, cuts, burns and other injuries from cutting metal, follow these rules:

- Read and observe safety precautions printed on metal-cutting discs and blades.
- Wear safety glasses, a face shield ($8 to $30) and hearing protection.
- Cover all exposed skin with gloves, long-sleeve shirt and pants.
- Allow freshly cut metal to cool before touching it.
- Wear gloves when handling metal that could have sharp edges.
- Securely clamp metal before cutting it.
- Never allow anyone near you while you're cutting metal unless they're wearing hearing and eye protection.

## ③ Cut aluminum with your miter saw

Making accurate cuts on aluminum rods, tubes and angles is easy with a miter saw and a blade designed to cut nonferrous metal (check the label). If the motor housing on your saw is open and could collect metal chips, tape a piece of cloth over the openings to protect the motor windings and bearings while you cut the aluminum. (Remember to remove it when the saw goes back into regular service or the motor will overheat.) Trapping the aluminum with a wood backer as shown reduces the danger of flying metal shards and makes it easier to hold the metal in place for cutting. This tip is especially important when you're cutting thin-walled pieces. Without the backing board, the blade will often catch on the metal and distort it and make it unusable.

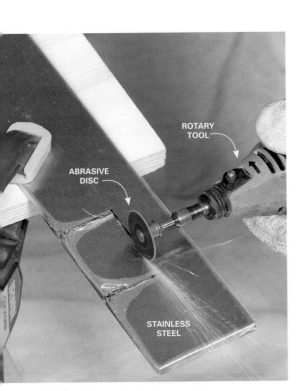

 **Cut stainless steel with a grinding disc**

There are many types of stainless steel, and some hard varieties are challenging to cut. For small jobs like cutting stainless steel backsplash tiles, a rotary tool fitted with an abrasive metal-cutting disc works fine. For larger jobs, mount an abrasive disc in an angle grinder.

**5** **Simply score and snap**

Siding contractors and roofers routinely score and snap aluminum siding and flashing to create straight, precise cuts. And you can use the same technique anytime you need a straight cut on aluminum or other light-gauge sheet metal, even steel. Clamp or hold a straightedge or square along the cutting marks and score a line with the tip of a sharp utility knife blade. Then bend the sheet back and forth a few times to snap it. You can use the same trick to cut steel studs. Snip the two sides. Then score a line between the cuts and bend the stud to break it.

**6** **Get into tight spots with an oscillating tool**

When access is tight, or you need to make a flush cut, an oscillating tool fitted with a metal-cutting blade will solve the problem. Corroded mounting nuts on toilets and faucets are easy to cut off with an oscillating tool. You can also use an oscillating tool to cut plumbing pipes, automotive bolts, nails and other metal objects in places where a larger tool wouldn't fit. Just make sure the blade is intended to cut metal.

USING DIY
TOOLS & MATERIALS

METAL-CUTTING BLADE

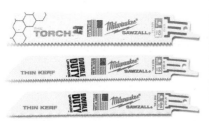

### 7 Cut smarter: Use a recip saw

The next time you reach for your hacksaw, grab your reciprocating saw instead. Mount a metal-cutting blade in your recip saw and you've got the ultimate power hacksaw for cutting bolts, rods, pipes and angle iron. A recip saw with a metal-cutting blade also works great for remodeling demolition when there are nails and pipes to cut off. Here are a few tips for cutting metal with a recip saw:

- Set your saw to straight rather than oscillating if there's a choice.
- Extend blade life by keeping the saw's speed slow.
- Choose a blade with 20 to 24 TPI (teeth per inch) for thin metal, 10 to 18 TPI for medium-thickness metal, and about 8 TPI for thick metal.
- Buy bimetal or carbide-tooth blades for longer blade life.

## MATCH THE BLADE TO THE METAL

With the right blade or grinding disc, you can cut almost any kind of metal. The key is to match the blade to the material.

There are two types of metal: ferrous and non-ferrous. (The term "ferrous" is derived from the Latin word "ferrum," which means iron.) Any metal that contains iron is a ferrous metal and requires a ferrous-metal-cutting blade. Steel angle iron, steel roofing, rebar and steel bolts are examples of ferrous-metal building materials. Most metal-cutting blades and discs are labeled for cutting either nonferrous or ferrous metal.

The two most common nonferrous metals DIYers need to cut are aluminum and copper. Nonferrous metals are usually softer and easier to cut than ferrous metals.

METAL LATH

DIAMOND BLADE

### 8 Cut metal lath and mesh with a grinder

Metal lath and hardware cloth can be cut with a tin snips, but there's an easier way. Mount a diamond blade in your angle grinder and use it like a saw to cut the mesh. We recommend using a diamond blade that's labeled as a ferrous-metal-cutting blade, but many tradespeople use a regular masonry diamond blade with good results.

# CHOOSING CAULK

## With a little knowledge, selecting sealant is simple

By **Mark Petersen**

**A**dmit it. You've been one of the lost souls standing in the caulk aisle, staring dumbfounded at the magnitude of caulk choices. This article will help you make sense of those ever-expanding choices and choose the right caulk for your project.

## FOUR COMMON FORMULAS

These types of caulk dominate the shelves at home centers. Labels don't always tell you what's in the tube, so we've included examples of each type in this article. But there are many more brands than the ones we show. All are available in various colors and paintable.

### Acrylic Latex: $2 to $5

Acrylic latex caulks are the easiest to apply and smooth out. They're also the only sealants that clean up with water. Look for versions labeled "siliconized" or "plus silicone." Adding silicone to acrylic latex improves adhesion and flexibility.

### Polyurethane: $6

Poly caulks are generally tougher than other sealants, making them a good choice for driveways and other areas that take a beating. But their gooey consistency makes them hard to work with. Check the label before painting; you may have to wait several days.

### Solvent-Based: $6 to $9

Many solvent-based caulks are great for roofing because they don't degrade in direct sunlight and can be applied to wet surfaces. But they're gooey and hard to apply neatly.

### Hybrid: $7 and up

Most hybrid caulks combine silicone and polyurethane for top-notch adhesion, flexibility and longevity. They're easier to apply neatly than polyurethane, but not as easy as acrylic latex. Most aren't labeled "hybrid," so we've pointed out the hybrids in the various photos. Cost is a clue: High-quality hybrids are usually the most expensive caulks on the shelf.

## EXTERIOR SIDING AND TRIM:

### Choose a hybrid or polyurethane

On your home's exterior, high-quality caulk is critical—it locks out water, protecting your home against rot and peeling paint. Although some inexpensive acrylic latex caulks are rated for exterior use, we recommend hybrid caulks because they offer better adhesion and flexibility. For matching the appearance of materials like stucco or rough-sawn wood, we like Vulkem, a textured polyurethane.

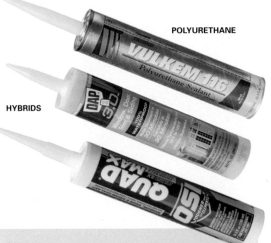

POLYURETHANE

HYBRIDS

### Expensive caulk is worth it

The most common reason for using caulk, whether indoors or out, is to prevent water penetration—and serious damage. That's why spending an extra five bucks on high-quality caulk is usually smart.

## INTERIOR PAINTING:
### Choose acrylic latex
This is the one project for which it doesn't make sense to spend a lot of money. For just a couple bucks, you can find a caulk that dries fast, is easy to work with, easy to clean up and can handle a little movement. Alex Plus is one good choice, but there are several others. If you have a large recurring crack in a wall corner or in a crown molding joint, choose a product with better flexibility such as a hybrid formula or Big Stretch acrylic caulk.

### A superior acrylic latex caulk
Like other acrylic latex caulks, Sashco's Big Stretch is easy to smooth out and cleans up with water. Unlike other acrylic latex caulks, it offers great adhesion and amazing elasticity. We tested Sashco's claim that it will stretch "more than 500 percent of its original size." Claim verified. Depending on the color and retailer, Big Stretch costs $7 to $12 per tube.

## KITCHEN AND BATH:
### Just check the label
Caulk in kitchens and bathrooms is often visible, so choosing a product that's easy to apply neatly is important. It also needs to be waterproof and mold and mildew resistant. Choose a product labeled with those traits. Acrylic latex kitchen and bath caulks are the easiest to work with, but hybrids generally have a longer life span.

HYBRID          ACRYLIC LATEX

### What about silicone?
Years ago, silicone caulk was a good choice for many jobs. Today, there are better options for almost every situation. So why is silicone still so popular? Here's what one manufacturer of caulks (including silicone) told us: "Silicone is what our customers saw their fathers use. It's what they're familiar with."

## CONCRETE AND MASONRY:

### Choose a specialty caulk

A caulk specially formulated for concrete and masonry will outperform general-purpose products. Most concrete and masonry sealants are polyurethane or hybrid formulas. But one acrylic latex product, Slab, also performs well, especially on concrete cracks that move a lot. Some concrete and masonry caulks are self-leveling and can be used only on level surfaces.

**FROM LEFT TO RIGHT: POLYURETHANE, HYBRID AND ACRYLIC LATEX**

## ROOFING:

### Choose solvent-based sealants

Any caulk that lives on a roof is going to get hammered by the elements. It needs to be able to survive extreme exposure to sunlight and temperature variations yet remain flexible. These two recommended products can actually be applied on wet surfaces!

**SOLVENT-BASED SEALANTS**

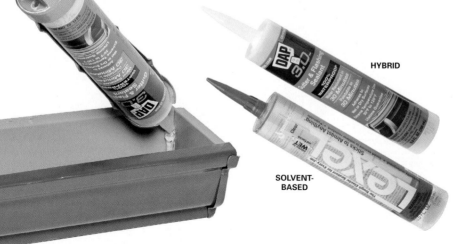

**HYBRID**

**SOLVENT-BASED**

## GUTTERS:

### Go with a hybrid or solvent-based product

It's no surprise that a product designed to seal gutters needs to be 100 percent waterproof. But it also needs to be tough—tough enough to handle the abrasion from debris and ice in colder climates. Most gutter sealants do a good job on metal, but not all will adhere to plastic gutters. Be sure to check the label.

# HandyHints®

## POCKET MAGNET

Here's a tip I discovered by accident. I'd been installing some rare earth magnets in a project, so I had a few in my pocket. When I stepped away from my workbench, I looked down and saw my 12-ft. tape measure attached to my pocket! It's not a lot of trouble to use the tape's clip, but having the tape measure stuck to your pocket is even easier.

I keep a few magnets stuck to my tape measure's clip so I don't lose them. This won't work with a 25-ft. tape; it's just too heavy. And don't put the magnets in the same pocket as your phone or credit cards.

—Brad Holden

RARE EARTH MAGNET

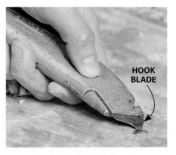

## MEASURE ACCURATELY— BURN AN INCH

The hook at the end of a tape measure is designed to slip in and out a little. That movement compensates for the thickness of the hook, depending on whether you're taking inside or outside measurements. But a bent hook or worn rivets can lead to inaccuracy. So when you need precision, bypass hook-related errors by holding the tape at the 1-in. mark and making your mark exactly 1 in. beyond the desired measurement.

## THE MONEY WRENCH TRICK

If you don't have the right size open-end wrench to fit a nut or bolt, just dig into your pocket and pull out your loose change. Shove the coins into the gap between the wrench jaw and the nut or bolt head until you get a snug fit.

—Gordon McKay

## COMPRESSOR CREEPER

Air compressors are heavy and cumbersome to haul around a shop or garage, so I put mine on wheels. I picked up this mechanic's creeper at a yard sale for $15. Now it's a breeze to roll, rather than carry, my compressor wherever I need it.

—Neal Halsey

HOOK BLADE

## HOOK-BLADE STAPLE PULLER

I've found the easiest way to pull staples is with a hook blade in my utility knife. A quick jerk in the middle of the staple usually does the trick. Once in a while, the staples snap in two and I have to pull them out with pliers. But that's better than pulling every single one that way.

—Neil Long

USING DIY TOOLS & MATERIALS

# SPECIAL SECTION
# 28 Things Homeowners
# Must Know

## Simple smarts that save time, money and trouble

"DIY is partly about know-how. But sometimes, being in the know is even more important. Knowing the right material to choose, remembering a clever trick or understanding the cause of a problem can make all the difference. Here are a few favorite tidbits of knowledge, picked up over 30 years of home ownership, maintenance and improvement."

—Gary Wentz, Editor-in-Chief

### Common leak, easy fix

Most plumbing valves—like the shutoffs under your sink or outdoor faucets—have a packing nut and a packing washer. And sooner or later, they'll leak. In most cases, the fix is simple: Just tighten the packing nut. If that doesn't work, remove the old washer and take it to a home center to find a match.

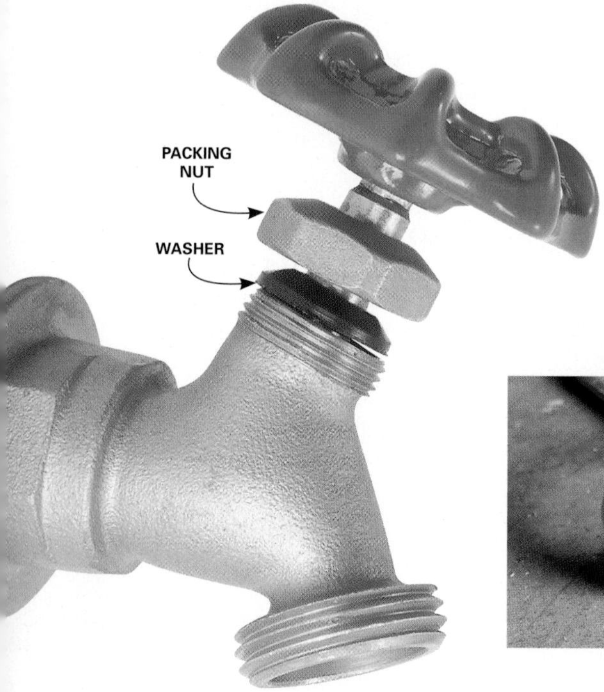

### Stay safe on the roof

Whether you're reroofing or just cleaning gutters, a roof harness can prevent tragedy. You can get a complete kit for less than $150 online.

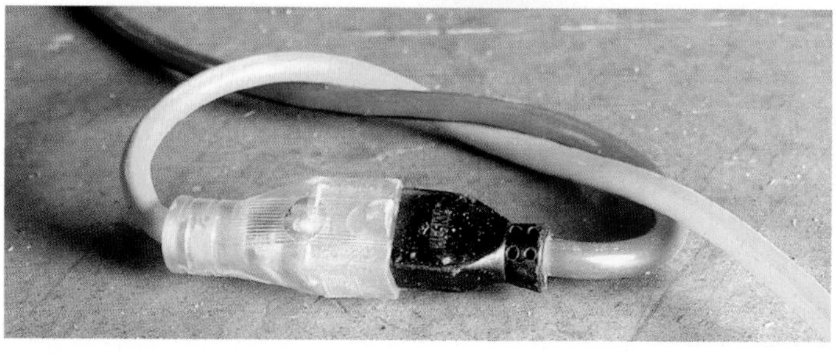

PACKING NUT

WASHER

### Solid cord connection

A knot keeps the ends of your cords from pulling apart as you drag the cords around.

WATER-BASED POLY      OIL-BASED POLY

CODE STICKER

## Oil poly vs. water-based

Neither is better than the other, and neither is tougher; durability depends on the formulation of the specific product. But there are important differences:

- Oil usually contains more "solids" and less solvent, which means you'll get a thicker buildup from each coat.
- Oil dries slower. That makes it easier to apply smoothly but also allows more time for airborne dust to create "whiskers" on the surface.
- Oil is yellowish, which can be good or bad, depending on the look you want. Water-based poly is colorless.
- Water-based poly doesn't fill the air with nasty fumes and cleans up with soap and water.

## Is treated wood safe?

Pressure-treated lumber used to contain arsenic. But arsenic was banned for residential use back in 2003, and today's treated wood is considered safe, even for food contact. Some common labels are ACQ, CA and MCQ.

## Avoid squeeze-tube caulk

Caulk is available in tubes that require a caulk gun and in squeeze tubes like the ones for toothpaste. When neatness counts, go with the gun, which allows better control of both placement and flow.

## Don't squish ants

The easiest way to wipe out an in-house ant colony is to set out ant bait. And if you do that, those ants crawling across your floor will be carrying toxic treats back to the colony. Let them help you!

## Make paint last

Here's the most common peeling situation for exterior paint: Over time, paint develops tiny cracks. Then moisture gets behind the paint, weakening the paint's bond and causing peeling. Left alone, that process spreads and accelerates. For you, that means days of tedious scraping before you can repaint. But you can avoid that by touching up cracks every year. It may feel like a waste of time to paint spots that don't look bad yet, but it will save you major work later.

# 28 Things Homeowners Must Know

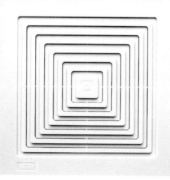

### Bath fans aren't just for odors

The most important job of a bath fan is to exhaust moisture. Excess humidity in a home causes many problems: mold and odors, condensation on windows, rot inside walls, even peeling paint inside and out. It's best to run your bath fan for at least 15 minutes after a bath or shower.

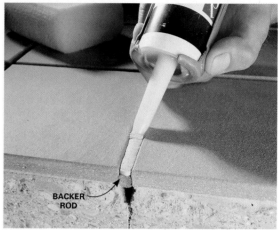

### Backer rod makes caulk last

When you're caulking a deep gap, backer rod has two benefits: It saves caulk, and more important, it makes a thinner caulk bead that will last longer. (A thick bead can't flex as easily and is more likely to fail as building materials move.) Backer rod is simply a foam rope available in various diameters. Get 20 ft. at any home center for about $5.

### Replace washer hoses

Washing machine hoses that leak or even burst are a common cause of water damage. Some insurance companies offer a discount of up to 10 percent on your premiums if you replace the rubber hoses on your washing machine with no-burst stainless steel hoses. In 10 minutes, you could save five times the cost of the hoses on your next bill, but this is a smart move even if your insurer doesn't offer a discount.

### Power outages can confuse your water softener

Your softener is probably set to clean and recharge the resin bed at night while you're sleeping. But after a long power outage, it might recharge as usual, not recharge at all or do it in the morning, delaying your morning shower and making you late for work. To reset the timer, check the owner's manual.

### Monetary measurements

A dollar bill is 6.14 in. long. But you don't have to memorize that; just remember that a buck is about 6 in. long and you'll always have an approximate measuring tool in your wallet.

### Toss out battered bits

Over the past 30 years, I've spent countless Saturday afternoons helping inexperienced friends with building projects. Here's a typical scene: I hear the telltale chatter of cam-out, walk over to my friend, scowl, yank the drill out of his hand and insert a fresh bit. Problem solved. As driver bits wear, cam-out becomes inevitable. So keep a supply of new bits and toss the old ones.

## The smartest move you can make before a vacation

Every insurance adjuster has a hundred stories like this one: The homeowners left town Friday and returned Sunday evening to find thousands of dollars in water damage. The moral of these stories is simple: Before going on vacation, turn off the main valve. In less than a minute, you can eliminate the most common cause of home damage.

## Keep batteries comfortable

When it comes to temperature, cordless tool batteries are fussy. For storage, 40 to 50 degrees F is optimal. That doesn't mean you have to create a climate-controlled storage space. But avoid the extremes that will gradually damage batteries. Don't leave them in your freezing garage all winter or in your car trunk on a sunny summer day.

## Bargain power tools

Online, you'll find several sources of "reconditioned" tools, sometimes at excellent prices. Several of us at *Family Handyman* have bought, saved and been completely satisfied. We have no bad experiences to report. Just be sure to add the shipping costs, which might lessen the bargain. And if you find a sweet deal, grab it. Supplies are often limited.

## Your beard may be a health hazard

Respirators (including "dust masks") are supposed to form an airtight seal against your face. But facial hair can prevent a reliable seal, allowing you to inhale dust or fumes. That's why OSHA says "respirators shall not be worn when facial hair comes between the sealing surface of the facepiece and the face." If you don't want to shave, the deluxe solution is a PAPR (powered air-purifying respirator), which can set you back $1,000 or more. For other options, search online for "respirator for beards."

## Many locks, one key

At most home centers, you can buy "keyed alike" locks in pairs, but what if you want three? Just look for a "key code" sticker on the package. The same code number means the same key. You can also rekey locks yourself. To see how, search for "rekey" at familyhandyman.com.

# 28 Things Homeowners Must Know

### An extinguisher can save your home

A fire extinguisher can mean the difference between a minor fire and total destruction. Experts recommend that you have one on each level of your home. Just remember that household extinguishers are meant for small fires. With a larger or fast-spreading fire, forget the extinguisher and get out of the house and call 911.

### No-skill pipe connections

Got a broken pipe? Before you call a plumber, consider this: Push-in plumbing connectors let you join pipes instantly just by shoving the pipe into the connector. No skills, knowledge or tools needed. Push-ins work with copper, PEX or CPVC plastic pipe. So if you need to replace a section of copper pipe, for example, you can simply cut out the bad section and replace it with a piece of PEX and a couple push-ins. Even a first-time plumber can manage that. Push-in plumbing connectors of various types and sizes are sold at home centers.

### Got a puddle? Look out!

Water heaters sometimes leak from the drain valve or relief valve. Those valves are easy to replace. But if a leak is coming from the tank, you've got serious trouble. The tank is lined with a thin coat of glass. Over years, that glass begins to crack, the steel begins to rust away and a puddle appears. Left alone, the tank will eventually rupture, causing an instant flood. It may take months for a leak to become a flood, or it may take days. But it will happen. Don't gamble. Replace that time bomb now.

### Sealing air leaks saves big

When you think of energy efficiency, you probably think of major upgrades like a new furnace or extra insulation. But before you go down that path, seal up air leaks. In most homes, especially older ones, sealing has a much greater payoff. And most air-sealing tasks are easy. To see how, search for "air leaks" at familyhandyman.com.

### Spend more on painter's tape

When buying masking tape, let price be your guide. More expensive tapes block paint better and release easier without harming surfaces. You might save $3 on cheap tape, but you'll regret the purchase.

## Change furnace filters—or pay

If you regularly change your furnace filter, you're saving on energy and repair costs. If you don't, the HVAC pros we work with would like to thank you for your generous support. Your dirty filters provide lots of repair work and sometimes even furnace replacement jobs.

## CO detectors are mandatory

Most appliances that burn fuel vent exhaust gases outside. But exhaust systems can fail, so CO detectors are the best way to stay safe. Install one on each level of your home.

Locate them in hallways near bedrooms but at least 15 ft. away from fuel-burning appliances. CO is roughly the same weight as air, so it neither rises to the ceiling nor sinks to the floor.

### Want more?

*100 Things Every Homeowner Must Know* will make you a smarter homeowner (even if you're already pretty smart). Buy your copy today at rdstore.com.

Also available wherever books are sold.

## Easy dishwasher maintenance

Most people don't even know it's there, but the filter inside a dishwasher tub needs occasional care. As it gathers debris, it gets partially plugged. That means poor cleaning of dishes, slow draining and rotten odors. Chances are, you can locate and remove the filter without any know-how. But if you need help, just search online for the make and model. After that, cleaning is an easy 10-minute job.

## "Frost-proof" faucets can freeze

If you leave a water-filled hose connected to an outdoor faucet, it can trap water inside the line and freeze, bursting the hose or the supply pipe inside your home.

# INDEX

*Visit **familyhandyman.com** for hundreds of home improvement articles.*

## A

Acrylic latex caulk, 274–275
Aerators, 214–216
Air compressors, 277
Air conditioning units
    leaks in, 200
    mini-split systems, 90–91
Aluminum
    cutting, 270
    welding, 81–82
    wiring, 70, 79
Angle grinders, 76, 84, 162, 269, 271–272
Antennas, router, 74
Ant removal, 279
Appleply, 30, 121
Apple tree cleanup, 247
Aprons, welding, 84
Argon, for welding, 81–82
Asbestos, 22, 50
Attics
    insulating pipes in, 111
    leaks in, 197, 200
Awls, 52, 162

## B

Backer boards, 204
Backer rods, 281
Backflow devices for
    sprinkler systems, 219, 221, 223
Back plates, cabinet
    hardware, 15
Ball valves, soldering, 92
Barn wood project, 160–164

Bath mat project, cedar, 148–149
Bathroom cleaners, 57
Batteries
    cordless brad nailers
        and, 266–268
    solar kit, 69
    storing cordless tool, 280
Beard safety, 281
Birch plywood, 30, 118–119, 121
Birds
    bird feeder backyard
        cantina project, 165–168
    birdhouse as hiding
        spot, 184
    placement of feeders, 210
Bits, 203, 281
Blades
    for cutting metal, 272
    engagement on lawn
        tractors, 239
    setting height of table
        saw, 182
Bleach
    to clean siding and
        trim, 58
    mold and, 23
    to purify water, 108
Bolts, as ladder hooks, 12
Boring rods, 244
Bottle caddy project, 169–172
Brad nailers, cordless, 263–268

Broadcast spreaders, 215–216
Bulbs, LED, 70
Bumpers, lawn tractor, 239

## C

Cabinets
    cabinet doors project, 130–135
    garage makeover
        project, 252–260
    renewing, 15
    swing-out storage in, 24–28
    warming up pipes in, 112
Cables
    basics on electrical, 77–79
    heat, 111–112
Caddy project, bottle, 169–172
Camp showers, 106
Carbon monoxide detectors, 101, 103, 283
Carpeting, mold under, 22–23
Cart project, compressor, 179
Cat litter container as
    hiding spot, 188
Caulk
    avoid squeeze-tube, 279
    choosing, 273–276
    before painting house
        exterior, 60
Cedar bath mat project, 148–149
Ceilings, dropped
    draft stopping, 20
    fire blocking, 19
Cement, 12, 234–236
Chairs as hiding spots, 188
Chimney flue planters, 248
Chimney leaks, 197, 200
Circular saws, 270
Cisterns, 105
Clamps
    convenient workbench, 183
    crimp, 245
    as handles, 63
    for welding, 84, 87
Clamshell diggers, 233

Clock as hiding spot, 185
Clutter, ditching, 10
Combination-core plywood, 121
Compressor cart project, 179
Computer recycling, 76
Concrete
    basics, 234–236
    block for retaining walls, 208
    caulk for, 276
    easy mixing, 201
Condensate pumps, 113
Control joints in cement, 236
Controllers, sprinkler
    system water, 246
Coping baseboard, 44–46
Copper wiring, 70–71
Cord connections, solid, 279
Cordless brad nailers, 263–268
Cores, plywood, 121
Corkscrew substitute, 11
Crate shelf project, 136–139
Crimp clamps, 245
Curve guides, 181
Cutting blade engagement
    on lawn tractors, 239

## D

Deburring tools, 84
Dehumidifiers, 106, 113
Dethatchers, 215–216
Diggers
    auger-style, 233
    clamshell, 233
    digging bars, 232
    posthole, 231
Digging holes, 230–233
Dishwasher maintenance, 282
Dolly, pallet, 181
Doors
    cabinet doors project, 130–135
    cleaning shower, 57
    garage, 112, 257
    jambs, miters for, 41–46
    security measures for, 13
Dormer leaks, 198
Draft blocking, 103

237

Draft stopping, smoke and
gases, 17, 20
Drawers
container storage
project, 29–33
hiding spots in, 185
stops for, 16
Drill presses, 204
Drop spreaders, 215–216
Dryer and washing machine
pedestal project, 34–40
Dry-erase boards, cleaning,
56
Dust masks, 47, 281

## E

Earplug tether, 180
Electrical cables, 19, 77–79
Electrical panels, 48, 75
Engines, lawn tractor, 241
Entertainment center,
garage, 252–260
Epoxy mixing surface, 182
Extinguishers, fire, 14, 280

## F

Fans, bathroom, 283
Faucets
indoor, 112
outdoor, 110, 283
Ferrous metals, cutting,
269–270, 272
Fertilizers, 217
Files, metal, 84
Filters, furnace, 282
Finishes, deck, 211
Fire blocking, 17–20
Fire extinguishers, 14, 280
Fire hazards, 70, 178
Fireplace usage during
power outages, 103
Flags, red, for extra-long
load, 251
Flappers, toilet, 98–99
Flashing, 191, 199–200
Flip-top bench project,
122–129
Floating shelves project,
156–159
Floors
draft stopping and
joists, 20
garage, 258–259
protecting, 48
Flux-core wire, 81

136

Food container storage
project, 29–33
Framing squares, 262
French cleat tool wall
project, 150–155
Frost-free sill cocks, 110
Furnaces
backup tips for, 101–103
filters for, 282
Furniture
door stops on, 53
ideas to enlarge a room,
10
shortening legs on, 183

## G

Garages
cleaning, 250
doors, 112, 257
floors, 258–259
makeover project,
252–260
Garbage bags for clothes
packing, 11
Garden tools, multi-
purpose, 209
Garden tractors, 238
Gauges
gas, 239
sheet metal, 84
Generators for furnace
backup, 102
Glasses, safety, 84, 88,
162, 270
Gloves
vinyl or nitrile, 175
welding, 84
Glue, ready-to-go, 181

Greenhouse, plastic
container, 249
Grocery bag shoe covers, 56
Gun tips, cordless brad
nailer, 265
Gutters
caulk for, 276
cleaning, 56
installing, 191

## H

Hair appliance storage, 54
Hammers, chipping, 84
Hand sanitizers, 105
Hanger bolts, installing, 182
Hangers, coat, for
wire-splicing, 71
Hard drives, damaging or
removing, 76
Harnesses, roof, 279
Heaters, propane and
kerosene, 103
Heating units, mini-splits,
90–91
Helmets, welding, 84
Hiding places, household,
184–188
Holes, digging, 230–233
Hole saws, 202–206
Hoses
replacing washing
machine, 281
winter tips for, 110, 210
Hour meters on lawn
tractors, 239
House painting and
staining, exterior, 58–61
Hybrid caulk, 274–276

## I

Ice dams, 197, 200
Ice scraping, easy, 190
Inlet screens, washing
machine, 95
Insulation
for fire blocking, 18–19
garage door, 112, 257
knob-and-tube wiring, 71
pipe, 111
Iodine, to disinfect water, 108
Irrigation systems
fixing, 218–223
installing, 242–246
for living wall project,
228–229

## J

Jackets, welding, 84
Jack-o'-lanterns, using hole
saws to carve, 206–207
Jambs, window and door,
miters for, 41–46
Jigs, framing, 84
Joints in cement, control, 236
Joists
fire-blocking and draft
blocking, 20
sealing rim, 111

## K

Keys
LEGO key station, 55
used as corkscrews, 11
Knob-and-tube wiring, 71

## L

Ladder hooks, 12
Landings, fire blocking, 18
Lath, tearing off, 47–50
Laundry room pedestal
project, 34–40
Lawn mowers, riding, 209,
238
Lawn restoration, 213–217
Lawn tractors, 237–241
Leaf blowers, for cleaning
out garage, 250
Leaks
air, 283
attic, 200
fixing common, 278
roof, 196–200
in sprinkler systems, 221
LED bulbs, 70
LEGO key station, 55
Living wall project, 224–229
Locks, keyed alike, 282
Lumber-core plywood, 121
Lumberyards, plywood at,
119

## M

Magnets
medicine cabinet, 54
rare earth in pocket, 277
rare earth stud finder, 11
tool bar, 201
toolbox label, 183
vent as hiding spot, 186
welding, 84, 87

160

Maintenance records, under-the-hood, 251

Main valves, shutting off, 280

Markers, as hiding spot, 186

Masonry and concrete, caulk for, 276

Mattocks, 231

Measuring stick, firewood, 249

Medicine cabinet magnets, 54

Medium-density fiberboard (MDF), 118–119, 121

Metal
buying, 87
-clad cables, 78
cutting, 269–272

Mice extermination, 191

MIG welding, 81

Mini blinds, cleaning, 57

Mini-split systems, 90–91

Miters, tips for tight-fitting, 41–46

Miter saws, 270

Mold myths, 21–23

Mowers, riding lawn, 209, 238

Mow-in-reverse mechanisms, lawn tractors, 241

## N

Nailers, cordless brad, 263–268

Nail guns, 52

Nails
brad, 52
lath, 50
nail pops, 16
prepainting heads of, 201

Nonferrous metals, cutting, 270, 272

Nonmetallic cables, 79

## O

Odors, mold and, 22

Organizers, shoe, 14

Oscillating tools, for cutting metal, 271

Outlets, ground plug placement and, 70

## P

Paintbrushes and rollers, 64–65

Paint cans
handles for, 63
openers for, 64, 66
straining, 63
tidy closing of, 66

Painter's tape, 182, 280

Painting
cabinets, 15
caulk for interior house, 275
exterior house, 58–61, 62, 279

Pallet dolly, 181

Paper towel storage, 51

Particleboard-core plywood, 121

Patio paver base panels, plastic, 192–195

Patio projects
bird feeder backyard cantina, 165–168
living wall, 224–229
Viking long table, 140–147

Paver base panels, plastic, 192–195

PEX fittings, 91–92

Pine, for barn wood project, 160–164

Pipes
crushed sprinkler system, 221
cutting plastic, 244
fire blocking for plumbing, 19
insulation for, 111
kinks in poly, 245
preventing frozen, 109–112
pulling, 243
purposely freezing, 93
push-in plumbing connectors for, 280
swing, 245

Planters
chimney flue, 248
for living wall project, 225–226, 229

Plaster walls
finding studs in, 11
tearing off, 47–50

Pliers, MIG, 84

Plows, vibratory, 243–244

Plywood, purchasing, 116–121

Polyurethane
caulk, 274
oil vs. water-based, 279
wipe-on, 173–178

Portland cement, 12, 234, 236

Posthole augers and diggers, 231–233

Power head as multi-purpose tool, 209

Power outages, staying warm during, 101–103

Power rakes, 215–216

Power tool online bargains, 280

Pressure washers, using on house exteriors, 58

Priming house exteriors, 61

Professionals, mold, 22

Projects
barn wood, 160–164
bird feeder backyard cantina, 165–168
bottle caddy, 169–172
cabinet doors, 130–135
cedar bath mat, 148–149
compressor cart, 179
crate shelf, 136–139
flip-top bench, 122–129
floating shelves, 156–159
food container storage, 29–33
French cleat tool wall, 150–155
garage makeover, 252–260
living wall, 224–229
Viking long table, 140–147
welding table, 85–88

Pruning, 210

Pumpkin carving with hole saw, 206–207

Pumps, condensate, 113

Push-in plumbing connectors, 280

PVC wye fittings, for holding hair appliances, 54

## R

Rag cutter, 180

Rainwater collection systems, 105

Ratchet straps, 250

Reciprocating saws, 272

Refacing cabinets, 15

Retaining walls, 208

Riding lawn mowers, 209, 238
*See also Lawn tractors*

Rim joists, sealing, 111

Roofs
caulk for, 276
leaks in, 196–200
safety, 279

Roots in sewer lines, 94–95

Rotary tools, 271

Routers, 72–75

## S

Safety
aluminum wiring, 70
beards and, 281
carbon monoxide detectors, 101, 103, 283
cement, 235
cutting metal, 270
glasses, 84, 88, 162, 270
roof, 279
welding, 88

Salt, deicing, 236

Sanding
disc cleaner, 180
house exteriors, 59
plywood, 119

Sawdust for oil spills, 251

Saws
chop, 86
circular, 270
hole, 202–206
metal-cutting, 86, 269–272
miter, 42–45, 270
reciprocating, 272

29

Scraping house exteriors, 59
Security measures, 13
Self-tapping fittings for irrigation systems, 246
Sheds, adding solar power to, 68–69
Shelves
    crate shelf project, 136–139
    fix sagging, 52
    floating shelves project, 156–159
Shims
    miter saws and, 42–43
    toilet, 113
Shoe covers, grocery bag, 56
Shoe organizers, repurposed, 14
Shovels, 231–232
Shower doors, cleaning, 57
Shutoff valves, fixing leaks at, 278
Siding and trim, caulk for, 274
Sill cocks, frost-free, 110
Soap dispensers, refilling, 57
Soapstone, 84
Soccer ball as hiding spot, 187
Sod, 231–232, 243
Sofa stops, 53
Soffits, fire blocking for, 18–19
Solar power kits for sheds, 68–69
Soldering ball valves, 92
Solvent-based caulk, 274, 276
Spatulas for gutter cleanup, 56
Spouts, motor oil, 251
Spreaders, seed, 215–216, 247
Sprinkler systems, fixing, 218–223
Squares
    framing, 262
    for welding, 84
Staining
    exterior house, 58–62
    plywood, 118
Stairs, fire blocking, 19
Staple pullers, 277
Stick welding, 83
Storage
    food container storage project, 29–33
    paper towel, 51
    shoe organizer, 14

swing-out, 24–28
water, 104–106
Stranded wires vs. solid wires, 79
Stretch wrap, for ratchet straps, 250
Stringers, stair, fire blocking for, 19
Studs, finding, 11
Sunblock tube as hiding spot, 187
Swing pipes, 245

T
Table project, Viking long, 140–147
Tape
    painter's, 280
    Teflon, 54
Tape measures, 277
Thermostats, 103, 110, 112
Thin-set cement, 12
TIG welding, 82
Tile shovels, 232–233
Tires, spare, as hiding spot, 186
Toilet paper holder as hiding spot, 187
Toilets
    draining, 113
    fixing, 96
    leveling, 113
    tune-ups for, 97–100
    water outages and, 106–107
Tongs, for cleaning mini blinds, 57
Toolbox labels, magnetic, 183
Tool wall project, French cleat, 150–155
Tractors, lawn, 237–241
Transmissions, types of lawn tractor, 240
Trash-bag dispenser, 51
Treated wood, 282
Trigger locks, hole saws and, 205
Truss-style joists, draft stopping, 20
Tubs, fire blocking for drop-in, 18

U
Underground feeder cables, 79
Utility knives, 277
Utility lines, 230, 243

V
Valve boxes, 246
Valves
    shutting off main, 280
    soldering ball, 92
Veneers, plywood, 120–121
Vents
    as hiding spot, 186
    inspecting plumbing, 91
    leaks from bath and kitchen, 200
    leaks in roof, 198
    vent boots, 199
Vibratory plows, 243–244
Viking long table project, 140–147

W
Walls
    finding studs in plaster, 11
    fire blocking for basement, 18
    fixing nail pops in, 16
    leaks in, 198
    liner for damaged, 12
    living wall project, 224–229
    protecting, 53
    retaining, 208
Washing machines
    cleaning inlet screens on, 95
    laundry room pedestal project, 34–40
    replacing hoses on, 281
Water
    for newly seeded lawns, 217

outages, 104–108
pressure, 221
shutting off, 111
Water controllers, sprinkler system, 246
Water heater leaks, 283
Waterproof coatings, basement, 63
Water softeners, resetting, 282
Weed killer, 212–215
Welding
    basics, 80
    MIG, 81
    safety, 88
    stick, 83
    TIG, 82
    tools and gear, 84
    welding table project, 85–88
Wi-Fi
    thermostats, 110
    tips for faster, 72–75
Window jambs, miters for, 41–46
Windows
    bars, 13
    locks, 14
    treatments, 10
Wine rack, easy-to-make, 53
Wire connectors, grease-filled, 246
Wireless range extenders, 73
Wiring
    aluminum, 70, 79
    basics, 77–79
    determining size of, 71
    knob-and-tube, 71
Wood
    sealing exterior, 61
    to use for Viking long table, 142
    See also Plywood, purchasing
Workbench project, 122–129
Wrench tricks, 277

Z
Zero turn radius mowers, 241
Zones, nonfunctioning watering system, 222–223

# ACKNOWLEDGMENTS

## FAMILY HANDYMAN

| | |
|---|---|
| Chief Content Officer | Nick Grzechowiak |
| Editor-in-Chief | Gary Wentz |
| Senior Editors | Mary Flanagan |
| | Travis Larson |
| | Mark Petersen |
| Associate and Contributing Editors | Mike Berner |
| | Brad Holden |
| | Rick Muscoplat |
| | Josh Risberg |
| Associate Creative Director | Vern Johnson |
| Senior Designer | Marcia Roepke |
| Graphic Designer | Mariah Cates |
| Photographer | Tom Fenenga |
| Managing Editor | Donna Bierbach |
| Production Artist | Mary Schwender |
| Lead Carpenter | Jeremiah James |
| Editorial Services Associate | Peggy McDermott |
| Production Manager | Leslie Kogan |

## ILLUSTRATORS

| | |
|---|---|
| Steve Björkman | Brad Holden |
| Matt Boley | Frank Rohrbach III |
| Jeff Gorton | |

## OTHER CONSULTANTS

Al Hildenbrand, electrical
Rune Eriksen, electrical
Tim Johnson, electrical
John Williamson, electrical
Les Zell, plumbing

For information about advertising in
*Family Handyman* magazine, call (646) 518-4215

To subscribe to *Family Handyman* magazine:
- By Internet:    familyhandyman.com/customercare
- By email:    customercare@familyhandyman.com
- By mail:    The Family Handyman
    Customer Care
    P.O. Box 6099
    Harlan, IA 51593-1599

We welcome your ideas and opinions.
Write: The Editor, Family Handyman
2915 Commers Drive, Suite 700
Eagan, MN 55121
Fax: (651) 994-2250
E-mail: feedback@familyhandyman.com